CORPORATE STRATEGY IN ACTION

The Author

Geoffrey Lewis is a Senior Lecturer at the Graduate School of Management, Monash University, Melbourne. He received a B. App. Sc. degree from the University of Adelaide, an MBA from the University of Melbourne, and his PhD from London University.

Before embarking on an academic career, he spent nine years in the Australian metals industry in the areas of research, production engineering, and corporate planning. This was followed by six years overseas experience including research, consulting, and teaching while at the London Business School and the International Management Institute, Geneva. After returning to Australia in 1982 he was a member of the Directing Staff at the Australian Administrative Staff College before joining the University of Melbourne in 1984. He has been a member of the Faculty at the Graduate School of Management at Monash University since early 1988. From August 1988 he will be a Visiting Associate Professor at the Darden Graduate School of Business at the University of Virginia.

Dr Lewis has worked as a consultant to a wide range of organizations in Australia, Europe and America. His current research and consulting interests are focused on the integration of the strategy process and organizational change activities directed at changing the culture of organizations.

> He said: 'One day perhaps I'll be able to explain — not explain, because it's difficult for me, isn't it, to put into words — but to make you see.
> Words are not what make you *see*.'

Arthur Brown to his brother Waldo in
The Solid Mandala by Patrick White.

Corporate Strategy in Action

THE STRATEGY PROCESS IN BRITISH ROAD SERVICES

GEOFFREY LEWIS

ROUTLEDGE
London and New York

First published 1988
by Routledge
11 New Fetter Lane, London EC4 4EE
29 West 35th Street, New York, NY 10001

Printed and bound in Great Britain by
Biddles Ltd, Guildford and King's Lynn

British Library Cataloguing in Publication Data

Lewis, Geoffrey, 1947-
Corporate strategy in action: the strategy process in British Road Services.
1. Great Britain. Road freight transport services. British Road Services.
Organisational change. Management aspects
I. Title
388.3′24′0684

ISBN 0-415-00410-1

Library of Congress Cataloging in Publication Data

Lewis, Geoffrey, 1947–
Corporate strategy in action : the strategy process in British Road Services / Geoffrey Lewis.
p. cm.
Bibliography: p.
Includes index.
ISBN 0-415-00410-1
1. British Road Services Ltd. — Management. 2. Organizational change — Great Britain — Case studies. 3. Strategic planning — Great Britain — Case studies. I. Title.
HE5663.Z7B85 1988
388.3′24′0941–dc19 88-30796
CIP

Contents

List of Figures

List of Figures *(continued)*

List of Tables

FOREWORD
By Edgar H. Schein

This study of a major strategic change in British Road Services Limited is remarkable in several respects. Perhaps what is most significant is that we have here an ethnographic study of senior management in action. One of the great problems in studying organizations has been the lack of information about what goes on in the executive suite, forcing us to theorize about such matters, and treating top management as a 'black box' whose workings could only be inferred from the output. Lewis has given us a chance to look into the black box, and has given us enough detail to really mull over whether our current theories can deal with the organizational realities that this research reveals.

Secondly, this study is remarkable for its level of detail. Some readers will be impatient with this and wonder why they have to read about so many meetings and so many political processes, yet it is precisely in this detail that we discover the reality and the complexity of how organizations really evolve and change. And it is the painstaking documentation that lends credibility to the kind of theory that Lewis puts forward.

The theory or the cognitive model used to explain the behaviour of this organization over the several years of the study is the third point to be mentioned. We have here one of the few studies that genuinely combines the models and theories that have come out of the field of strategy with the models and theories that have come out of the fields of organizational psychology, sociology, and anthropology. Much has been written about organizational culture in recent years, but very little detailed research has been done to show how culture really operates when one examines its role in constraining or facilitating organizational change.

The cognitive model that Lewis uses will no doubt be evolved further as more research is done, but it is a useful weaving together of a great many threads that have been until now left dangling. The thorough review of the strategy and culture literature that is used to build the model and analyse the data is most helpful in providing a road map through this difficult area.

A fourth point worth noting is the explicit recognition of first and second order change. Much has been written about this, but not much ethnographic data has been marshalled to show the contrast between adaptation and metamorphosis or transformation. The integration into this model of political processes, and the many illustrations of the operation of those processes makes for a richer and more credible analysis.

The analysis of strategy as both a process and a solution, as something that has rational analytical as well as organizational social processes involved in it is a useful reminder that the monolithic models proposed by some writers on strategy are at best oversimplifications and at worst distortions. We see in Lewis's study the complex interplay between process and solution, and we see the many iterations that an organization goes through before it has achieved a new direction that is more than an incremental adaptation.

Finally, this study illustrates what is possible in organizational research if we legitimize more clinical and ethnographic approaches. Lewis is to be congratulated for his energy and dedication in seeing a project like this through to conclusion, and our field is enriched as a result.

Edgar H. Schein,
Cambridge, Ma.,
15 November 1987.

PREFACE

This book examines the ways in which managers address the issues of strategic choice and organizational change. It presents the findings of a two-year longitudinal research study of strategic change in a major group of companies in the UK transport industry. The author's involvement ranged from attendance at Board meetings to observing the daily working life of the management team and enabled him to trace the development of a new strategic direction. The extensiveness and seniority of the management level at which the research was conducted make it unique.

That top management were able to change the strategic direction of the business should perhaps be taken for granted — for this surely is the function of top management. The management of strategic change is, however, one of the most complex processes confronting managers. Existing theories of the strategy process provide little guidance to managers who wish to bring about strategic change.

The book aims to redress this weakness in the strategy literature by presenting a theoretical model of the process, grounded in empirical research, which will provide a foundation on which managerial practice can be built.

The Research Setting

The book is based upon a study of British Road Services Limited (BRS), which at the time of the study[1] was a group of eight regional companies with 150 branches operating a wide range of national road transport services. In 1979 the group's revenue was over £150 million, and it employed almost 10,000 people. The group was one of several comprising the state-owned National Freight Corporation (NFC) which, although controlling less than 10 per cent of the market, was by far the largest organization in the British road transport industry.

British Road Services Limited was established as part of the British Transport Commission in 1948 following the nationalization of the transport industry. At that time BRS effectively had a monopoly on the long-distance haulage segment of the industry. In 1953 the road transport industry was denationalized, but the conservative government was unsuccessful in divesting BRS and was left with a substantial, though fragmented, organization. The organization later underwent a series of major changes, mostly as a result of government legislation, including the 1968 Transport Act, under which the National Freight Corporation (NFC) was created.

Following the appointment of Peter Thompson as group co-ordinator in 1972, BRS was restructured into eight legally separate, regional companies operating autonomously within agreed financial constraints. Concomitant changes were made by Thompson in the product-market strategy of BRS. Until this change the role of BRS in the road transport industry had essentially been the same since the organization was established in 1948, that is, primarily a long-distance road haulier involved in what is known as general haulage. The new product-market strategy was to change the emphasis of the group's activities from its traditional haulage work to new areas such as contract hire, truck rental, distribution, and warehousing.

In 1976 another change was made to the management structure of BRS. Peter Thompson was promoted to the position of Chief Executive of the NFC and was succeeded as BRS group co-ordinator by David White, the managing director of one of the regional companies.

By 1977, five years after the introduction of the new strategy and structure, BRS's rapidly declining general haulage fleet was still losing money. It was becoming clear to BRS management that the rate at which new activities could continue to grow was insufficient to compensate for the planned decline in general haulage. Cash constraints imposed by the government resulted in increasing pressure on profit and capital availability, and this was manifested in a number of ways, including pressure for the accelerated decline of general haulage. The rate of general haulage decline became the focus of a fundamental strategic disagreement between Peter Thompson and BRS management, which stemmed from basically different views: Thompson believed that the selective reduction of the activity would reveal a profitable core of business; BRS management argued that if general haulage were declined at a faster rate than new products grew, overall financial performance would decline because organizational contraction would jeopardize the group's key strength, a national network of marketing and operating locations.

This created a dilemma for the management of the organization. After five years, Thompson's strategy had run its course, and a new strategy had to be found that satisfied the conflicting demands of improved financial performance and the avoidance of organizational contraction. It was the study of the decision-making process through which this dilemma was resolved that provided the focus for the research presented in this book.

As pointed out by David White in his note, this was only one of a broad range of issues that were being managed within BRS at this time. At the centre of these issues was David White, who was responsible for managing a large, complex organization in a turbulent industry. A high level of economic uncertainty, government pressures, industrial relations tensions, changing technology, and increasingly sophisticated competition were impinging on BRS. The organization's background and decentralized corporate structure made managing more complex than in many other similar sized businesses. These broader issues, and David White's record of achievement in building BRS's financial performance and strategic capability in these difficult circumstances, is not recorded here but should not go unmentioned. The successful privatisation in 1982 of the NFC, of which BRS was the largest group, attests to this achievement.

The Theoretical Issues

The BRS study examines a wide range of theoretical issues concerning the nature of strategic change. Can strategic change, for example, be best understood as an incremental, evolutionary process or as a dramatic organizational transformation, and what are the managerial implications of these different perspectives?

The book addresses a number of the major inadequacies of existing theoretical approaches. The essence of the strategy process is the managerial choices and actions which allow an organization to adapt to its environment. Normative strategy theories describe these choices and actions in terms of analytical and political processes through which strategies are formulated and implemented. Management, particularly at the more senior levels, however, is as much about uncertainty and the incalculable as it is about well-understood and carefully analysed strategies. This uncertainty about cause-effect relationships in managerial decision making is well established in the literature (Thompson 1967).

This issue is often overlooked by political theories of organizational decision making. Even when agreement exists about preferred outcomes, strategic choice usually involves more judgment than computation. There are matters that managers don't know about and things that can't be known, including cause-effect relationships. This is the nature of the decisions that managers confront in reality as distinct from the laboratory situations that have been the focus of most Decision Theory research. The analytic decision paradigm, which has provided the theoretical underpinning for most models of the strategy process, fails in the context of these complex decision problems. More recent models of the strategy process have enhanced power for describing and explaining the decision-making behaviour of managers in actual organizations. Considerable conceptual problems remain, however, because even these more sophisticated models have been developed within the assumptions of the analytic paradigm (Steinbruner 1974).

The book presents a new model of the strategy process based on assumptions outside the analytic paradigm. Cognitive theory provides the theoretical foundation for a metamorphic model that proposes two forms of organizational change: incremental development and metamorphic change. Incremental development involves adjustments to marginal environmental variations. As a result of either external performance pressures or proactively managed strategic change, these essentially stable periods are interrupted by bursts of metamorphic transformation. The book examines the pattern of organizational processes and behaviours associated with metamorphic change.

The nature and role of diversity, power, and conflict in the strategic decision-making process are considered within the framework of this metamorphic model of strategic change. Cognitive theory is used to conceptualize organizational culture in a way that provides more analytical incisiveness and power. The model allows much of the empirical work on the management of strategic decision making and change (Mintzberg et al. 1976; Quinn 1980; Pettigrew 1985) to be examined within a new theoretical framework. Implications for the management of organizational culture and politics as elements of the strategy process are considered.

The Research Method[2]

Pettigrew (1972, 1985) argues that a major reason for the failure of most theories of organizational decision making is that they are founded on inadequate empirical research. Research which purports to be concerned with decision-making processes should be founded on a process-oriented methodology. That this methodology presents practical problems of organizational access and costly, intensive data collection techniques does not weaken the fundamental soundness of Pettigrew's point. The methodology adopted for the BRS study responds to Pettigrew's call for intensive, process-oriented research and the extensiveness and seniority of the management level at which the research was conducted make it unique.

The analysis presented in the book is based upon qualitative data collected within a longitudinal research design using the technique of participant observation. Data were collected continuously over a period of two years using the following sources:

- observation of meetings, including all Group Policy Committee meetings, most group and company planning and control meetings, and a wide range of management meetings at group, company and branch level;
- discussions/interviews with all of the senior managers at group and company level;
- a wide range of documents, including group and company strategic reviews, corporate plans and budgets.

Intensive data collection over such an extended period of fieldwork resulted in a large amount of material, the major element of which was half a million words of fieldnotes.

The conceptual framework of the strategy process which has been developed is of course subject to the limitations of the research, which derive from the unavoidable weaknesses of qualitative methodology. Problems of reactive effects and selective perception and interpretation cannot be overlooked but were minimized by careful development and management of the participant-observer role and by a multimethod/multisource research design.

The difficulties associated with the analysis and interpretation of qualitative data are severe, and were related to the underlying methodology as well as the nature of the data. Because of the approach adopted — inductively searching for a theoretical framework which explained observed reality, rather than collecting data specifically to test a preconceived theory — the process of analysis and interpretation evolved as the material and ideas developed. In practical terms this meant that the analysis had to be built up one step at the time, layer by layer with increasing conceptual abstraction.

The final stage of the analysis involved linking the interpretation of the data with theories and concepts from the literature to develop more generalized concepts — 'grounded theory' (Glaser and Strauss 1967).

Qualitative methods are still burdened by a poor image compared with the more 'rigorous' quantitative approaches, but the methodological foundations upon which they rest are gradually becoming more widely accepted:

> The label qualitative methods has no precise meaning in any of the social sciences. It is at best an umbrella term covering an array of interpretive techniques which seek to describe, decode, translate and otherwise come to terms with the meaning, not the frequency, of certain more or less naturally occurring phenomena in the social world (Van Maanen 1979:520).

Findings based upon a single case are difficult to validate in the traditional scientific sense. The validity of the theoretical conclusions reached can be judged largely in terms of the accuracy of the data collected and the reasonableness of the interpretation of that data.

Problems of generalizing the conclusions are inherent in the methodology — to what extent does the analysis of a single organization justify general conclusions about the nature of the strategy process? This problem does not, however, detract from the validity of the conclusions; it simply reflects the inherent limitations of exploratory research.

The conceptualization of the model of the strategy process that is presented in the book draws on my continuing research and involvement with managers as a consultant and educator. My experience subsequent to the BRS research has been important in refining and validating the theoretical conclusions presented in the book.

The Plan of the Book

There are difficulties associated with the presentation of qualitative data. It is hard to maintain the sense and chronology of events while integrating the analysis of the data and the theoretical conclusions that have been drawn from them. To make it easier for the reader I have presented the theoretical model first and placed the data and analysis within this conceptual framework.

Chapter 1 establishes the theoretical framework within which the research has been undertaken. A number of conceptual weaknesses associated with traditional theoretical approaches to strategy are discussed. The nexus between strategy and organizational change is explored and the nature of strategic change is considered. In this chapter I argue that cognitive theory provides a conceptual foundation on which a new model of the strategy process can be built.

Chapter 2 develops a new model of the strategy process. Using cognitive theory as a conceptual foundation, a metamorphic model of strategic change is developed. The model proposes two forms of organizational change: incremental development and metamorphic change. Incremental development involves adjustments to marginal environmental variations. As a result of either external performance pressures or proactively managed strategic change, these stable periods are interrupted by bursts of metamorphic transformation.

Chapter 3 presents a strategic analysis of BRS from its creation in 1947 until 1979 when the field research was completed. The analysis examines the series of fundamental changes the organization underwent. These changes identify a series of 'eras' which constitute a pattern of periods of stability interrupted by periods of discontinuity or transformation.

Chapter 4 examines the period 1972-76 in more detail. During this period a number of crucial strategic decisions were made which influenced in a fundamental way the product-market strategy and the structure and management style of the organization. This brought to the organization an internal consistency which had not previously existed. A coherent organizational culture was beginning to emerge, but within it were the seeds of a strategic dilemma that would eventually have to be confronted.

Chapter 5 describes the nature of the strategic dilemma which emerged because of a fundamental incompatibility between a major part of the business's activities and the recently introduced organization structure and management style.

Chapter 6 discusses the diversity of management perceptions and preferences which existed regarding the strategic dilemma. This diversity, combined with the dispersed management power structure, provided the rudiments for political processes which were influential in the resolution of the dilemma.

Chapter 7 examines in detail the decision-making process which resulted in the development of a new strategy.

Chapter 8 presents the theoretical conclusions and develops further ideas regarding the management of strategic change.

Appendix 1 provides background on the senior managers of BRS and NFC who were involved in the events described.

Appendix 2 provides detail on each of the regional companies and demonstrates the degree of diversity that existed within the BRS group.

Appendix 3 details the major events which took place in the strategic decision-making process described in Chapter 7.

Appendix 4 discusses the research processes, including some of the methodological issues and problems associated with the analysis and presentation of the research material.

Notes

1. The study extended from 1976-79. BRS has since undergone major changes including privatisation in 1982 under the Thatcher government.

2. A more detailed discussion of the methodology and techniques adopted can be found in Appendix IV.

NOTE
By David White, Deputy Chairman of the National Freight Consortium plc

In August 1987, I was asked to write this note. It seems a long time ago that the events as described took place.

BRS continues to be a very profitable company and contributes the largest amount to the new privatised National Freight Consortium — which, in itself, has been a great success story.

Strangely enough general haulage — although renamed, still remains a product within the BRS Group and is profitable.

The book, I feel, concentrates too much on one product and does not reflect the true balance of all the success that was being achieved by the team of management (the Group Policy Committee, or GPC) in other product areas.

The book also refers constantly to conflict — although memories fade, I do not remember the events in that way. My recollection is quite clear — I was fortunate, as the Chairman of the GPC, to lead a team of managers who all had their own strongly held views on many subjects — as I did.

I believe the team was united throughout in the belief that when all the debate and argument was done, what was good for the profitable health of the company as a whole, was the most important single factor.

Most of the people mentioned in the book are still with the National Freight Consortium and are contributing to its success — long may the situation continue.

I was, and am, proud to have been involved in BRS — it was, and is, a great company with a degree of comradeship that has been unsurpassed in my working life.

ACKNOWLEDGEMENTS

The BRS research was started in 1976. In the ensuing period I have had the support of many people in many important ways. Without the commitment and efforts of these people this book would not have been written.

First, David White and the other managers of BRS, who for a period of more than two years allowed me to share their often stressful working lives. They good-humouredly tolerated my persistent questioning, and they showed an intuitive understanding and sensitivity that made it possible for me to be part of their world while standing apart from it. That they consented to the research at all is to their great credit; that they continued to support it so fully only adds to my indebtedness. I have tried to capture and explain their world in a way which they will understand — because it is after all their world, and ultimately it is their responsibility to shape it.

I would also like to express my gratitude to those people who have influenced my thinking about managing organizations, most of whom I know only through the written word. Of those who have influenced me in a more direct way I would particularly like to thank my doctoral supervisor, Dr Stuart Timperley of the London Graduate School of Business, and Professors Charles Handy, John Hunt, Denis Pym, and Ed Schein.

My thanks also go to the many people who have helped in some direct way in the preparation of my doctoral dissertation and subsequently this book. Joy Lewis transcribed over a thousand pages of field notes, and Jane Keller typed the dissertation manuscript, both of them with a sense of commitment far beyond anything I could have reasonably expected. Bill Byrt of the Melbourne Graduate School of Management provided valuable comments on the structure of the book. Betty Thuan, a doctoral candidate at the Melbourne School of Management, helped with indexing and final editing.

I would like to particularly recognize the contribution of Linda Tullberg of McKinsey and Company's Melbourne office whose criticisms and suggestions have helped in the refinement of many of the concepts presented in the book.

Finally, I wish to thank my wife Mardi who, for the last ten years has had to compete for time with 'the BRS study'. She made it possible in ways that only she knows, and without her encouragement and support it would not have been possible. It is to Mardi that this book is dedicated.

1
THE STRATEGY PROCESS — THEORETICAL ORIENTATIONS

The BRS research was undertaken to address certain conceptual weaknesses that were perceived to exist in the area of strategic management. Traditional approaches to strategy have tended to view it as a process through which the top management determine the organization's 'mission' and the means by which it will be achieved. These approaches suffered fundamental problems with the conceptualization of 'organizational goals' and failed to predict or explain observed organizational processes — managers did not seem to behave as the theory said they should. Organizational change as an inherent part of the strategy process has received little attention in the strategy literature. Traditional approaches treat organizational change as being essentially non-problematic. It suggests that, having decided what needs to be done, managers simply apply managerial and administrative procedures to achieve the desired result. Practising managers know that organizational change is central to the strategy process and perhaps the most complex and difficult aspect of the managerial task.

What is strategy?

The failure to develop a coherent and commonly accepted conceptual framework in the area of strategy has been discussed regularly in the literature. In a review of the definitional problems associated with the concept of strategy, Shirley suggests that:

> Every emerging discipline goes through a shake-out period during which there is significant disagreement — confusion, even — over fundamental concepts. Such is the case with the field of study that has become known as corporate strategy and policy (Shirley 1982:262).

Camerer argues:

> The usual approach to the development of a new language of strategy and policy is an exhaustive 'literature review' or catalogue of definitions used by others; typically reviewers then try to put out the fire with gasoline by synthesizing these diverse working definitions into a 'new', 'improved' super-definition (Camerer 1985:2).

Although most commentators are not so scathing, the lack of a coherent conceptual framework which can be subjected to rigorous testing by researchers, and communicated to practitioners, is generally recognized as a major problem.

There does appear to be emerging within the literature, however, a framework for theorizing about strategy, and although this framework has yet to develop rigour and analytical incisiveness, progress is being made. Much of the debate in the literature hinges on two fundamental conceptual dichotomies. These are more than mere definitional differences, they represent fundamentally different perspectives on the nature of the phenomena being studied.

The first dichotomy is whether strategy is considered to be a process or the outcome of that process, that is, a solution. The second aspect is sometimes referred to as the content of strategy (Pettigrew 1985:19). This distinction has been discerningly captured by Bower and Doz (1979) with what they term 'positional and managerial views of strategy'. Within this framework a definitional difference can be drawn between 'strategy as a pattern of administrative and positional outputs in the relationship of the organization to its environment, and strategic management which operates on the process which generates this pattern of output' (Bower and Doz 1979: 156,157).

This dichotomy is consistently and clearly evident throughout the literature and would appear to be useful rather than problematic. Camerer's concern about the lack of 'Deductive theorizing, with more attention to a game-theoretic definition of equilibrium and to recent ideas from economics' (1985:1) can be seen as a challenge to researchers in the field with a particular focus of concern, without implying the demolition of the work of researchers with a different theoretical interest. Theoretical progress will be enhanced by different research methodologies being brought to bear on different research issues.

The second fundamental dichotomy is between the view of strategy as a economic/rational phenomenon or as an organizational/social phenomenon. This distinction can be applied to both elements of the first dichotomy: that between strategy as a process, and strategy as an outcome. Applied to the process aspect of strategy, we can observe a clear trend in the literature from the early Business Policy approaches,[1] which were intentionally prescriptive and based on models of rational individual decision making, to more descriptive models,[2] which attempt to account for the reality of organizational decision making, including complex social and political processes.

The early work in the field was almost exclusively devoted to economic/rational models of the firm, which stressed strategy solutions based on purely economic arguments. This approach continues to be strongly represented in the literature, with increasingly sophisticated models and techniques being applied.[3]

It is only recently, however, that the organizational/social perspective has been applied to the notion of strategy as an outcome or a solution. Miles and Snow's (1978) typology includes features of the organization's structure and style as well as the product-market characteristics normally associated with strategy types. The capability of the organization in terms of its structure, systems, and management style can be seen as constituting a strategic solution, which may or may not be successful, depending on external factors, such as the nature of industry competition.

This notion of organizational capability constituting a — or perhaps the — strategic solution underlies much recent popular management literature. One interpretation of the success of Japanese business is based on this argument: competitive success derives not from carefully analysed and thought-out strategies, but from an organization's inherent capability to compete. This argument is convincingly presented by Pascale (1984) in a study of Honda's entry to the US motorcycle market. The proponents of 'strategy as an economic/ rational solution' (BCG Report: Strategy Alternatives for the British Motorcycle Industry 1975) analysed the situation in terms of volume-related cost reductions, and the consequential relationship between market share and profitability. Pascale's study of what happened showed that Honda's success was the result of the commitment of its managers to make the venture a success, and their ability to experiment, adapt and learn (1984:48) rather than to a brilliantly conceived strategy. Pascale concludes:

> We tend to impute coherence and purposive rationality to events when the opposite may be closer to the truth. How an organization deals with miscalculation, mistakes, and negative events outside its field of vision is often crucial to success over time (Pascale 1984:48).

The concept of strategy as a solution defined in terms of organizational capability is at the heart of the McKinsey 7-S model (Pascale and Athos 1981), Peters and Waterman's best-selling book, *In Search of Excellence* (1982), and the current preoccupation with organizational culture in the management literature.[4]

The various perspectives of strategy that derive from these dichotomies can be summarized in the form of the matrix shown in Figure 1.1.

	Economic/Rational	Social/Organizational
Strategy as a Process	I e.g. Normative business policy models	II e.g. Pettigrew's political process model (1973)
Strategy as a Solution	IV e.g. Strategy types models Galbraith and Schendel (1983)	III e.g. *In Search of Excellence* Peters and Waterman (1982)

Figure 1.1 Schematic diagram of perspectives on strategy

Integrated models of the strategy process

There has been an obvious trend in the strategy literature, particularly that concerned with decision-making processes and the management of those processes, towards conceptual treatments which attempt to integrate the economic/rational and social/organizational perspectives.[5]

Normative business policy models of the strategy process (Ansoff 1965; Christensen et al. 1965; Steiner 1969; Andrews 1971; Argenti 1974; Glueck 1976) are based upon the idea that organizations respond to the changing environment by formulating carefully analysed and well thought through 'strategies' that take account of certain environmental and organizational pressures and constraints. These normative business policy models of the strategy process could be represented in simplified diagrammatic form as shown in Figure 1.2.

This approach to strategy is intentionally prescriptive and based upon models of rational, individual decision making (Dewey 1910), and therefore shares its origins with Decision Theory. The decision theorist is primarily concerned with constructing models which will determine what decisions should be made, rather than predicting the actual behaviour of individuals, much less organizations, in real decision situations.

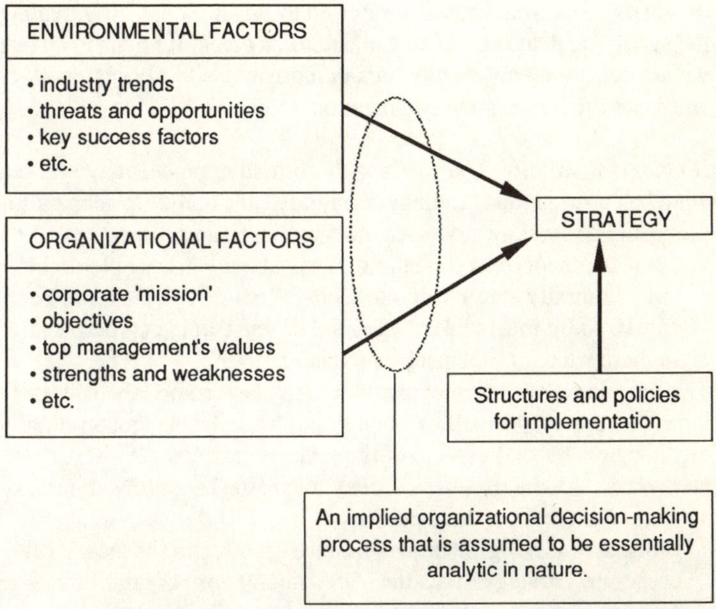

Figure 1.2: Simplified normative business policy model

Integrated models of the strategy process have been developed because of the failure of more narrowly based approaches to address several fundamental issues:

The conceptualization of organizational goals and values A fundamental theoretical problem that continues to plague normative, narrowly based analytical approaches to the strategy process is that of the conceptualization of organizational goals. Models based upon this approach assume that organizational goals and values can be identified by the decision makers (whose identity is not specified but clearly central to the issue anyway), and that, once identified, provide the criteria used in selecting from alternatives. The concept of organizational goals and values constituted in this way is inherently problematic because it involves the reification of the organization — giving the status of concrete reality, particularly the power of thought and action, to what is essentially an abstract social construct. Simon (1964:1) argues that 'it is difficult to introduce the concept of organizational goals without reifying the organization — treating it as something more than a system of interacting individuals'. Silverman has also referred to this difficulty: 'by treating the "goals" and "needs" of organizations as given, it seems to us that we are attributing apparently human motivations to objects: in other words we are reifying the organization' (1968:223).

'Ecological validity' The traditional, normative models have lacked what has been termed 'ecological validity', the ability to account for the reality of strategy processes observed in organizations:

> . . . if the theory has something to say about what people do in real, culturally significant situations. What it says must not be trivial, and it must make some kind of sense to the participants in these situations themselves (Neisser 1976:2).

The development of integrated models has come about largely through these difficulties being addressed by incorporating organizational/social aspects of the strategy process. As a result, the perspective of the Business Policy theorists has evolved to take account of these theoretical problems:

> Singularly lacking or de-emphasized in the current theory of corporate strategy are the behavioural or organizational aspects, or more generally what might be called the social systems aspects, of strategy formulation. Thus far, what has been focused on and emphasized in the theory are the intellectual-analytical aspects . . . One plausible explanation of why the current theory of corporate strategy has thus far remained aloof from social system relationships lies in the influence of formal decision theory . . . (Guth 1976:375).

There was a need for a more behaviourally oriented approach, one that took account of the complexities of a system that includes human emotions, differing perceptions of reality, divergent goals and values and a great deal of inherent uncertainty at all levels.

Behavioural theories of organizational decision making recognized the fundamental problems inherent in the normative approaches and suggested that the strategy process involved political as well as analytical elements; that is, processes associated with conflict arising from a diversity of interests, policy demands, and power structures through which these conflicts are resolved and policies agreed. Hence, the normative model was elaborated to include political processes through which a diversity of interests and preferences are accommodated and which result in goals associated with a predominant group (usually top management, but in theory any powerful coalition). These 'organizational' goals provided the criteria for what remained essentially an analytic process.

Subsequent approaches have attempted to treat the problematic nature of organizational goals by considering individual and organizational values. This raises the question, however, of how individual and organizational values are related without re-introducing the problematic of reification: simple summation of individual values is clearly inadequate. The concept of 'organizational culture' — shared beliefs and values and the artefacts and behaviours that reflect and re-affirm them — has been introduced into the strategy literature in an attempt to deal with this problem.

More recent theoretical approaches to the strategy process are integrated in the sense that they view the decision-making process as involving analytical and political processes within the context of organizational culture. Grinyer and Spender (1979) make a direct link between strategic decision making and organizational culture (although they use the term 'pattern of beliefs' or 'recipe' rather than culture). Building on the work of Hedberg and Jonsson (1977), they develop a model of the way changing patterns of beliefs are integrated into the strategy process:

> The company's commitment to a particular recipe (pattern of beliefs) was reinforced by its success, and became institutionalized in procedures, behavioural patterns, skills, capital equipment, and a network of external relations. This created considerable inertia, so that when the recipe became obsolete and financial performance declined, salvation was sought in more aggressive implementation and tighter financial controls, which produced a temporary recovery, while slack was consumed, but could not stop the downward trend. Only persistent crisis — and in one case, impending closure — eventually induced the necessary fundamental re-orientation through the adoption of a revised recipe brought in by the senior executives (Hedberg and Jonsson 1977:12).

The point here is that the culture of the organization constrains organizational behaviour, including strategic choice, to a defined area. The nature and content of both analytical and political processes are constrained by the culture: 'The pattern of diverse beliefs can be visualized as a multiplicity of constraints defining a feasible solution space within which the firm's strategy must be located' (Grinyer and Spender 1979:130). At the same time, these constraints, or boundaries, are constantly shifting as a result of analytical and political processes.

This framework provides a linkage between the economic/rational and the social/organizational approaches to strategy as an output or solution (see Figure 1.3).

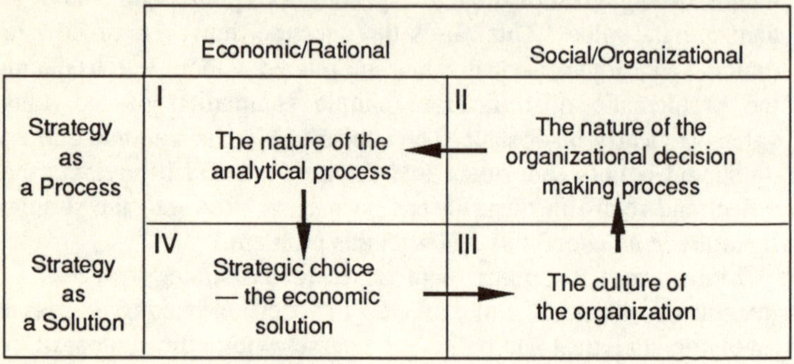

Figure 1.3: The link between 'strategy' and 'culture'

Because the culture of the organization constrains strategic choice within the boundaries of certain economic/rational solutions, strategy as a social/organizational solution becomes a crucial constraint on the strategy process — 'we know that organization structure and processes of compensation, incentives, control and management development influence and constrain the formulation of strategy' (Andrews 1980:27). That this aspect of strategy has been recognized by some of the original theorists in the Business Policy field is an indication of the extent to which the approaches to strategy as a process have moved from the normative, economic/rational view to a more integrated perspective incorporating social/organizational processes.

Major strategic initiatives imply a change in the culture of the organization, and a key aspect of managing the strategy process involves the management of organizational culture. Although Grinyer and Spender (1979) provide some insights, they do not examine in any detail the processes through which shared patterns of beliefs and values change. A conceptual framework for the way that beliefs and values are created and changed at the collective level is crucial to the further development of an integrated model of the strategy process.

The links between the nature of the organization — its culture — and the strategic choices made are extremely complex. The complexity and subtlety of the linkages are revealed by the BRS research and other empirical studies,[6] and are essentially a function of the change processes which are at the core of the strategy process. A new strategy requires the decision makers to view the world, the industry and the enterprise's place within it differently. It also requires new patterns of behaviour and change at a personal level. The development and formalization of strategy and these cognitive and behavioural changes are inseparable parts of a complex, unfolding process. For managers to even contemplate a strategic shift indicates that substantial cognitive change has already occurred. The crucial strategy process issue is to understand how these changes take place, and how they can be managed.

Strategy and the management of organizational change

Strategic management has evolved in response to the challenge of the increasingly turbulent environment in which enterprises and their managers exist (Ansoff 1984). If organizations are to have a dynamic interchange with their environment, whether it is on the basis of carefully planned proactive strategies, or just reluctant adaptation, it is axiomatic that organizational change is involved. It is curious, therefore, that the subject of the management of organizational change has not received more attention in the strategy literature.

The traditional, normative models of strategy implementation assume that organizational change follows the process of strategic choice (formulation); in practice the dichotomy between strategy formulation and implementation is artificial (Bower and Doz 1979). Contemporary formulations of the normative, business policy approach recognize strategy formulation and implementation as being dynamically linked. These links, however, tend to be viewed in a rather mechanical way:

> In real life the processes of formulation and implementation are intertwined. Feedback from operations gives notice of changing environmental factors to which strategy should be adjusted. The formulation of strategy is not finished when implementation begins. A business organization is always changing in response to its own makeup and past development (Christensen, Andrews, and Bower 1973:619).

The traditional view of strategy implementation assumes first, that organizational change follows the process of strategic choice; and second, that the process of change is essentially non-problematic. Managers, having decided what needs to be done, use administrative procedures to bring about the necessary action. Bower and Doz (1979), in an excellent discussion of this issue, argue that the dichotomy between strategy formulation and implementation, in reality, does not make much sense:

> In fact, it is not possible to deal sensibly with the analytical problem of formulating a strategy for a company without basing it on an assessment of the current posture of the company and its possible moves. Because the processes that determine and constrain the company's economic and financial posture are administrative in nature, a feasible strategy can be formulated only on the basis of an administrative understanding of what the company is and what the leverage points are within it. By assuming complete plasticity of the organization in terms of transfer of resources, corporate planning models may be a useful analytical tool. But they do not allow the development of an overall workable strategy grounded in reality (Bower and Doz 1979:154,155).

Rooted in many of the traditional approaches to strategy implementation is a traditional, structural philosophy of management that assumes that organizational change can be brought about by structural means — changing the breakdown of tasks and the allocation of authority, reporting relationships, reward systems, and formalized practices and procedures (Perrow 1973).

> The implementation of strategy is comprised of a series of subactivities which are primarily administrative. If purpose is determined, then the resources of a company can be mobilized to accomplish it. An organizational structure appropriate for the efficient performance of the required tasks must be made effective by information systems and relationships permitting coordination of subdivided activities. The organizational processes of performance measurement, compensation, management development — all of them enmeshed in systems of incentives and controls — must be directed toward the kind of behaviour required by organizational purpose (Andrews 1980:27).

Underlying this approach to change are the same basic assumptions about human rational choice behaviour that form the basis for normative theories of the strategy process. A great deal of change can be accomplished this way, in the right circumstances. But if the process of strategic choice involves managers developing new 'frames of reference' — new perspectives on the world and perhaps themselves — a more sophisticated approach to the management of change is required. Although the disciplines of organizational behaviour and organization development are vitally concerned with these questions of change, theoretical development in the strategy area has drawn very little upon these disciplines:

> The organization development literature has rarely been used to inform thinking about strategic change, even though recent writing by, for example, Beckhard and Harris (1977) and Beer (1980) could be used with profit to grapple with some of the practical problems of creating and managing strategic change (Pettigrew 1985:19).

The works of Mintzberg et al. (1976) and Quinn (1980) are rare exceptions. Similarly, very few theorists from the field of organization development have adopted a strategic perspective of change. Again there are important exceptions, for example, Berg (1979) and Tichy (1983). Unfortunately, neither writer adopts a perspective that is easily linked to the mainstream of the strategy literature. Pettigrew's major study of strategic change in ICI is unique in consciously placing itself at the nexus of organizational change and the strategy process. From his review of the literature, Pettigrew (1985) concludes that 'the highly rational and linear process models' are inadequate and different approaches to the study of strategic change need to be developed.

Pettigrew presents researchers with the most pressing challenge in the field of strategic management: the development of an integrated model of strategy in which strategic change is conceptualized in terms of processes that have been established on the basis of empirical evidence and can serve as a guide to action for those whose role it is to manage strategic change.

The BRS research supports the contention that strategy, in the context of a real organization, and from the perspective of the organization's managers, is concerned with the management of complex and diverse organizational processes. In terms of the model presented in Figure 1.3, this is consistent with the view of strategy as an integrated process involving analytical, political, and cognitive elements.

This is more than an issue of arbitrary definition. The BRS research shows how strategic outcomes are determined by the decision-making process — in effect, cells III and IV in Figure 1.3 are the product of cells I and II. The means (the process), determine the ends (the strategic outcomes), and the implication for management is that the strategy process must be managed. Strategy cannot be managed as an abstract analytical activity separate from the complexity of organizational processes.

Implicit in the strategy process are fundamental organizational changes. As the BRS data will demonstrate, the formulation of a new strategy involves more than the adaptation of the organization to a changing environment. In BRS a dilemma arose because certain beliefs and values about the organization, the environment, and the nature of the relationship between the two, constrained incremental change. The managerial frame of reference or cognitive structure failed, no longer providing workable solutions. The dilemma was the manifestation of the dissonance between the organizationally defined reality and the environment. A new strategy required a shift in the collective cognitive structure of the decision makers: the core shared beliefs and values of the organization failed. The strategy process could therefore be seen as a process of cultural change, and strategic management as the management of this process.

What makes change strategic?

Perhaps the most fundamental question in the area of strategy is what makes something strategic? What distinguishes a strategic decision from an operational one? What distinguishes strategic change from everyday organizational change? In a review of the definitional problems surrounding the strategy concept, Shirley (1982) concludes that there is a complete absence of consensus about what types of decisions are strategic in nature.

The various definitions of the term 'strategic' usually encompass notions concerning scope, time horizon, scale, and irrevocability. A decision that effects the future of an organization and involves a considerable and an irreversible allocation of resources would usually be considered strategic. Pettigrew, for example, says: 'Strategic is just a description of the magnitude of change . . .' (1985:439). The difficulty is that many apparently inconsequential, everyday decisions turn out to have strategic implications. The 'big strategic decisions' are usually the end result, or even simply the manifestation, of a process, the origins of which are uncertain and, at least on the surface, not particularly strategic.[7]

Unfortunately the area of management suffers from an overabundance of words that enter the managerial vocabulary on a wave of popularity and then, as a result of imprecision and overuse, quickly degenerate to having little specific meaning. This has been true of terms like 'strategic' and 'organizational culture'. In contemporary management parlance, there is a danger that everything, and therefore nothing, is strategic. In discussing 'strategy', whether from a theoretical or practical viewpoint, there is a definitional problem.

One way of dealing with this problem is to see if various types of change can be identified. This may then allow a particular type of change to be distinguished as strategic. Throughout the diverse array of theories of social and organizational change, one theme is consistent — social systems evolve and develop not in a steady continuous way, but in stages, with stable periods of steady incremental change interrupted by short periods of rapid and profound change.[8]

The idea that change takes two fundamentally different forms is developed in the literature of a wide range of disciplines. In the area of psychotherapy, Watzlawick et al. (1974) have presented the case succinctly on the basis of both theory and empirical observation. These authors refer to first-order and second-order change and exemplify the two types of change using a mathematical analogy (the Theory of Groups and the Theory of Logical Types):

> Group Theory gives us a framework for thinking about the kind of change that can occur within a system that itself stays invariant; the Theory of Logical Types is not concerned with what goes on inside a class, i.e., between its members, but gives us a frame for considering the relationship between member and class and the peculiar metamorphosis which is in the nature of shifts from one logical level to the next higher. If we accept this basic distinction between the two theories it follows that there are two different types of change: one that occurs within a given system which itself remains unchanged, and one whose occurrence changes the system itself (Watzlawick et al. 1974:10).

An important conclusion can be drawn from the postulates of the Theory of Logical Types, namely that 'going from one level to the next higher entails a shift, a jump, a discontinuity or transformation — in a word, a change — of the greatest theoretical and practical importance, for it provides a way out of a system' (Watzlawick et al. 1974:9,10).

The notion of gradual, evolving change punctuated by periods of transformation is implicit in the stage models of corporate growth (Chandler 1962; Greiner 1972). More recently, these approaches to the overall pattern of change (Starbuck 1971; Leontiades 1980) have been labelled 'metamorphosis' models of change, capturing the idea that organizations go through periods of change that are so dramatic and discontinuous that they undergo a 'change of form'. Miller also makes this distinction between evolutionary and revolutionary change. He argues that revolutionary change involves quantum leaps 'radically transforming many elements of the structure, while change is incremental or evolutionary when it is piecemeal or gradual' (1982:133). Organizations have tradition-bound periods punctuated by non-cumulative revolutionary breaks.

This model of organizational change suggests that the strategy process is concerned with metamorphosis, the change from one form of organization to another. It also suggests that the nature and scope of choices and actions in the metamorphic change process are fundamentally different from those associated with incremental change.

Metaphors that might prove useful in exploring this special type of change are available. Perhaps the most commonly known metamorphic transformation is that of the caterpillar to a butterfly (see Figure 1.4). The curves shown in Figure 1.4 indicate the life-cycles of the caterpillar and butterfly. It is not intended to imply that a predeter-

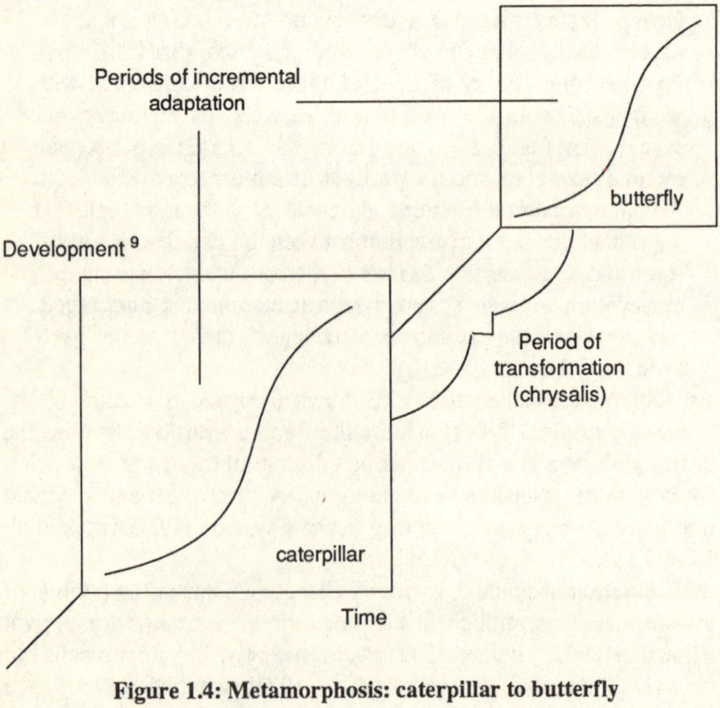

Figure 1.4: Metamorphosis: caterpillar to butterfly

mined life-cycle or pattern of development holds for the general case.[9] In the context of the study of organizations, the term 'development' needs to be defined idiosyncratically. In many cases it would equate with growth, although the notion of increasing complexity is perhaps more consistent with a general theory of the strategy process.

In the metamorphosis of the butterfly, the chrysalis stage involves a dramatic and complex reorganization of the structure and function of the organism. It is not an incremental and predictable progression. Bizarre things happen. Old structures and links break down, and completely new ones are formed. Old functions disappear, and new ones emerge. All this takes place in a cocoon that shrouds the dramatic changes from view. The process of strategic change in the life of a butterfly is not the moment it emerges formed from the cocoon; the strategic change is the strange metamorphosis that takes place in the chrysalis, and of which the butterfly is the final, dramatic manifestation.[10]

Interestingly, Tunstall alludes to this metaphor in describing the strategic change that confronted AT&T following governmental intervention in the US telecommunications industry: 'AT&T will experience a metamorphosis that would challenge the most boastful caterpillar' (1983:25).

In a review of these approaches to the overall pattern of change, Pettigrew points out a number of problems with these attempts to explain organizational change:

> One has to be doubtful about the simple determinism of stages, about implied notions of progressive linear development to higher levels of growth or greater 'maturity' and the reification explicit in statements about the firm behaving, rather than individuals or groups producing an effect which could be labelled as the firm behaving. However a potentially valuable feature of such metamorphosis models of change is the explanatory role played by environmental disturbance in creating change (Pettigrew 1985:445).

The problems of determinism and linearity stem from borrowing too heavily from the biological metaphors from which some of these models have been derived. These models can only be given more explanatory power if the processes that drive the two forms of change and trigger a shift from one form to the other are understood. The metamorphosis analogy is useful for describing the nature of organizational change, but it does not provide the necessary theoretical framework for understanding why such a pattern of change should exist, and it tells us little about the processes.

Although there are conceptual dangers in taking metaphors too far, it would seem useful to examine strategic change in organizations using this biological model. Strategic change in organizations seems to share many characteristics of the biological model: to outsiders the change is often not apparent until it is revealed by some dramatic manifestation — a major acquisition revealing a new strategic direction, the wholesale reorganization of the management team, a fundamental restructuring of the organization. These are the butterflies emerging from the chrysalis of organizational change. This metamorphic model of the strategy process suggests two fundamentally different forms of organizational change. The first involves incremental adaptation to environmental variation. The second involves a transformation, or metamorphosis, in the face of rapid environmental change or discontinuity. It is this metamorphosis, this change in form, which would seem to constitute the essence of strategic change.

Within the organization, the process of change often does seem bizarre and chaotic; understanding and prediction seem to break down. This is often attributed by members lower in the organization to the incompetence or bad motives of top management. But top management may also become disoriented when the established frame of reference fails and a new one has yet to be comprehended. As Berg (1979) observes, the old emotional structure no longer protects organizational members from anxiety; the established way of explaining the world and relating to one another comes into question: things are not the way they were, and it is not clear how they are to be in the future. Berg points out that these periods of rapid and dramatic change are infused with emotion; 'rational' behaviour does not help because its basis — a shared, coherent frame of reference — has failed in the face of changing circumstances.

Hence, the focus of concern when studying the strategy process should be the way that people deal with their complex, uncertain, and ambiguous world; and, more particularly, the mechanisms that managers use when making decisions. Cognitive theory argues that in order to experience and cope with the complex, confusing reality of the environment, individuals form simplified, structured beliefs about the nature of their world.

These belief structures determine the nature of decision-making processes. When cognitive theory is applied to the apparently straightforward view of the strategy process as managerial choices and actions aimed at ensuring that the organization successfully adapts to its environment, the implications are profound (Bower and

Doz 1979:159). The essence of strategy is a fundamental shift in the cognitions of the decision makers. Therefore a better understanding of the strategy process, and more effective management of strategic change, hinges on the development of a theoretical framework that has as central to it the cognitive structures of decision makers. Underlying the two basic forms of change are frames of reference that are shared by the members of the social entity. These have been described variously in the literature as cognitive structures, schemata, cognitive maps, ground rules of social interaction, emotional structures, recipes, shared beliefs, values and attitudes, or basic assumptions, or in the more recent management literature, organizational culture.

The discontinuous and rapid change that takes place during the period of metamorphosis entails a fundamental shift in the collective cognitive structure or frame of reference (see Figure 1.5). This is not an elaboration or development of what was held in the past but a fundamental departure — in Kuhn's (1970) terms, a paradigm shift.

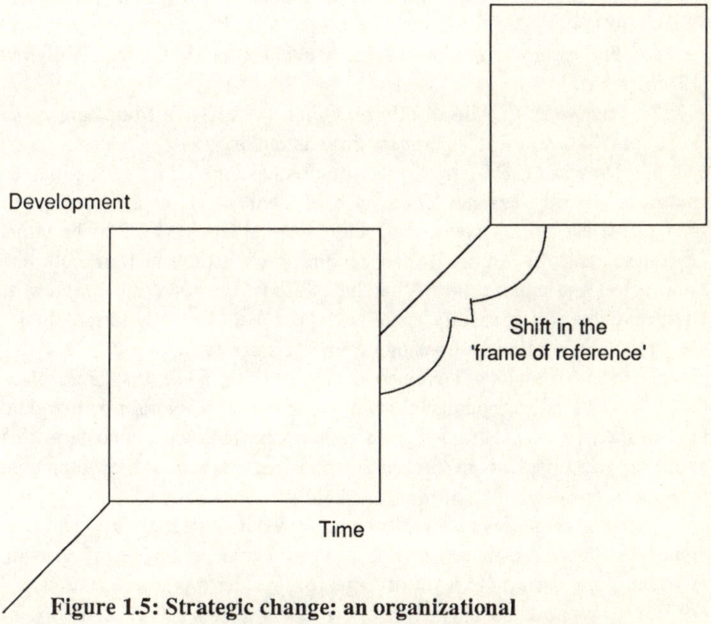

Figure 1.5: Strategic change: an organizational metamorphosis involving a shift in the frame of reference or collective cognitive structure

Cognitive theory provides a theoretical foundation on which the analysis of the BRS data has been based. The new model of the strategy process developed on the basis of the BRS study is presented in the following chapter.

Notes

1. Christensen et al. (1965); Ansoff (1965); Steiner (1969); Andrews (1971); Argenti(1974); Glueck (1976).

2. Simon (1957); March and Simon (1958); Cyert and March (1963); Bower (1970); Pettigrew (1973, 1980); Mintzberg et al. (1976, 1978); Quinn (1980.)

3. Boston Consulting Group (1973); Henderson (1979); Arthur D. Little, Inc. (1974); Royal Dutch Shell (1975); Hofer and Schendel (1978); Porter, (1980); Strategic Planning Associates, Inc. (1981); Rumelt (1974).

4. For example, Deal and Kennedy (1982); Hickman and Silva (1985); Schein (1985).

5. These integrated approaches include Pettigrew (1973, 1977, 1979, 1985); Murray (1979); Butler et al. (1979); Mintzberg et al. (1976, 1979); Horvath and McMillan (1979); Bower and Doz (1979); Quinn (1980); and Fahey (1981).

6. For example, Quinn (1980); Mintzberg et al. (1976); Pettigrew (1986).

7. The work of Allison (1971), Quinn (1980), and Mintzberg et al. (1976) provide empirical support for this contention.

8. Darwin's (1859) theory of evolution has implicit in it the notion of continuous, steady change. This has been challenged by the concept of 'punctuated evolution' proposed by Eldredge and Gould (1972). The terms 'evolution' and 'revolution' have become well established in both the sociological and organizational literature. Eisenstadt, in a critical review of alternative theories of social change points out that 'The very idea of stages suggests a non-continuous transition from one stage to another' (1978:4).

9. The continuous, incremental growth or variation that takes place during periods of environmental stability involves elaboration or marginal modification to an established base. Within the biological metaphor, this could be conceived as an evolving process of growth and development through a life-cycle.

10. Although this case has been presented convincingly by Land who argues that 'there is a ubiquitous and irreversible procession . . . (of) growth, at which point, at a new level of organization, the process repeats itself' (1973:12). Without actually developing the argument, Land's theory of transformation suggests two kinds of change — the first is continuous and gradual, the second is discontinuous, abrupt, and constitutes a major transformation or metamorphosis. Land treats development as being synonymous with growth.

2
A COGNITIVE THEORY OF THE STRATEGY PROCESS

This chapter advances a new model of the strategy process. The model is based on the analysis of the unique empirical study presented in the following chapters. Using assumptions outside the analytic paradigm, the strategy process is conceived in terms of fundamental shifts in the cognitive structures of decision makers.

Cognitive theory provides the theoretical foundation for a metamorphic model that proposes two forms of organizational change: incremental development and metamorphic change. Incremental adaptation involves adjustments to marginal environmental variations. As a result of either external performance pressures or proactively managed strategic change, these stable periods are interrupted by bursts of metamorphic transformation.

The pattern of organizational processes and behaviours associated with the two forms of change are discussed. The model accounts for the role of organizational politics and culture in the strategy.

Theoretical foundations of the metamorphic model

The essence of the strategy process is the managerial choices and actions that allow an organization to adapt successfully to its environment. Contemporary theories describe these choices and actions in terms of analytical and political processes through which strategies are formulated and implemented. These models of the strategy process are based on the analytic paradigm, sharing a set of basic working assumptions derived from the concept of rational choice. Studies of decision making in organizations have found, however, that the analytic paradigm does not describe actual decision-making processes (Beyer 1981:196), and in complex decision situations fails to explain actual decision outcomes (Steinbruner 1976).

An examination of the assumptions implicit in the analytic paradigm suggest the reasons for its failure. In order for the paradigm to hold true the human mind must operate so that decision makers (Steinbruner 1974):

- scan the environment comprehensively for all relevant information;
- calculate outcomes explicitly and integrate values so that overall optimization is achieved; and
- expand problems upward and laterally to include a more general conception of objectives (values) and environmental interactions.

These assumptions are contradicted by cognitive psychology. There is general agreement among cognitive theorists on five basic principles (Steinbruner 1976:103):

- the mind is an inference mechanism that actively imposes order on highly uncertain or ambiguous situations by developing a structure of core beliefs;
- the mind operates in such a way as to keep core beliefs consistent and unchallenged; this constrains the ordering of memory and the processing of new information; the core belief structure is composed of an integrated pattern of beliefs, each held at some level of consistency;
- the human mind is in contact with its environment, the important features of which impose themselves; hence the mind is constrained by reality in important ways;
- in order to be able to cope with the complicated set of interacting beliefs, constrained by internal consistency and external reality, cognitive inference mechanisms work to keep the structure of core beliefs as simple as possible; and
- the mind resists change to its core belief structure because changing one element may require a wholesale shift in the structure if internal consistency is to be maintained.

The diagram in Figure 2.1 is a schematic representation of the cognitive inference mechanism of the mind. Cognitive theory explains why the failure of the analytic paradigm is most apparent in situations involving uncertainty and trade-offs between values. In these complex decisions, the inference mechanism of the mind is faced with a conflict between external reality and the maintenance of an internally consistent core belief structure. The analytic paradigm does not recognize the existence of this core belief structure. It assumes that the mind is not constrained by the need for internal consistency and can readily integrate values, recognize alternative outcomes, and be sensitive to all pertinent information.

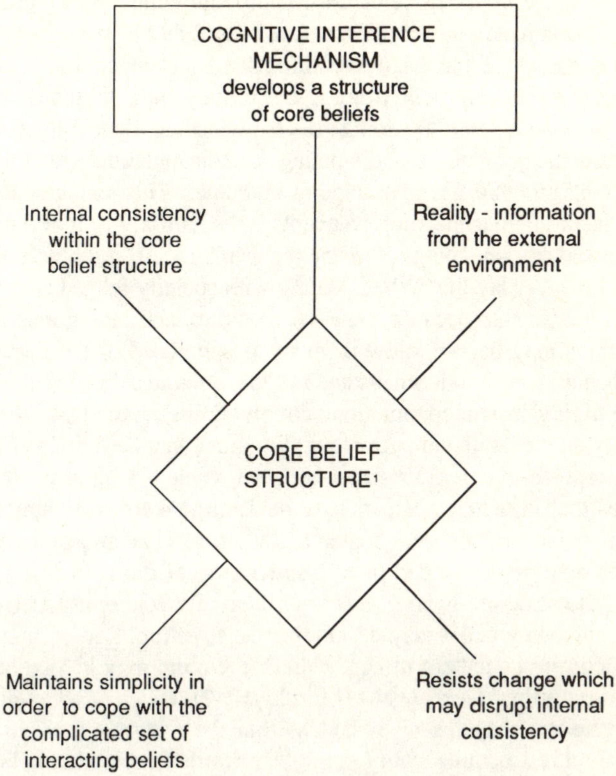

Figure 2.1: The elements of cognitive processes

Cognitive theory argues that the integration of values violates the principle of consistency. In order to integrate values, the mind must recognize and maintain values that are inconsistent. The consistency principle suggests that the mind will respond to the complex situation in one of two ways, depending on the degree of uncertainty or ambiguity. Under conditions of a high degree of uncertainty, the mind will refuse to recognize that a trade-off is required and will ignore the relationship between the values. Under these circumstances the decision maker will remain insensitive to pertinent information rather than confront value inconsistency. When information coming from the environment is sparse or ambiguous, the impact of reality is weakened. Denial by an internally consistent inference mechanism that has been proved by past experience is relatively easy. It is the high degree of uncertainty and ambiguity that allows the decision maker to remain in a state of ignorant bliss.

The nature of the cognitive inference mechanism is such that decision makers constantly struggle to impose unambiguous meaning on events. In so doing they use categorical rather than probabilistic judgments, anticipating specific outcomes rather than assigning probabilities to a range of outcomes. This tendency to impose unambiguous meaning on events is the natural result of built-in, unconsciously operating inference mechanisms that are highly functional in everyday life. When dealing with socially related situations this is reasonable because, however complex and ambiguous these situations may be, we know them to be composed of the decisions and behaviours of individuals and not just random events.

In highly structured situations, involving little uncertainty or ambiguity, however, the impact of reality is such that the mind is forced to recognize the relationships between values. Cognitive theory argues that in these circumstances, decision makers will choose between values rather than make a trade-off. This choice between values may involve a complete restructuring of the core beliefs because the structure is an interacting, internally coherent pattern and changing a key belief may destabilize the structure. Rather than face restructuring its pattern of core beliefs, the mind may invoke 'autistic restructuring' mechanisms (Murphy 1947), which allow reality to be denied in the face of evidence from the external environment. The mind restructures reality rather than restructure its core beliefs.

The diagram in Figure 2.2 is a schematic representation of cognitive decision processes under conditions of uncertainty.

A cognitive theory of the strategy process

Although the important role of cognitive factors in decision making has been recognized for some time (Simon 1957; March and Simon 1958), a crucial theoretical issue remains inadequately treated. Simply assuming that processes that operate at the level of the individual can be applied to organizations, without conceptualizing the way this comes about, introduces the problematic of reification.[2] What meaning do cognitive structures have when applied at the level of organizations?

McCaskey (1982) discusses the notion of collective conceptual maps in terms of the social process of constructing reality and argues that the coherence of a social group depends on developing a common map. This shared view of the world becomes the group's

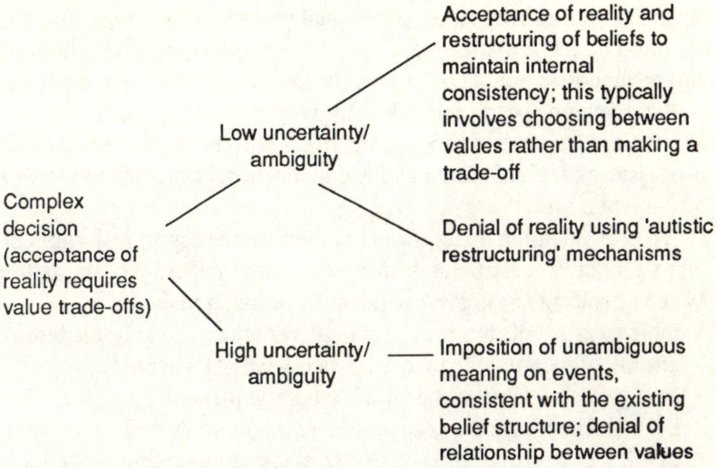

Figure 2.2: Schematic representation of cognitive decision processes under varying conditions of uncertainty

reality and it's slow to change it. McCaskey offers little explanation of how collective maps are formed other than to say that the process involves 'the interaction, perhaps collision, of several subjective readings of the surrounding world'(1982:22).

The notion that a collective set of beliefs about the world and how it functions influences organizational decision making has been incorporated in the strategy literature through the concept of corporate, or organizational, culture.[3] The more completely the cognitive structures of top management, or organizational elite, are shared, the more coherent and pervasive will be the 'organizational culture'. A set of behaviours and organizational processes will act to reinforce the established cognitive structures, and thus re-affirm and reflect the culture of the organization. The organizational processes of selection and socialization, ritual, ceremonies, and language perform the functions of reaffirming values and rewarding conformity.

An intuitive response to the concept of collective cognitive structures is that it is inconsistent with the observed political behaviour that arises from a diversity of individual interests. Even within a collective cognitive structure, however, a genuine diversity of interests may exist that will result in processes and behaviours of an essentially political nature. The relationship between organizational culture and political processes has been the focus of much of Pettigrew's work (1985). He argues that organizational culture can shape, as well as reflect, organizational power relationships, and that a central concept linking political and cultural aspects of continuity and change is legitimacy. Perhaps the most comprehensive treatment of this issue has been undertaken by Pfeffer (1981), who argues that the impact of a diversity of interests will be mediated through processes of legitimization and rationalization in organizations with a coherent culture.

The organizational behaviours and processes associated with collective cognitive structures are essentially cybernetic in nature. When operating in the cybernetic mode decision makers:

- monitor a small number of critical variables and rely on limited information coming from established feedback channels;
- keep goals separate and deal with them sequentially;
- keep problems narrowly focused and fragmented; and
- employ a repertoire of routines, or standard operating procedures, to deal with marginal variations in the environment.

This cybernetic mode of operation, shown schematically in Figure 2.3, is explained by cognitive theory.

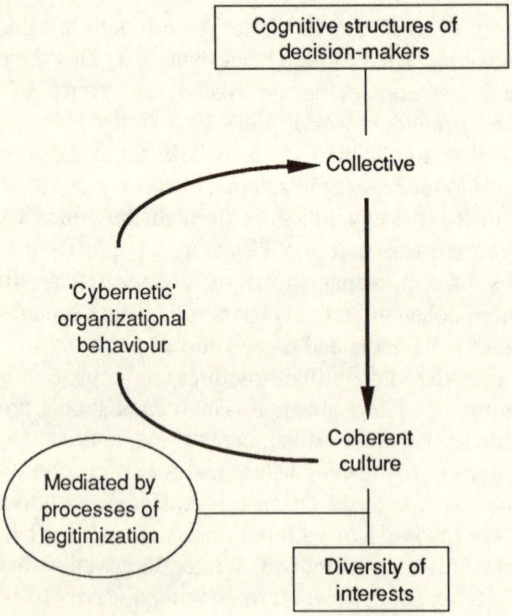

Figure 2.3: The cybernetic mode of organizational behaviour

Cybernetic behaviour is the outcome of organizational processes that reflect and maintain the collective cognitive structure. To be consistent with the principles of cognitive functioning these processes must:

- maintain the internal consistency and simplicity of collective cognitive structures;
- enable an organizationally enacted reality that has a sufficient level of consistency with the externally imposed reality;
- enable change that may disrupt internal consistency to be resisted.

There is considerable evidence that an organization maintains a cybernetic mode of operating long after it fails to be effective in successfully adapting to its environment (Metcalfe 1979). Beyer (1981), in her review article on ideologies and decision making in organizations, draws on a number of sources in making this point. The processes might make the organizational response too simple to deal effectively with the environmental complexity, with a consequent failure in adaptation. McCall (1977) observed that incongruities critical to adaptation may be missed or misinterpreted because they do not fit within the existing collective cognitive structure. By using cybernetic processes to deal with uncertainty and complexity, organizations may be warding off the very things they need to survive (Pondy and Mitroff 1979). Thus, as Weick (1979) has pointed out, organizations need to develop ways of enriching as well as simplifying their environments. This is the paradox of the cybernetic mode of organizational decision making — the essential processes of simplifying in order to cope with complexity and uncertainty filter out the information necessary for survival in changing circumstances.

The processes that build a coherent organizational culture give an organization the ability to act collectively and with certainty,[5] but they have within them the seeds of organizational failure. Cognitive theory explains why these processes fail under certain conditions. Core belief structures are interacting and internally coherent. Partial change is extremely difficult to accommodate because any change that disrupts the internal consistency of the structure will be resisted. In organizations where decision makers have developed collective cognitive structures the scope for change within the constraint of internal consistency is extremely limited.

The limited scope of cybernetic decision processes, and the difficulty of finding the energy to change standard operating procedures, will tend to prevent dramatic shifts in organizational behaviour, even in the face of continuing failure. Incremental adaptation is the inevitable consequence of cybernetic processes based on monitoring a small number of critical variables and a reliance on an established repertoire of responses. Cybernetic processes fail, however, under conditions of 'lethal discontinuity' (Ashby 1952). When environmental uncertainty cannot be controlled, organizational disaggregation (Steinbruner 1976) and the repetition of ineffective standard operating procedures perpetuate the problem. Successful adaptation in the face of environmental discontinuities requires the restructuring of core beliefs and a range of standard operating procedures outside the organization's experience or capability.

The organizational behaviours and processes associated with collective cognitive structures will maintain stability and continuity but can only cause the existing collective cognitive structure to be further shared and refined. They can enhance the coherence of an existing culture and play an important role in incremental, non-strategic change. Metamorphic change, however, requires a transformation of the collective cognitive structure of key decision makers. This can only come about through a different pattern of organizational processes: 'strategic organizational behaviour'.

Cybernetic decision theory (Steinbruner 1976) provides one of the elements of a theory for the metamorphic model of the strategy process. The process of incremental decision making and growth can be explained simply in terms of cybernetic theory. The metamorphic model takes cognitive theory as its point of departure and develops a model of the strategy process which encompasses two fundamental mechanisms:

- A cybernetic process operating within the framework of a collective cognitive structure. This cognitive structure defines desired effects, effective causes, and beliefs about cause-effect relationships. The process is effective in circumstances where the environment can be decomposed into manageable elements and results in incremental routine adaptation to marginal environmental variation.
- A metamorphosis that results in the transformation of the collective cognitive structure of decision makers. This metamorphosis is triggered by certain conditions (environmental discontinuity and external performance demands, or strategically proactive management) and involves a complex strategic decision process comprising analytical, political, and belief based elements. The outcome of a successful strategic decision-making process is a new collective cognitive structure, which provides a framework within which the organization can again operate cybernetically.

The second form of change involves three overlapping phases:

- a breakdown of the collective cognitive structure and the supporting cybernetic behaviour, due to the failure of the structure to meet the demands of changing circumstances;
- a transformation during which a new cognitive structure emerges — the new cognitive structure enacts the organization and its environment in such a way that the demands of the new circumstances are successfully dealt with, and the new structure exists in the minds of the key decision makers but is not shared throughout the organization;
- progressively spreading this new cognitive structure so that it becomes shared throughout the organization — the new collective cognitive structure provides the framework within which the organization can again operate cybernetically.

Breakdown of the collective cognitive structure

The pattern of organizational behaviour associated with strategic change results from the failure of the decision-makers' collective cognitive structure to cope with changing circumstances.

The catalyst for the failure can take two basic forms:

- environmental discontinuity, which makes it impossible to meet external performance demands while operating within the existing collective cognitive structure; and
- strategically proactive management, which challenges the existing collective cognitive structure.

The initial response of decision makers is to search for solutions within the established cognitive structure. Typically, in large organizations, standard operating procedures are activated through the formal planning and control structure. These procedures, which are often prescribed by established policies, are not supported by analysis but are based upon 'scanning of the organization's existing memory' (Mintzberg et al. 1976:255).

This initial response of activating standard decision procedures is essentially cybernetic in nature. The form of this initial response is determined by the power structure of the organization. In organizations with a concentrated power structure, there will be a tendency for each routine to be implemented by decree. Where external performance demands exist, successive failure of the implemented routines will lead to:

- the decision makers eventually questioning their own cognitive structure, and consequently the emergence of a new strategy, or

- the removal of the decision makers, or
- the failure of the organization.

In organizations with dispersed power structures, the activation of standard decision procedures is usually accompanied by the political processes of legitimization and rationalization. When confronted with a policy proposal that is counter to their preferred position, decision makers typically respond by proposing alternative policies from within the collective cognitive structure. The alternatives reflect the perceptions and preferences of the various individuals concerned and are the outcomes of individual decision processes. These processes are themselves cybernetic in nature, conditioned by the need to keep intact the established cognitive structures.

When decision makers have exhausted the repertoire of standard operating procedures, they are faced with a dilemma.[6] The collective cognitive structure then comes into question. This stage of the decision-making process would be considered to constitute formal problem recognition. This analysis suggests that it simply reflects the progressive breakdown of the collective cognitive structure which, until this time, has been guiding managerial action. Being confronted by a dilemma acts as a catalyst for strategic decision making by triggering organizational processes out of the cybernetic mode.

Grinyer and Spender's (1979) concept of a 'feasible solution space' is consistent with this conceptualization. They define a feasible solution space in terms of a 'recipe', or in terms of cognitive theory, a collective cognitive structure. Management is confronted with a dilemma when a solution to a problem cannot be found within the feasible solution space.

The situation is very complex in multilevel organizations with dispersed power structures, as in the case of large, diversified companies. The need for a different strategic focus at the corporate, business, and functional or area level suggests that variations may occur between the cognitive structures of managers at each level. The evidence presented in the following chapters supports this contention. A strategic issue had to be resolved between three levels of management — the Chief Executive, the Group Managing Director, and the Managing Directors of regionally based, autonomous operating companies. The research shows that although a solution may exist within the cognitive structure of one level of management, this solution may lie outside the cognitive structure of another level. The Chief Executive's proposed solution to the strategic issue was outside the company Managing Directors' feasible solution space. The dispersed power structure meant that the implementation of the proposals made by the Chief Executive depended on the active support of the company Managing Directors. If it had not been for the dispersed power and the consequent political behaviour, the Chief Executive's 'solution' would have been imposed on the organization. This solution would have come from the Chief Executive's existing cognitive structure and therefore would not have constituted strategic change within the metamorphic model of strategy.[7] It was the combination of a strategic issue which did not have a solution within the overlap of the feasible solution spaces of the various decision makers, and a dispersed power structure which created a dilemma.

The model of the decision-making process proposed by Mintzberg et al. (1976) includes 'authorization routines', where upward agreement is sought but does not provide for 'approval routines', where downward agreement is required. It is reasonable to expect these 'approval routines' to be an important feature of the strategy process in any organization where power is substantially dispersed vertically.

Strategic dilemmas are the catalysts that trigger the strategic mode of behaviour. The established decision-making structures and processes embody the cognitive and power structures that are at the heart of the dilemma. A solution to the dilemma therefore demands that the nature of the decision-making process changes dramatically.

A key step in the strategy process is to remove the process from the constraints of the formal decision-making structure in which the cybernetic mode of behaviour is anchored; consultants are engaged, task forces, working parties, or some other form of special committees are formed; new planning systems or techniques are introduced.

This step in the strategic decision-making process has been identified by Mintzberg et al. — 'We find evidence for a formal diagnostic step, for example, the creation of an investigating committee or task force' (1976:254). Quinn also points to the importance of establishing information gathering networks outside the formal structure — 'Since people sift signals about threats and opportunities through perceptual screens defined by their own values, careful executives make sure their sensing networks include people who look at the world very differently than do those in the enterprise's dominating culture' (1980:5).

Although these processes are often extremely complex, they tend to more closely approximate a normative analytical mode. The predominantly analytical nature of these activities indicates the key role support staff and consultants can play in the strategy process and the way top management can use these mechanisms to inject the desired degree of analysis — 'factual evaluation is carried out, generally by technocrats, followed by managerial choice by judgment or bargaining' (Mintzberg et al. 1976:258).

In BRS the strategic dilemma resulted in the formation of a working party. The working party was given the brief of examining certain aspects of the issue and developing a range of alternative solutions. In effect this would have involved developing and maintaining a series of contradictory cognitive structures. In the event, the working party went through a self-contained decision process, and in the process developed a single, internally coherent cognitive structure. The result was a set of specific recommendations rather than a range of alternatives. This is consistent with findings of Mintzberg et al. that 'only one solution emerged from the design process . . . the decision makers were confronted with simple sets of proposed courses of action rather than conflicting alternatives' (1976:256). It seems that the cognitive mechanisms of those involved in analytical decision making drag the process back into the cybernetic mode because of the need to develop and maintain simplified, internally consistent cognitive structures.

The emergence of a new cognitive structure

Once the collective cognitive structure has broken down the decision process moves into a new phase. The focus of the process becomes the generation of new solutions. Typically a wide range of alternative solutions will be proposed. The nature of these proposals is largely determined by the past experience and current concerns of the people involved. In organizations with dispersed power structures, the attempt to gain approval to alternative proposals usually involves a dialectical process (Mitroff and Emshoff 1979) of policy formulation, proposal, rejection, and reformulation. Mintzberg et al. (1976) have termed this aspect of the decision-making process a 'failure recycle'. It is through this dialectical process that a coherent strategy gradually emerges. As Mintzberg points out, 'Inherent in it (strategic decision making) are factors causing the decision process to cycle back to earlier phases . . . By cycling within one routine or between two routines, the decision maker gradually comes to comprehend a complex issue' (Mintzberg et al. 1976:265). Hence, the approval process constitutes a comprehension cycle, and it is through this recycling process that new cognitive structures emerge (see Figure 2.4).

The failure recycle that is the key to the comprehension cycle, and hence the formation of new cognitive structures, only occurs be-

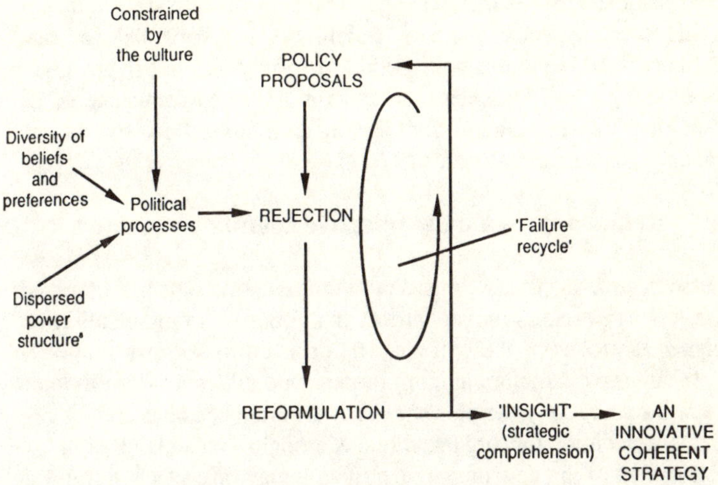

Figure 2.4: The comprehension cycle

cause the dispersed power structure and culturally based processual constraints make possible the expression of the diverse preferences through the rejection of policy proposals. We see here the complex interaction between analytical, political, and belief-based processes which are at the centre of strategic organizational behaviour.

As suggested by Mitroff and Emshoff, 'conflict is needed to ferret out and to challenge the underlying assumptions that each policy makes' (1979:3). Through the approval process, underlying differences are confronted and a coherent, viable strategy emerges.

Mintzberg et al. suggest that political activity 'generally manifests itself in the use of the bargaining routines among those who have some control over choices' (1976:262). What these researchers fail to identify is that this political activity is one of the major 'inherent factors causing the process to cycle back to earlier phases' (1976:265); that is, political activity plays a crucial role in generating the comprehension cycles essential to the effectiveness of the strategy process.

Policy proposals raised during the decision-making process usually have clear and inevitable implications in terms of the structure of the organization, and therefore for the status, power and careers of various individuals and groups. The strategy process is therefore inherently political. Several writers have stressed the functional role that political processes can play in organizations. Burns argues that 'Political action is the necessary instrument for the accomplishment of internal change which to an outsider is the inevitable consequence of a new situation' (1961:266). Salancik and Pfeffer make the same point more forcefully: 'Political power far from being a dirty business, is, in its most naked form, one of the few mechanisms available for aligning an organization with its own reality' (Salancik and Pfeffer 1977:3).

Reforming — a new collective cognitive structure

Once a new, internally consistent cognitive structure has emerged, the strategy process moves into its final phase. Communication becomes the focus of the process. The decision makers who hold the new cognitive structure attempt to persuade others to share the new view. Progressively the new cognitive structure becomes collectively held throughout the organization. Although some elaboration or refinement of the new cognitive structure may take place during this process, its essential core structure remains intact.

It appears that when a fairly simply and internally consistent cognitive structure in the form of a new, coherent strategy that provides a solution to the dilemma emerges, it can be easily 'explained' and communicated. Resistance stemming from differing preferred outcomes then becomes blatantly political, and therefore not legitimate or able to be rationalized within the culture of the organization. Diversity of interests become easier to manage, and to some extent can be left unresolved ('quasi resolution of conflict' [Cyert and March 1963]).

The BRS study shows that once a viable strategy is identified the agreement of top management is fairly easily gained. The central issue becomes that of formally securing the commitment of line management. Dealing with resistance after a new cognitive structure has been clearly articulated is relatively easy, although it often involves a high level of interpersonal tension. Standard managerial actions (transferring and promoting people who are prepared to champion the new cause, changing systems and reward structures to support the new approach, and so on) can be employed.

A metamorphic model of the strategy process

This metamorphic model presents a view of the process of strategic change which is fundamentally different from that implied by normative theories of the strategy process. A schematic representation of the model is shown in Figure 2.5.

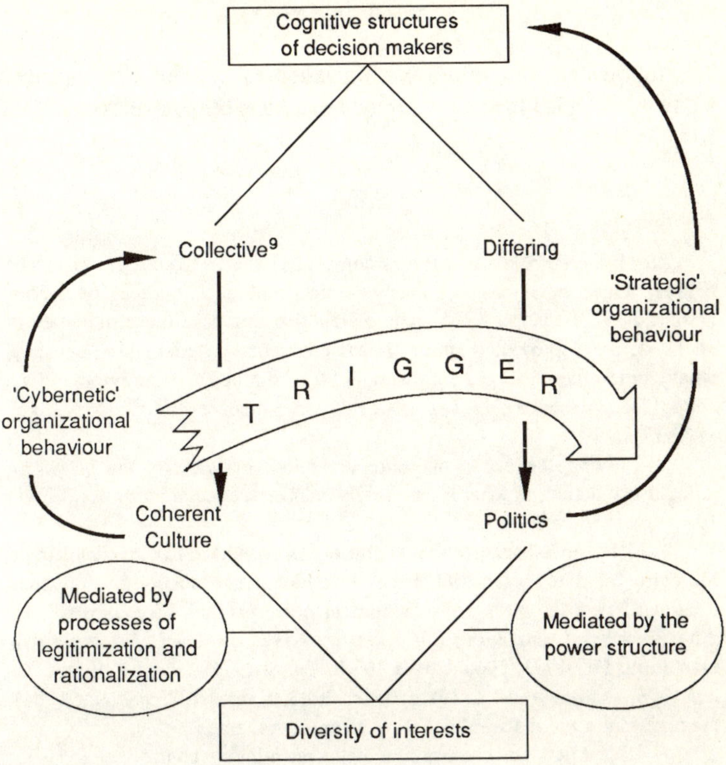

Figure 2.5: Schematic representation of strategic change processes

Using assumptions outside the analytic paradigm, the strategy process is conceived in terms of fundamental shifts in the cognitive structures of decision makers. Cognitive theory provides the theoretical foundation for the model which proposes two forms of organizational change: incremental adaptation and metamorphic change. Incremental development involves adjustments to marginal environmental variations. As a result of either external performance pressures or proactively managed strategic change, these stable periods are interrupted by bursts of metamorphic transformation.

Within the framework of the metamorphic model strategic change involves three basic phases:

- a breakdown of an established collective cognitive structure;
- the emergence of a new cognitive structure; and
- reforming — a new collective cognitive structure.

* * * *

The following chapters present a detailed analysis of the empirical study upon which the metamorphic model has been developed.

Notes

1. The core belief structure is composed of ordered sets, or clusters of beliefs, which have been variously termed schemata, or cognitive maps (Axelrod 1973; Neisser 1976). The beliefs that compose these schemata or cognitive maps provide a more or less coherent way of making sense of what would otherwise be a confusing array of signals. A cognitive map 'is a cognitive representation of the world and ourselves in it' (McCaskey 1982:17).

2. Giving the status of concrete reality, particularly the power of thought and action, to what is essentially an abstract social construct (Simon 1964:1; Silverman 1968:223).

3. The term 'organizational culture' has been used in the management literature for many years but, because it has lacked adequate conceptual treatment, its usefulness as a theoretical construct has been limited. Although varying formulations of the concept have been employed (e.g. Goffman 1959; Fox 1971; Harshbarger 1973; Handy 1976; Silverzweig and Allen 1976; Pettigrew 1977, 1985; Baker 1980; Kanter 1983; Schein 1984), the notion of a set of shared beliefs is a common theme.

4. Cybernetic mechanisms achieve uncertainty control by focusing the decision process on a few incoming variables while eliminating entirely any calculation of probable outcomes. The decision maker is assumed to have a set of 'responses' and decision rules that determine the course of action to take having received information to which he is sensitive; that is, decision rules associate a given action with a given range of 'values' for the critical variables in focus. The 'responses' are action with a given range of 'values' for the critical variables in focus. The 'responses' are action sequences, of the character of a recipe, established by earlier experience. They are programs that accept and adjust to very specific and very limited kinds of information (Steinbruner 1976:66).

This is a very specific, and narrow, use of the term 'cybernetic'. It follows Steinbruner's (1974) usage and does not intend to imply the broader range of processes subsumed under the term 'cybernetic' as used in General Systems Theory (Dell and Goolishian 1981).

5. To the extent that it improves the ability of an organization to act in a unified way, a shared culture makes possible the optimal expression of its distinctive competence (Gagliardi 1986:124).

6. Doubts about the prevailing world usually begin with the appearance of dilemmas. A dilemma is a problem or question that cannot be

solved or answered within the prevailing world view and therefore calls it into question (Ackoff 1981:13).

7. Defined here as a fundamental shift in the cognitions of the decision makers.

8. In organizations with concentrated power structures, e.g. entrepreneurial companies, strategic change may occur without political processes. In these organizations the faithful follow the shifts in the cognitive structure of the leader — they simply believe, or at least conform. The doubters and heretics are ejected.

9. Because of the nature of human cognitive processes and the concomitant organizational cybernetic behaviour, the extent to which cognitive structures are shared tends to be discrete rather than continuous. Collective cognitive structures are reinforcing and self-supporting, but when they fail in the face of an unyielding environment, they fragment. Hence, cognitive structures tend to either be shared to a substantial degree or not shared at all.

3
THE STRATEGIC DEVELOPMENT OF BRITISH ROAD SERVICES

The first twenty-five years of British Road Services' history were characterized by the countervailing influences of imposed government policy and the management philosophy and style of the acquired small hauliers from which BRS was forged. Government policy, driven by a desire to integrate the nation's road transport activities, imposed a highly centralized structure and bureaucratic style on the organization in its formative years. It soon became apparent that this approach was doomed, and the organization drifted towards the more entrepreneurial style of the small haulier.

Changes in government policy subsequently confirmed a more commercial orientation. Although the strategy of national integration was effectively abandoned, a large, professionally managed organization had been created. This organization operated a wide range of road transport activities within a framework of corporate plans and national product policies. A distinctive organizational culture was emerging, but the management philosophy underlying its strategy, structure and management style lacked clarity and was not widely shared among the managers.

During the subsequent decade strategic changes were initiated by successive chief executives. These changes improved the consistency between the strategy, structure, and management style of the organization.

The strategic development of BRS is analysed in terms of a series of eras. These eras constituted a pattern of periods of stability and incremental change within a well-established managerial frame of reference. These eras were interrupted by periods of discontinuity and transformation during which the collective cognitive structure that had guided managerial thought and behaviour failed and came under challenge.

Strategy as a process of organizational transformation

The new strategy that was the focus of the research reported in this book involved a fundamental redefinition of BRS' role in the transport industry. In effect the mission of the organization was redefined. This mission, like the new strategy, was the outcome of the complex interaction of a wide range of influences, including changes in the business environment and the organization.

Throughout the life of the organization a number of developments in its basic elements occurred:

- *Management Population.* The original management population of BRS was almost entirely composed of small hauliers whose businesses had been acquired under the1947 Transport Act. The management philosophy[1] they brought with them was essentially entrepreneurial, and in many ways diametrically opposed to the highly formalized approach implicit in the policy imposed by the government. The population gradually changed to a more professional management group as the acquired hauliers adapted to the more complex, formal organizational environment in which they worked. Further, the acquired hauliers were gradually replaced by new managers, an increasing number of whom were university graduates or from outside the haulage industry.
- *Technology.* The technological base of the organization changed very little. Vehicles became larger, the British motorway system developed, articulated lorries became predominant in long- distance haulage, and materials-handling equipment developed (containerization, forklifts, tail-lifts, etc.). All of these changes had an impact, but the nature of the tasks involved and the work flow changed only to a limited extent. Road haulage and the associated activities remained essentially the same. BRS tended to adopt new equipment or methods in step with the industry, but dramatic technological innovation was not a significant feature of either BRS or the industry.

  Technological changes, however, did change the nature of the market to the extent that distribution patterns and cost structures encouraged the growth of warehousing and distribution services at the expense of traditional ad hoc transport arrangements — road transport tended to become in some ways a more standardized service.

  Computer technology was introduced into BRS for accounting purposes before it was generally adopted by the industry, largely because it was one of the few road transport companies of sufficient size to justify the capital cost involved, and perhaps the only one with a large, standardized accounting system. Information technology was used primarily for accounting/administrative purposes and, until 1979, operational applications were limited to operations research modelling.

- *Structural Configuration.* Given the nature of the business in which BRS was involved, a branch structure was fundamental. Moving goods from one location to another necessitated a network of operating locations across areas where business was undertaken. The branch structure was originally based upon the depots of the 3700 acquired haulage companies. Although the number of branches was continuously and systematically reduced, the basic organizational configuration of a branch structure remained unchanged.

The structural arrangements used to co-ordinate and control the operating branches underwent a number of changes, however, although some form of regional or area structure was always used between the operating branches and the headquarters. There was a trend for the number of intermediate levels between headquarters and the branches to decline over the years. Further, from its inception, the organization moved towards increased decentralization of decision-making authority. Initially this was because the acquired hauliers resisted the highly centralized management structure originally imposed on BRS. Subsequently top management generally encouraged decentralization. The moves to branch profit centres, branch ownership of resources, and legally separate regional companies were critical in this trend to decentralization.

Originally, managerial control was based on bureaucratic mechanisms (operating procedures, policies, a 'Management Manual'), but these were gradually replaced by financial budgeting and reporting procedures. These planning and control systems became increasingly elaborate and were a key feature of the management philosophy of the organization.

Certain of these contextual changes can be traced through the development of the organization from its creation in 1948. BRS went through a series of clearly identifiable periods, with distinctive characteristics associated with each. One of these was the role it played, either by design or by default, in the industry. The organization went through several periods of transformation associated with role transitions (Table 3.1). These transformations were the result of the interaction of numerous influences.

An era of monopoly

British Road Services was formed following the nationalization of the British road transport industry in 1947. Under the Transport Act of that year, ownership of the entire inland transport system, embracing road haulage, the railways, buses, and inland waterways, was vested in the British Transport Commission. The operations of the various transport activities were placed in the hands of subordinate 'executives'. The Road Transport Executive, later split into the Road Passenger Executive and the Road Haulage Executive, controlled the road holdings. Thus, long-distance road haulage was brought under the control of a nationalized monopoly and all companies with a preponderance of operations involving carriage of freight over 40 miles were acquired by the British Transport Commission. These companies formed the basis of BRS.

The initial strategy, structure and management style of BRS were fundamentally linked to government policy and the rationale for nationalization. Under the 1947 Act, the British Transport Commission was charged with providing 'an efficient, adequate, economical and properly integrated system of public inland transport'. The reasons for nationalization advanced by the Labour Party at the time included:

- economies of scale — technological economies could only be achieved by integration and central control;
- elimination of wasteful competition — because fixed costs formed a high proportion of total costs, correct allocation of traffic between various modes of transport could only be achieved through common ownership;
- provision of socially desirable services — central, unified control would ensure services to rural and sparsely populated areas;
- protection of the 'larger national good' — some industries were too strategically important to be left in private ownership (Thompson and Hunter 1973: 10).

Hence, the policy imposed by the government introduced to BRS a management philosophy with a strong orientation towards service to industry and consumers of transport rather than the free-enterprise aspirations of profitability and growth. BRS had an effective operating monopoly over a large sector of the industry, and profit was therefore considered to be neither economically relevant nor ideologically appropriate. Efficiency was conceived and measured purely in terms of costs.

Beyond these formally stated reasons for nationalization, four

Major Periods	Role in the Industry	Key Influences for Changes
1. *Monopoly* (Nationalization) (1947-1953)	BRS created as a highly centralized organization with the objective of integrating and co-ordinating long-distance road transport.	1947 Transport Act (Government intervention in the industry) established a monopoly situation in the long-distance road haulage industry.
2. *Destabilization* (Denationalization) 1953-1956	A period of role transition with the objective of returning the industry to the pre-nationalization situation by disposing of BRS.	1953 Transport Act (Government intervention in the industry) re-established competition in the industry, although some licensing restrictions remained.
3. *Commercial Development* (the Transport Holding Company era) 1956-1968	The remnants from decentralization re-organized and given the mandate of commercial viability within the highly competitive road haulage industry; product-market strategy not artificially constrained and differentiation of activities began, but BRS remained essentially a large general haulier based on a national network of Branches and central co-ordinating structures.	1. Failure of the 1953 Act due to the changing nature of the industry. 2. 1956 Transport Act consolidated the remaining BRS organization. 3. 1962 Transport Act (continued Government intervention) established the Transport Holding Company. 4. The emergence of a distinct BRS culture resulted from the growing professionalization of the acquired hauliers. 5. Major changes in the management population commenced.
4. *Rationalization* (the Len Payne era) 1968-1972	A period of role transition — severe contraction of general haulage activities and questioning of the role as a large general haulier; increasing decentralization and abandoning of natural structures and systems for the co-ordination of general haulage.	1. 1968 Transport Act (continued Government intervention) established the National Freight Corporation. 2. NFC rationalization policies. 3. General haulage profitability crisis in late 1969s. 4. Inherent conflict between BRS haulier culture and centralized structures for co-ordinating activities. 5. Len Payne appointed as BRS Managing Director. 6. Incompatability between major elements of the organization become increasingly apparent.

Table 3.1: An overview of the stategic development of BRS ***(continued)***

Major Periods	Role in the Industry	Key Influences for Changes
5. *Diversification* (the Peter Thompson era) 1972-1976	Formal recognition of the discontinuation of the national general haulier role; rapid diversification into other transport activities and continued decline of general haulage. Confirmation and informal implementation of the role which was emerging during the previous periods. Major role becoming that of 'total transport service' operator.	1. Appointment of a new Group Co-ordinator (Peter Thompson) and the subsequent strategic and structural initiatives. 2. Continuing problems of general haulage profitability. 3. The imposed performance valuation criteria and capital constraints.
6. *General Haulage Dilemma* (the David White era) 1976-1979	A period of role transition. Thompson's strategy implemented but limitations in terms of significant diversification opportunities and a core of profitable general haulage business threaten a major contraction of the organization. Considerable internal conflict while search for a solution to this dilemma proceeds.	1. Peter Thompson promoted to Chief Executive of the NFC, David White appointed BRS Group Co-ordinator. 2. The limitations of Thompson's strategy of diversification and general haulage decline are recognized and the implications of organizational contraction are perceived as unacceptable. 3. The decentralized power structure makes the imposition of policies for accelerated general haulage decline difficult. 4. NFC cash crisis makes change imperative.
7. *Technological Integration* (continuation of the David White era)	Dual role in the industry — a new general haulage strategy emerges alongside the maturing 'total transport service' role. The new strategy is based on information technology which allows BRS to adopt a key integrating role in the haulage industry. The strategy conceived as providing a range of 'service products' to small hauliers. Compatibility between strategy/structure/ control systems with general haulage is also achieved, but co-ordination is accomplished with information technology — each Branch Manager is left autonomous to act on the information provided by the central information system.	The nature of the strategic decision-making process stimulated by the general haulage dilemma and NFC cash crisis resulted in an innovative, viable solution being formed. *This decision-making process was the focus of the research reported in this book*

influences were crucial to the decision to nationalize the road transport industry:

- the highly fragmented and apparently disorganized nature of the industry;
- the continuing losses of the railways (which were also nationalized under the 1947 Act) and, more specifically, the fact that these losses were largely attributed to competition from road transport;
- the relatively successful control of the industry that had been exercised during the war years indicated the strategy implicit in the Act was feasible;
- the government's ideological position on state ownership.

The government's ideological position would have been in itself sufficient, but the other influences made the road transport industry an issue of some priority, and they had an important effect on the way in which the Act was conceived and implemented.

The industry had always been highly fragmented with most operators owning only one or two vehicles, and the owner-driver typifying the long-distance sector of the industry. The industry had therefore been unable to achieve economies of scale. The high level of competition, combined with a lack of management sophistication, resulted in generally low profits. Many owner-drivers (and also the larger operators) quoted rates for return loads that were not economic and had the effect of depressing the overall rate structure of the industry. Standards and service levels in the industry reflected its economics and tended, as a result, to often be unsatisfactory.

These problems were exacerbated by demand also being fragmented, much of the traffic being low in volume and irregular. The systems for the marketing and purchasing of transport capacity were primitive, usually relying on word-of-mouth, past experience, or 'random search'. Clearing houses had established themselves in an attempt to capitalize on this situation but gained a bad reputation because of frequent cases of questionable reliability and honesty.

In many respects, the fragmented haulage industry was a direct response to the market, the owner-driver having the operating flexibility and economic structure to provide the necessary service to the fragmented market. Large users of transport often established their own fleets and further destabilized the industry by back loading at low rates based on marginal costs.

The road/rail competition, the second factor, had led to the earliest political intervention in the industry. The first attempts by government at co-ordination or rationalization were through regulation by means of the 1933 licensing provisions. This resulted in greater stability in the industry but did little to overcome the problems of matching, in total and in geographic distribution, the demand for transport and available capacity.

The third factor derived from more immediate experience. During the Second World War direct control over the industry had been exercised by the Road Haulage Organization. For the first time central control replaced the laissez-faire market. Under the special wartime conditions, this approach proved to be relatively successful. Although the government's state ownership policy was the primary driving force behind the 1947 Act, the success of the wartime approach to running the industry had a major influence on Labour thinking.

The stated objective of the Act, namely an integrated transport policy, including the co-ordination of road and rail services, gave a clear indication of the way the politicians thought the 'problems' of the industry could be overcome: state ownership would provide the framework within which fragmentation and road/rail competition could be dealt with using a central organization to unify and coordinate the industry along the lines developed during the war years.

Hence, in contrast to the highly decentralized arrangement of the industry, the Road Transport Executive set up a three-tier system of management, with a headquarters under which were 9 divisions, 30 districts, 227 groups and some 1000 depots. The tendency to overcentralization has been blamed on the railway dominated viewpoint prevalent within the British Transport Commission (Thomson and Hunter 1973:219), but it is likely that the highly centralized and hierarchical style of management that operated during the war also influenced the early days of the Road Transport Executive.

Government policy was also a strong force. The highly centralized management and operating structure initially established by the Road Transport Executive reflected the ideas of central control and direction of the industry implicit in the rationale for nationalization. This strategy was doomed for two reasons:

- The fragmented nature of the market. The transport market was not significantly altered by the nationalization of the industry and, unlike the wartime circumstances, it was not directly subject to government control or planning.
- The highly centralized and bureaucratic approach to management conflicted strongly with the philosophy and style of the operating management acquired with the hauliers.

The Act required the acquisition of thousands of small operating units. A beginning was made in 1948 by the voluntary transfer under private arrangements of about 400 of the largest road haulage companies. These formed the core of BRS and provided a framework into which the compulsorily acquired firms were integrated.

By 1952, the Road Haulage Executive had managed to acquire over 3700 separate undertakings with 42,000 vehicles, together with 80,000 employees, and amalgamated them into the operating company BRS (Thompson and Hunter 1973: 219). One of the reasons acquisition took three years was that 87 per cent of the transactions required the full legal machinery of compulsory purchase (Reid and Allen 1975:133).

Putting the Act into effect, that is, providing 'an efficient, adequate, economical and properly integrated system of public inland transport', required the amalgamation of thousands of individual operators into a single organization. Perhaps more importantly, it also involved building a management structure and developing operating systems that would provide for the integration and coordination of the supply side of the industry and somehow match this to the still highly fragmented market. From 1948, when the acquisition of private fleets began, the Road Transport Executive faced major problems, most of which reflected the structure of the industry and the characteristics of the acquired firms. The problems of creating the single operating organization were enormous. The highly fragmented and unorganized nature of the industry is described by Walker:

> Road carriers before nationalization were small. Twenty vehicles were owned on the average by the 400 largest undertakings acquired voluntarily and an average of only 10 by the 3300 undertakings condemned to compulsory acquisition. A yard in a back street, an open shed in which to do running repairs, and for duty as an office the front parlour or back kitchen of a neighbouring terrace house satisfied their simple needs. Business records could be kept in the owner's head with the assistance at most of a clerk to keep the books, and the routine to run the 10 to 20 vehicles which made up the fleet of the ordinary haulier demanded little more staff than a girl to type the letters and answer the phone when the owner was out. An embarrassingly large number of hauliers, it appeared, did not own but leased their premises under surprisingly short tenancies, and the lessors (who might, of course, have been the hauliers under another title) were often unable or unwilling to make over the premises on acquisition. British

> Road Services when such an undertaking was to be taken over, might find that they had acquired nothing but vehicles. Traffic was gone, drivers were gone, premises were gone, and the vehicles stood waiting in the street for want of accommodation (Walker 1953:99).

Countervailing influences

When the executive endeavoured to operate the highly centralized structure, they found the entrepreneurs whose firms had been compulsorily acquired, and who were now often managing regional units, were not prepared to conform to the bureaucratic structure. The executive soon learned that essential business contacts could not be maintained and adequate levels of service could not be provided within a rigidly centralized management structure. In 1951 BRS started to move towards decentralization with a two-tier system of division and districts, each division being a self-contained entity of about 1000 vehicles.

BRS announced that 'the operational groups comprised in each District would be small enough to ensure the personal service which had always been so valuable a feature of road haulage' (BTC Annual Report 1951:123).

Hence, from its inception the organization was subject to two distinct and generally countervailing influences:

- politically imposed policy, and
- the characteristics of the industry.

The strategy, structure and patterns of behaviour and practices of the organization were subject to formal policies imposed by political edict, but they were also strongly influenced by the market, technology, the nature of the business, and the management population.

The policy embodied in the nationalization Act and implemented through the Road Transport Executive had clear implications for the organizational characteristics of BRS. The organization was based upon a highly centralized structure and a bureaucratic management style with authority and responsibility clearly defined and attached to roles within the management structure. Communications were predominantly written and a 'Management Manual' set out the correct procedures and practices, with changes in policy communicated by 'Management Advices'. The prescribed role of a manager was essentially that of bureaucrat, to execute the rules and regulations as specified within the formal authority structure. This structure and management style were consistent with the strategy of integrating long-distance inland transport by means of central co-ordination and control. Co-operation within and between the various modes of transport was to replace the previous highly competitive system.

The industry from which the newly established organization was created, however, presented major countervailing forces. First, the management population of the organization was drawn almost exclusively from the previously existing free-enterprise haulage industry. These people inevitably brought into the organization the attitudes, values, and patterns of behaviour that had developed within the small haulier milieu. In spite of the bureaucratic model embodied in the formal policy, the organization introduced a management philosophy and style that could best be described as 'entrepreneurial'. These managers were generally oriented towards an informal, highly decentralized, even fragmented authority structure. They also brought with them well-entrenched beliefs and values about the operation of the industry. Profitability was central to the private haulier, but his time horizon was often relatively short, so that vehicle replacement, servicing of capital, and the maintenance of facilities were typically inadequately provided for in pricing calculations. There was a strong day-to-day operational emphasis, with satisfaction being largely derived from 'beating the opposition', 'doing sharp deals', overcoming crises, and the immediate feedback of short-term results. There was a strong general orientation towards risk, and risk and uncertainty were probably considered to add to the excitement of being a private haulier. This attitude to risk was unwittingly transferred to BRS with the operating practices they employed. The structure and philosophy inherent in the imposed policy and the actual acquired culture of BRS, therefore, were initially diametrically opposed.

The industry also exerted a second major influence on the organization through the characteristics of the market. The highly fragmented demand for transport and the long-established practices that had developed in response, militated against the policy of integration and central co-ordination of the industry. Local knowledge and flexibility were essential to provide the services to which the market was accustomed, and which it still demanded. These qualities were not characteristic of a monolithic bureaucracy.

The outcome of these countervailing forces was a situation intermediate between the imposed government policy and the previously established industry characteristics. The Road Haulage Executive quickly recognized that the centralized, bureaucratic structure was out of step with the management philosophy and style that had been acquired with the private hauliers. The executive also found that the rigidly centralized management structure and bureaucratic control mechanisms could not meet the demands of the fragmented and laissez-faire market. In spite of the high degree of imposed central control, many of the management and operating staff responded to the market as they had done in the past, adopting practices that were familiar rather than those that were in keeping with formal policy. As Thompson and Hunter point out, 'It was expecting a lot for highly independent, individualistic, down-to-earth hauliers to become junior managers in a massive and, at least initially, highly centralized organization like BRS' (1973:26).

The initial resilience of the established culture of the acquired private industry appears to have been greater than the bureaucratic influence the centralized organization brought to bear. The tension between the established culture and the imposed organization was undoubtedly exacerbated by the resistance, and even open hostility (displayed by both the market and the ex-owner managers), to the idea of nationalization and to the concept of a single long-distance road haulage organization. The movement towards decentralization, and the gradual evolution of an organizational culture more akin to that which characterized the industry before nationalization, was inexorable and almost immediate.

> Rather than BRS 'rationalizing' the industry by its presence and competition, as sometimes happened after the formation of a large company in a small-scale industry, the reverse tended to happen. BRS reverted to the customs and practices of the industry and did relatively little to change them . . . If BRS has taken advantage of some of the potential economics of large scale such as those given by the intricate network of regular services, for the most part it has moved determinedly in the other direction. Geographical and functional decentralization, the practice of not engorging acquired companies, and slimming down of the management structure, and the refusal to expand into various sectors of the industry, all help to show an acceptance of the economies of small scale (Thompson and Hunter 1973:256).

By 1951 BRS had started moving towards a decentralized management structure and greater emphasis on local branch autonomy. This suggests that the Road Haulage Executive had recognized the pressures and requirements of the market, and the nature of the culture they had inherited. Indeed, from its inception, in spite of incessant political interference, the organization showed a continuing trend to decentralization, and it is possible that this was because the organization was adapting inevitably to the characteristics of its management population and the market. As a result, the management philosophy and style, and later the structure, became inconsistent with the strategy implicit in the Act, and this combined with the unchanged nature of the market meant that the integration of the industry based upon central co-ordination was doomed.

Over time, however, significant changes did occur as a result of the policy imposed by the government. A large, national road transport organization was created and began to have a significant effect on the way the industry operated. Some rationalization of the industry undoubtedly occurred. Manufacturers and traders who had previously contracted a variety of small hauliers on an ad hoc basis now consolidated their traffic and either operated their own fleets or employed the nationalized haulier. In either case, traffic was consolidated, which allowed the rationalization of long-distance road haulage by combining various small or irregular movements into major traffic flows. BRS was also able to segment the market according to the type of operation involved, customer need, and other factors, and specialized activities such as bulk-liquids transport and contract hire began to develop.

Contract hire, in particular, started to grow in size and status and took on a new role in the industry. Attitudes within the organization towards this activity changed dramatically. The private haulier had generally been against contractual arrangements, as one BRS manager explained: 'Before nationalization a salesman would have been sacked for entering into a contract.' The disappearance of the myriad of small hauliers, however, meant that consignors had to consolidate their traffic and deal with a single organization, and under these circumstances longer-term fixed arrangements at agreed prices became more attractive. Concomitantly, the pressures within BRS towards more formal and predictable management and operating practices encouraged the adoption of contractual arrangements.

The policy of central control also brought about some changes in BRS to the attitudes and operating practices in the traditional general haulage sector. The consolidation and rationalization of the traffic flows allowed BRS to establish a considerable number of regular trunk services,[2] and the policy of central co-ordination encouraged co-operation between the various BRS branches. The policy stressed co-operation rather than competition, and the elaborate bureaucratic control systems reinforced it. The managers of operating branches were expected to assist with the overall co-ordination of transport and to forego any advantage for their own unit for the good of the whole organization. The performance of managers at all levels was judged on compliance with the policies and detailed rules and regulations and, with time, this had a big influence on the behaviour of managers.

These countervailing influences changed the industry. Specialized services were developed to satisfy particular segments of the market, and the management philosophy became similar to that of more sophisticated industries. The management philosophy that emerged was more suited to the larger organizational setting and oriented to longer-term profitability and viability, and to the reduction of uncertainty through contractual agreements. Associated with the 'contract hire culture' was the acceptance of a functional management structure and the constraints of operating within national product and marketing policies.

A distinctive organizational culture was evolving from the countervailing influences. Government policy led to a top management philosophy, the key elements of which were:

- a strategy of nationally co-ordinated long-distance road haulage activities;
- a centralized management and operating structure;
- a bureaucratic style of management based on a rigid hierarchy and control through procedures that standardized operating practices.

Counterpoised against this top management philosophy was the acquired entrepreneurial road haulage culture, which created an operating management philosophy with these features:

- a strategy of short-term, vehicle-by-vehicle profit maximization;
- a highly decentralized operating structure;
- an informal management style based upon direct supervision and reliance upon operators' skill and local knowledge.

Commercial development

In its 1951 election manifesto, the Conservative Party promised to 'free' road transport and, following its return to government the reversal of the nationalization policy was embodied in the 1953 Transport Act. The new Act abandoned the principle of an integrated transport system and purported to embody the principles of competition and decentralization.

The 1953 Act did not recognize, however, that BRS had acquired these principles with the private hauliers who now constituted the management population of the organization. By 1953 BRS had moved far from the 1948 structure; indeed, the culture was much closer to the market orientation of pre-1948 than the politicians realized. Clearly the Conservatives' ideological position on free enterprise and the market economy made denationalization of great political importance, and freeing up entry to the long-distance sector was a substantial change to the industry.

Customers of BRS, however, were not eagerly awaiting the return to free enterprise, as the Conservative government apparently supposed. Many were satisfied with the service they received and found advantages in dealing with an organization with a network of branches and services throughout the country. Further, many BRS managers also appreciated the advantages that came from a national haulage organization. They enjoyed their roles as professional managers in a large, well-known organization, and preferred to stay in its employ rather than reinvest in their own, small-scale operations. Hence, despite the efforts made to divest the assets of BRS, three years after the 1953 Act, the organization remained more or less intact. It was still by far the largest road transport organization in the country. The government was faced with organizing the remnants of BRS, which it attempted to do under the 1956 Transport Act.

By this time, the government acknowledged that BRS would have to keep the trunk and parcels services and some involvement in contract hire. Legislation to this effect resulted in BRS being left with some 16,000 vehicles by the end of 1956, and so it remained by far the largest operator in the industry.

During the 1950s, the competitive position of the railways continued to deteriorate. In a 1960 White Paper, the government agreed that the problems were partly caused by the diverse commitments of the British Transport Commission, and that the railways should be formed into a separate, more manageable unit. The government appointed a special advisory group, the Stedeford Committee, to review the operations of the railways. The findings of this committee resulted in the 1962 Transport Act, which finally ended attempts to integrate the inland transport system under a unified management structure, although integration of road and rail transport continued to be a political issue.

The 1962 Act further decentralized the nationalized transport sector by separating the various transport holdings. The British Transport Commission was dissolved and replaced with five separate boards responsible for Railways, London Transport, Docks, Inland Waterways and Road Transport. The road haulage operations were combined with provincial bus, tourism and sundry manufacturing interests to form the Transport Holding Company (THC).

With the establishment of the Transport Holding Company in 1962, the move towards the decentralization of the management structure of BRS was sanctioned officially as part of the formal policy. The conferring of free-ranging terms of reference appropriate to what was now a state-owned enterprise rather than a nationalized industry enabled the individual companies in the THC to be given full operating responsibility. A further important change in Government policy was the injunction to the THC to perform in financial terms as though it were a private company. Thus two aspects of the management philosophy originally introduced in 1948 by the acquired private hauliers, namely a highly decentralized management structure and a straightforward profit orientation, were now established as formal policy.

Shortly after the establishment of the THC, British Road Services Ltd was restructured because of the need for a high degree of flexibility and freedom to respond to rapidly changing circumstances and to customers' needs:

> With such things in mind, a process of reorganization was set in motion after the Holding Company took over, of which the chief objects were to give greater freedom and responsibility to the local units (Districts) . . . at the same time providing them with their own commercial and financial targets. Under these units there are some 160 branches, with an average of 40 vehicles each; each branch has its own Manager and its own district accounts . . . a first step was . . . to provide British Road Services Ltd with its own Managing Director and to reconstitute the Board (THC Annual Report 1963:17).

The restructuring involved replacing the division/district structure with fourteen districts (including the London Contracts District). The policy of decentralization had given the district and branch managers a considerable degree of autonomy, although a well-developed functional staff had been established at BRS headquarters, with executive directors responsible for finance, engineering, contracts, development, staff, marketing and special duties. The precise titles of the functions varied, but these areas continued to be represented at the headquarters over the years.

The rationalization of general haulage

Political debate about the transport system continued. Shortly after the 1962 Act, the system of regulation of the road haulage industry again came under challenge. In 1963, the Geddes committee was established by the Minister of Transport to examine the system. The committee concluded that the licensing system had failed to achieve the government's objectives, and that the whole system should be abolished. The following year a Labour government was elected, which later published a series of white papers on a national plan for transport. The Geddes committee and white papers culminated in the 1968 Transport Act, which completely changed the licensing and control structure of road haulage.

Through the 1968 Act, Labour politicians continued to seek legislative and regulatory co-ordination of the industry. The Transport Act 1968 once again reorganized the state-owned road-transport industry and continued attempts to integrate road and rail. Under this Act, the Transport Holding Company was replaced by the National Freight Corporation (NFC) as the central management entity of state-owned road transport interests. The management philosophy at this time was revealed by the belligerently self-sufficient and commercial slogan that the NFC adopted as its objective — 'Non-monolithic, non-bureaucratic, and non-subsidized: a commercial public Corporation'. Joining the Road Haulage Association (RHA) was an important symbolic act by BRS. The RHA was made up of private hauliers that had traditionally been hostile to Government interference of any sort. For some time after nationalization, much of the industry considered BRS as a sort of 'lame duck' common carrier, more akin to the railways than to the rest of the road transport industry. By joining the RHA, BRS was aligning itself publicly with the privately owned sector of the industry and, although it had to avoid being seen to take a position on what could be construed as political issues, it began to play a significant role in the road transport lobby.

Throughout BRS, the changing perception of the role of the organization in the industry was symbolized by the increasing emphasis on profit as a measure of efficiency, and perhaps, more importantly, but only later, as a measure of individual performance at all levels in the organization. In a paper presented shortly after the 1967 White Paper, C. W. Quick Smith, chief executive of the Transport Holding Company, argued strongly for the importance of profitability:

> It is profit as a measure of efficiency that is of such significance from an organizational point of view and it is the company structure that best lends itself to breaking activities down into reasonably small self-accounting units so that unprofitable

activities can be identified and remedied or abandoned; so that profitable activities can be developed and expanded; so that successful managers can be recognised and redeployed to make greater use of their potentialities; and so that less successful managers can be transferred to units where demands are commensurate with their capabilities (Quick Smith 1967:155).

Organizationally, the NFC continued the THC's policy of giving the operating companies a high degree of autonomy. This meant that the main groupings were run as separate businesses, and the operating companies within these groups came together only for accounting purposes. In its first annual report the National Freight Corporation quoted the White Paper's philosophy concerning organization:

The role of the NFC Board will be to set the framework within which its various subsidiaries will operate rather than to manage them. Freight transport is not a single, indivisible industry; its numerous parts vary enormously. Flexibility is therefore essential, and the new Board will be given the task of devising the structure most appropriate to its many-sided activities (NFC Annual Report 1969:3).

The 1968 Act officially changed the organization's financial accountability from full commercial profitability to balancing cash flow. The emphasis on profitability, however, was by then well entrenched at all levels of management and had become the established way of judging managers' performance.

During the 1960s, total profit responsibility was given to the operating branches, but the old, centralized control system for traffic operations, under which individual branch managers did not have complete control of their vehicles, still existed. In the words of a BRS branch manager 'In those days, tramping[3] was really tramping — once the driver reported (to the outbased branch), the vehicle was under the control of that branch'. Vehicles and trailers were not owned by the individual operating branches but were on the central asset register, and the branch manager did not have control of the vehicles for which he had profit responsibility. The chief executive of BRS had decided that unprofitable branches should be closed but, as a BRS manager pointed out — 'he could only do that if he knew which branches were unprofitable'. The control of operating assets was fundamental to the concept of branches as profit centres.

The increased autonomy of branch managers was part of a broader change in the notion of the role of branch managers. Comments made by a BRS company director aptly describes the change:

> In those days people were not encouraged to make decisions, any problems went straight up the line and down again. There was a Management Manual — that was a bible, the rules of the game with Management Advices notifying any changes — it took away all power of decision. It was more of a civil service approach, completely uncommercial. This attitude changed: branch managers are encouraged to take the responsibility at the sharp end to run the branch like a business.

When Len Payne joined the organization, initially as finance director and then in 1968 as managing director, he brought with him a management style oriented towards financial control and branch profit responsibility. A policy of rationalization based upon withdrawal from unprofitable general haulage activities[4] was implemented. Payne continued to use the financial reporting system as the key to ensuring management control. He regularly reviewed performance within a framework of meetings with each of the district managers and their accountants. This framework of review meetings was well established in BRS, a system of quarterly review meetings at branch and district level having been established during the time of the British Transport Commission.

Payne's policy of savagely cutting unprofitable general haulage operations led to a new approach to managerial control. Until the late 1960s, BRS was operating general haulage using the control system developed by the British Transport Commission. The operating assets (vehicles, trailers, etc.) were centrally owned, and operations were centrally co-ordinated by way of a variety of operating policies. The manager responsible for implementing Payne's general haulage rationalization policies was John Farrant, then head of operations, who expressed the following view of these operational arrangements:

> The HQ operational control made very little difference to general haulage, there was an emphasis on traffic balancing, priority of loading, traffic exchange points — all this was in the Management Manual which was upgraded and elaborated.
>
> They tried to make more efficient use of the national network of branches but were always behind the private sector on efficiency, productivity, documentation. There was over-control and conformity; but the system was regarded highly. It inevitably cracked up because of rigidity and the complexity of operating the system, all the documents. At the same time there was an emphasis on the bottom line at branch level; before this there was the 'common good' approach, where

branches were judged on their contribution to the overall profit.

The priority of loading had always been fiddled by the selection of traffic and by claiming 'special customer requirements', et cetera. — the traffic control points were completely powerless. Also, there was an unofficial subcharging process — all this led to a breakdown of the co-ordination of the traffic movements. People trusted the Management Manual and the complex charging system. For example, 'mythical mates', 'ghost doubleshunts', all these practices and charges were laid down in the Management Manual. One of the things that caused the trouble, a major influence on the breakdown of the general haulage co-ordination system, was the suitability of the equipment, for example, foodstuffs carried one way and steel on the way back, and so the sheets and ropes had to be changed over. Also the national tariff — the pink sheets — meant that charges could not be recovered; often an overall profit was being made but there was enormous divergence between branches . . . an enormous business in 'monopoly money', of inter branch charges . . . all this led to a gradual movement away from trunking and move into tramping, and that was the death of general haulage; we lost all the advantage of a national organization but had all the disadvantages of inefficiency. Trunking died out over five years.

At the branch level, the feeling was that if that was the attitude of the Transport Holding Company — you get fired if you don't make budget, et cetera — that is, a move from paternalism to a results orientation. At this time, the mid-sixties, there was a massive inflow of new blood because all the original branch managers were coming up for retirement — it was panic stations, lots of trainees were brought in. So the age profile, all over fifty-five, led to the reaction of recruitment which resulted in a change in attitudes, a different relationship between the local management and higher up. The change was with Payne who took a harder line on firing branch managers.

Payne applied the criteria of financial success, and I tried to introduce a new approach to general haulage. I said, with Payne's concurrence, that traffic control points were a dead duck, we should make operators responsible for the fleet they operate, measure the operation on revenue not tonnage or mileage — we tried to educate the operators to think in terms of money. The branches were encouraged to take a 'wheeler-

> dealer' approach on the rates; we cut out priority of loading, introduced Policy Statement No. 7 in which resources and assets were allocated to the individual branches. A change in the philosophy, we ignored the interdependence of branches — in practice the interdependence had gone anyway, it was just a formal recognition. (Interview with a BRS company managing director.)

It seemed that almost a quarter of a century after its establishment, the organizational culture had drifted back to the industry origins from which it had been forged. The strategy of national co-ordination of general haulage through a centralized operating structure supported by a bureaucratic control system had been abandoned. Local operating unit autonomy had been re-established and, with it, a control system based on financial performance. The general haulage industry had returned to its pre-nationalized fragmented and entrepreneurially driven state.

Behind this obvious reversion, however, was the creation of an organization unique in the British road transport industry. Not only was it incomparably larger and had a national network of branches, it operated a diverse range of road transport related activities and was managed professionally by a group of people who were oriented to achieving agreed financial goals within a framework of corporate plans and national product policies.

A distinctive organizational culture had evolved, but it lacked robustness and coherence. The management philosophy underlying the key aspects of its strategy, structure, and style lacked clarity and definition and was still not shared by a significant proportion of managers.

Following the election of a Conservative government in 1970, the industry was again faced with uncertainty, resulting from the Conservative policy to disengage from state ownership. In the event, for the first time since 1947, a change of government did not result in legislation requiring reorganization of the nationalized road transport industry.

The era of product-market diversification

In 1972, Peter Thompson was recruited to fill the position of group co-ordinator of BRS, reporting to the chairman of the National Freight Corporation. Shortly after his appointment, the BRS group was restructured into eight legally separate, regional companies operating autonomously within agreed financial constraints. The original structure of BRS had been highly centralized and hierarchical but had, over time, gradually become more decentralized. The 1972 reorganization was the natural culmination of this trend.

A central feature of the restructuring was the creation of a Group Policy Committee (GPC) as the key co-ordination and policy mechanism of the group. The GPC, under the chairmanship of Peter Thompson as group co-ordinator, was composed of the regional company managing directors and the group functional controllers. The role of the GPC was central, because virtually all major decisions were either made, or were at least ratified, by the committee.

The second major aspect of the 1972 changes was a fundamental change in the product-market strategy of BRS. Until this change, the role of BRS in the road transport industry had been the same as that established in 1948, that is, primarily a long-distance road haulier involved in what is known as 'general haulage'. The new strategy involved the diversification of the group's activities away from the traditional activity as fast as the growth of new activities such as contract hire, truck rental, distribution and warehousing would allow. Some of these activities were not new, but previously they were not treated as separate products. The new product-market strategy was the result of an evaluation instigated by Peter Thompson who concluded that BRS suffered inherent disadvantages in general haulage in relation to smaller hauliers because of their lower overheads and labour flexibility.

The changes introduced by Peter Thompson brought about to a large extent the alignment of the strategy and structure of the organization. During the 1960s, the operating branches had been given profit-centre status, and this had discouraged the interbranch co-operation and co-ordination essential to a national, integrated general haulage operation. The nature of the new activities was such that, although they were marketed as national products, the operational management could remain at the local level. Branch managers were no longer subject to the conflicting expectations of maximizing branch profits while optimizing traffic movements between branches, as had been the case with the traditional general haulage strategy. The general haulage activity remained 'unaligned', but as the new strategy assumed the continued decline of general haulage, this too, was consistent.

In 1976, the group co-ordinator was promoted to the position of chief executive of the NFC, and was succeeded by David White, one of the regional company managing directors. The group co-ordinator had reported directly to the chairman of the NFC and his promotion to chief executive effectively created another level in the hierarchy. David White's role (the title group co-ordinator was subsequently changed to group managing director) was intermediate between the regional company managing directors and the chief executive, who continued to exercise a direct influence over BRS strategy.

As group managing director, White saw strong product management in the group as a key success factor for BRS. The regional company managing directors' view was that product management should be limited to the companies, with only essential functions being represented at the group level. This attitude was rather difficult to justify, however, given that the strategy of diversification was based on national products. The diversification activities were all developed using national policies on pricing, advertising, corporate image and the country-wide servicing of customers. Although national policy co-ordination was the function and responsibility of the Group Policy Committee, there remained an obvious need for national product management — the development and co-ordination of national product policies across the regional companies required group product management.

The managing directors resented the influence exerted by the group and jealously guarded their right to run their own companies. Regional company autonomy was much talked about and constantly used to counter influence attempts by group managers. The managing directors' perception that under the new group managing director, BRS was tending towards increased centralization was a function of both the changing balance of power and the channels through which power was exerted.

The general haulage dilemma

In 1977, five years after the introduction of the new management structure and product-market strategy, BRS's rapidly declining general haulage fleet was still losing money. It was becoming clear to BRS top management that the rate at which new activities could continue to grow was insufficient to compensate for the planned decline in general haulage. Cash constraints imposed by the government had resulted in increasing pressure on profit and capital availability, and this was manifested in a number of ways, including pressure for the accelerated decline of general haulage. The rate of general haulage decline became a fundamental strategic disagreement between Peter Thompson and BRS management. The disagreement stemmed from the following two — basically different —

views: Thompson, as chief executive of the NFC, believed that selective reduction of the activity would reveal a profitable core of business; BRS argued that if general haulage was reduced at a rate faster than new products grew, overall financial performance would decline because organizational contraction would jeopardize the group's key strength, a national network of marketing and operating locations.

In many ways, a more fundamental structural issue than the trend to centralization was the problem of the incompatibility between the structure and general haulage. This problem was clearly recognized within BRS and was articulated openly when the general haulage dilemma was first confronted. The most obvious solutions involved changing the structure to make it compatible with the requirements of general haulage. The difficulty was that structural changes would have involved co-ordination and control across regional company boundaries and this was unacceptable to the managing directors. Indeed, BRS's previous experience indicated that such arrangements would not necessarily result in satisfactory performance in general haulage.

Each of the regional company managing directors held certain views about the management of general haulage, but very few of them shared Thompson's belief that the activity could be pared down to a profitable core. They did, however, share the perception that the continued decline of the activity would result in a significant organizational contraction. Organizational shrinkage could have been considered by the NFC as an unfortunate expedient necessary to achieve their financial objectives, but to the management of BRS it was a direct threat to their careers.

This complex array of perceptions and preferences, within the constraints of NFC cash and general haulage profits, created a dilemma. After five years, the 1972 strategy had run its course, and a new strategic initiative that satisfied the conflicting demands of improved financial performance and the avoidance of organizational contraction had to be found. The general haulage dilemma resulted in a situation where the chief executive was insisting that the group managing director apply certain general haulage policies within the BRS group, and the managing directors were refusing to accept these policies. This could not continue — some resolution had to be found, but this resolution was dependent upon a solution to the problems underlying the dilemma. A general haulage strategy had to be developed that would significantly improve the profitability of the activity with limited capital investment, and be compatible with the decentralized management structure. The complex sequence of events that had led to this situation is summarized in Figure 3.1.

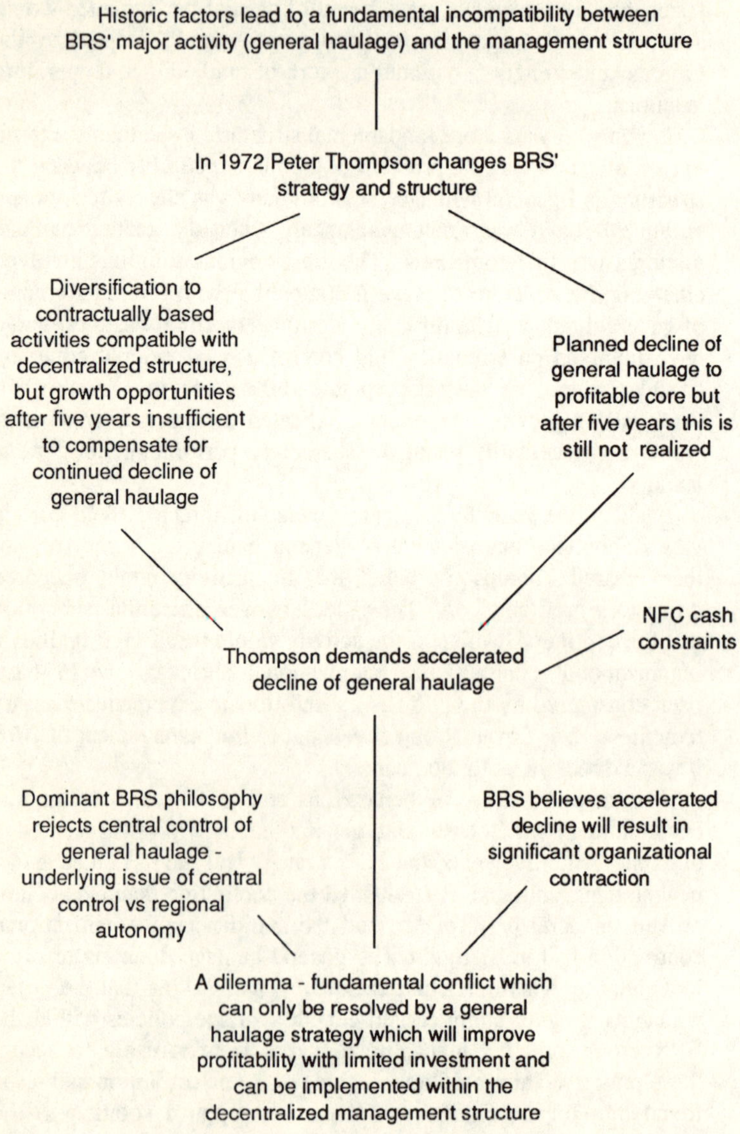

Figure 3.1: An overview of events leading to the general haulage dilemma

The emergence of a new general haulage strategy

The incompatibility between the strategy and structure within environmental and contextual pressures and constraints generated a dilemma which acted as a catalyst for the strategic decision-making process.

The decision-making process initially took the form of a series of policy proposals that could be summarized in this way:

Proposer	**Policies**
Chief Executive	Accelerated decline of general haulage
Group Managing Director	Product management of general haulage at Group level
Company Managing Directors	Management action at the individual company level

David White, as group managing director, was, in effect, the role of mediator between two fundamentally different views of the general haulage problem and its resolution. To act as mediator in this strategic issue he had to rely on the formal channels available to him, namely the planning and control system links with the chief executive, Peter Thompson, and the managing directors, and the Group Policy Committee link with the managing directors as a group. A great deal of informal activity was associated with the decision-making process, but ultimately the outcomes of these activities were reflected within the formal decision-making structure.

Over a period of six months, White arranged Group Policy Committee agreement to an inter-company working party. This was crucial in the decision-making process because it moved the general haulage dilemma out of the formal decision-making structure and brought the processes of analysis and evaluation under group control. The designated reporting relationship of the working party was through the GPC, but it was managed in such a way that it was isolated from the GPC. The managing directors received some information from their representatives on the working party, but the amount of information varied and was limited in all cases. Control of the working party was exercised by the group planning managers who assumed a managerial function as well as making a significant contribution to the analytical process.

While the work of the general haulage working party proceeded, the existing 1972 strategy provided the basis for the various elements of the 1978 planning cycle. The performance of general haulage continued to be a major source of criticism in review meetings with the NFC. The formation of the working party reflected BRS's belief that it was possible to develop new strategic alternatives that offered the promise of long-term revitalization of general haulage. Apparently, Thompson, however, did not believe that revitalization of general haulage was viable, or even desirable, and continued to press White to improve the profitability of the remaining general haulage business through policies of aggressive pricing and the severing of loss-making business.

Early in 1979, the group planning managers included a new concept in the strategic review document. The concept of service products rather than resource products, was crucial to the formulation of the new strategy. The new strategy was being forged out of a basic realization that in some way general haulage had to be maintained at a minimum level if organizational shrinkage were to be avoided. The new strategy had to assure the revitalization of general haulage but in a way complementary with the strategy of diversification and the structure of autonomous operating units. The strategy had also to involve low risk and not be cash demanding. The concept of service products, to a large extent, met these criteria. A large volume of revenue could be generated at fairly assured, if small, margins, and the existing fleet could be operated at breakeven at worst.

Six months after the working party reported its findings to the Group Policy Committee, the group managing director was still struggling to obtain agreement to a solution of the general haulage dilemma. The structure of the organization was such that the group managing director was forced to move back and forth between the Group Policy Committee and the NFC, in an attempt to find a solution that was acceptable to both parties. Thompson was tending to stick to his 1972 strategy and to treat any new initiatives from the group as variations on this theme. Meanwhile, the managing directors were resisting any suggestions that smacked of central control or in any way threatened regional company autonomy.

It appeared, however, that a strategy was crystallizing in the group managing director's mind, the key being a computerized information system that would allow central control and co-ordination without threatening the autonomy of the company managing directors. Activities could be managed and operated on a local branch basis with the information system providing co-ordination between the operating units. Central management and control could therefore be kept to a minimum, and co-ordination could be achieved without the imposition of a centralized management structure.

With the chief executive's assent and the tacit approval of the Group Policy Committee, the group managing director proceeded to implement the strategy. The 1980 NFC Annual Report reflected the changing strategic stance of the BRS:

> BRS offers a total physical distribution service, provides a wide range of freight transport and warehousing, and specializes in contract hire and truck and trailer rental. It has been moving increasingly into services to the transport industry, such as BRS Rescue and in 1980 extended these to include Datafreight. This is a computer-based information system designed to facilitate and reduce empty running, thus making a substantial contribution to fuel-saving (NFC Annual Report 1980:6).

The Annual Report might have added that this computer-based information system, in conjunction with a national network of operating branches and transport management expertise, offered BRS the potential to play an integrating role in the industry — the role originally designated when the organization was established under the Transport Act of 1947.

Shifting managerial 'frames of reference'

The pattern of strategic development observed in BRS is consistent with the metamorphic model of the strategy process presented in the previous chapter. BRS experienced a series of stable periods, or eras, during which change took the form of incremental adaptation to marginal environmental variations. These stable periods were interrupted by periods of dramatic change, which appear to have been unstable and difficult.

As BRS moved from one era to the next, and underwent a series of transformations, the management philosophy shifted. This shift in management philosophy was reflected in the changing strategy, structure, and management style of the organization. The frame of reference, or collective cognitive structure, with which management viewed the world changed fundamentally — the way they perceived the industry, the organization, and the relationship between the two, underwent a series of transformations (Figure 3.2).

The first period of transformation resulted from the clash of the countervailing influences of imposed government policy and the management philosophy and style of the acquired small hauliers from which BRS was forged. This basically unstable situation had

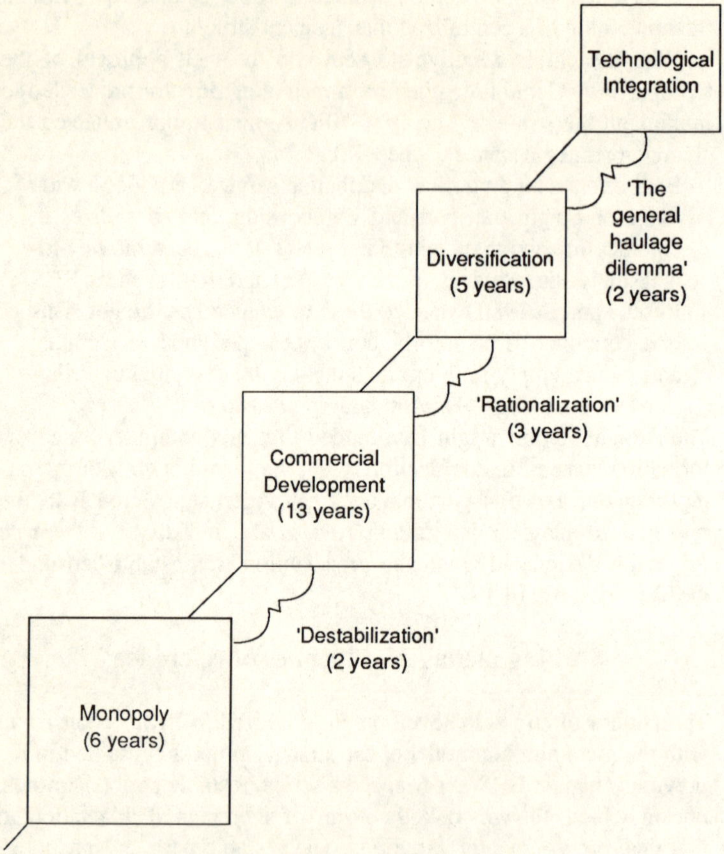

Figure 3.2: Shifts in the managerial frame of reference

been created by the 1947 Transport Act which established the 'monopoly era'. In effect government policy attempted to impose a cognitive structure on a group of managers who already had a strongly established collective cognitive structure. With the formation of the Transport Holding Company, greater consistency between government policy and the management philosophy was established. A coherent culture based upon a collective cognitive structure was beginning to emerge.

The second period of dramatic change followed the appointment of a new chief executive who imposed a particular view of the organization's strategy. This unstable period paved the way for the era of diversification during which internal inconsistencies were addressed and to a large extent rectified. The organization was again beginning to coalesce around a collective cognitive structure.

Limited data are available on the actual process of change during these two periods of transformation. The third period, 'the general haulage dilemma', was the object of the extensive research that forms the empirical base of the book. The next chapter examines, in detail, the period immediately preceding this third transformation — the 'era of diversification' during which a new collective cognitive structure was established. The remaining chapters examine the period of transformation in detail and analyse the processes involved.

Notes

1. The term 'management philosophy' is used in a colloquial sense to indicate the beliefs and values held about business and managerial issues. The term is consistent with the more technical term 'cognitive structures' used elsewhere.

2. Trunk services, or 'trunking', is a mode of road transport in which vehicles are dedicated to particular routes and usually operate on the basis of a regular schedule.

3. Tramping is the most basic mode of road transport. Vehicle routing and scheduling are essentially determined by the availability and destination of traffic. In effect the vehicle's destination is determined by the traffic available, so that the driver goes from place to place without knowing what the next load or destination will be.

4. 'General haulage' is a generic term applied to non-specialized road transport activities, including tramping, trunking, and round-trip journeys. More specialized services, such as contract hire, distribution, truck rental, warehousing and parcels delivery are usually referred to specifically, and would not fall within the term 'general haulage'.

4
THE ERA OF DIVERSIFICATION

Major changes occurred within BRS between the years 1972 and 1976 following the appointment of a new chief executive from outside the organization. The decentralized structure was reinforced by the formation of regional companies, each with its own board and managing director. A new style of management was introduced by way of mechanisms such as 'bottom-up' corporate planning and a Group Policy Committee. A new product-market strategy was articulated that explicitly favoured diversification towards a broad range of transport services at the expense of the traditional general haulage activity.

These changes brought an internal consistency to the organization's strategy, structure, and management style that had previously not existed. Management action was finally forging a coherent organizational culture from the wide range of factors that had influenced the organization since its inception. At the core of the culture was a collective cognitive structure — a set of beliefs and values that were shared predominantly by the managers of BRS. This collective cognitive structure was reflected in, and reaffirmed by, a fabric of behaviour patterns and artefacts. These behaviour patterns and artefacts have been described in terms of the BRS's strategy, structure and systems, and management style.

The formation of regional company structure

In January 1972, a new co-ordinator was appointed to the BRS group. The incumbent, Peter Thompson, had previously held senior management positions in the transport activities of a number of major British corporations. After a six-month period of evaluation, he announced that the organization would be restructured from ten districts into seven regional companies.

The changes introduced by Thompson were within the framework established by the NFC, and clearly emphasized the need for a high degree of autonomy for the operating units. The appointment of a 'Group Co-ordinator' rather than a managing director prepared the way for the formation of the BRS regional companies. The NFC management philosophy regarding this organizational issue was presented clearly in the 1971 Annual Report:

> The NFC remains convinced that a company based structure, with the responsibility placed firmly on the managing director of each company and with each company clearly defined as a profit centre, best suits road transport and the business of the Corporation. Economy of scale and size, valuable in such areas as finance, investment, buying, large scale contract negotiations, remain suspect at the operating level in road transport, where smaller units frequently show levels of flexibility, adaptability, initiative, selectivity and profit, denied to larger, more general, more 'commodity dispensing' companies. The change from the conglomerate nature of its predecessor (the Transport Holding Company) to an intensively freight orientated organization, marketing total distribution and intermodal packages, requires however, at least in the short term, and if a concerted initiative is to be taken, rather more central co-ordination than that which suited the THC. Our aim must be to get the best of both worlds.
>
> The most significant change, however, was the appointment of Group Co-ordinators, each of whom was given responsibility for overseeing the profit, performance and health of a group of companies. The Co-ordinator does not encroach on the day-to-day affairs of his companies or seek to inhibit the company managing directors. His role is rather to set, stimulate and monitor the pace for his companies, keeping their operational, commercial and personnel requirements in perspective and priority, co-ordinating their needs with the centre, and providing a direct link with the Chairman in his capacity as Chief Executive of the corporation (NFC Annual Report 1971:32, 33).

The restructuring was accompanied by a substantial change in BRS senior management. The impact of the reorganization on the senior management of BRS can be judged from the organization charts in Figure 4.1.

Of the ten district managers (London Contracts District had been merged with the South Eastern District in 1971 in a separate move),

1972 Organization

BRS Group Co-ordinator P. A. Thompson

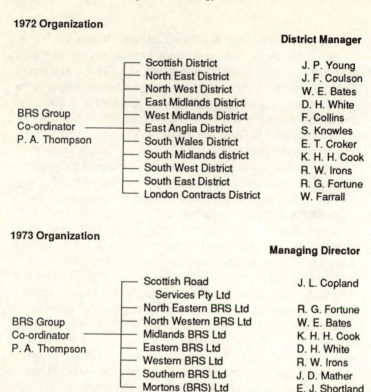

	District Manager
Scottish District	J. P. Young
North East District	J. F. Coulson
North West District	W. E. Bates
East Midlands District	D. H. White
West Midlands District	F. Collins
East Anglia District	S. Knowles
South Wales District	E. T. Croker
South Midlands district	K. H. H. Cook
South West District	R. W. Irons
South East District	R. G. Fortune
London Contracts District	W. Farrall

1973 Organization

BRS Group Co-ordinator P. A. Thompson

	Managing Director
Scottish Road Services Pty Ltd	J. L. Copland
North Eastern BRS Ltd	R. G. Fortune
North Western BRS Ltd	W. E. Bates
Midlands BRS Ltd	K. H. H. Cook
Eastern BRS Ltd	D. H. White
Western BRS Ltd	R. W. Irons
Southern BRS Ltd	J. D. Mather
Mortons (BRS) Ltd	E. J. Shortland

Figure 4.1 Senior management changes in BRS 1972-73

only five became regional company managing directors. Several of the older district managers were made redundant or retired. The general pattern was that the younger district managers were selected as managing directors:

> Peter Thompson brought about a revolution in BRS; he kicked out all the general haulage men and created a young team; he kept Wilf Bates because of the incestuous nature of the North West, and Wilf was doing a good job in general haulage. Wilf Bates was the odd man out, he had a general haulage background. There was no obvious successor to Wilf, and the district's profits were very strong, so Thompson decided to keep the North Western profits going while the other companies went through the transition. (Interview with a BRS company managing director.)

The situation was not quite as clear cut, however, as this interview indicates. A number of the managing directors had spent most, if not all, of their working lives in the general haulage side of the transport industry.

Major changes were also effected at group management level, with the senior staff being reduced from nine to four members (Figure 4.2). The reduction in BRS headquarters senior staff was powerfully symbolic of the philosophy and style of the new group co-ordinator of the BRS group.

1971 (December)

Group Managing Director	L. S. Payne
Directors	W. E. Macve A. J. Wright T. R. V. Bolland
Assistant Managing Directors	W. C. Webster J. D. Mather
Director Contracts	R. V. Cole
Executive Director - Finance	J. K. Watson
Executive Director - Engineering	W. V. Batstone
Executive Director - Development	C. A. F. Gotteri
Head of Marketing	K. P. H. Fielding
Head of Operations	J. Farrant
Head of Staff	G. F. Mee

1973 (January)

Group Co-ordinator	P. A. Thompson
Services Controller	R. V. Cole
Finance Controller	J. K. Watson
Head of Marketing	K. P. H. Fielding
Head of Personnel	G. F. Mee

Figure 4.2 BRS Group management changes during 1972

Changes to the planning and control system

The restructuring into regional companies and the slimming down of headquarters management were only two aspects of the wide ranging changes introduced by Thompson. In terms of direct impact on the behaviour of the senior management group, and therefore the management style of BRS, significant changes were also effected through the planning and control system.

Basic financial controls such as the reporting of revenues and costs, credit control, annual budgets, and the central control of capital and cash had been fundamental elements of the BRS system. The actual form of the financial system was modified as the organization underwent change.

Changes in the way the financial reporting system was used as a management control mechanism, however, were more important than the changes in its form. As the organization became more decentralized, the role of 'bureaucratic' devices, such as the 'Management Manual' as a mechanism for ensuring uniformity and co-ordination between the organizational units, gradually diminished.

Under the old structure, the divisional managers were extremely powerful and gained a high degree of autonomy as the originally all-powerful central control waned. Although capital and cash were centrally controlled, the profit and cash positions of the divisions were generally such that they could provide replacement and development capital on a self-financing basis. This financial self-sufficiency gave the divisions a great deal of independence. The locus of power had shifted from headquarters to the divisions, which used the financial reporting system, in the form of branch 'Trading Returns', to monitor and control the branch managers. Centralization of the accounting system at this organizational level resulted in divisional management being in the position of 'controlling the control system'. Without accounting staff support, the branch managers were not generally in a position to challenge, or manipulate, the system that was being applied to them. When the divisions were disbanded in 1963, the District managers took on this powerful role within the control system.

Hence, although the structure of the financial reporting system remained essentially the same, its use as an instrument of managerial decision making and control changed. As the managerial and operational autonomy of the organizational subunits continued to grow, the need for control by the centre by way of the financial reporting system increased:

> Gradually the control from the top loosened, but not significantly until 1964 with the establishment of the Transport Holding Company, the division/district reorganization, and the appointment of a new managing director. The spirit changed when the new managing director, Len Payne came . . . the branch relationship with the Districts revolved around Trading Returns. Len Payne tidied up the paperwork, two teams went

> to all the branches to examine the situation regarding control information — the OPS 20 vehicle control sheet was introduced to plan the utilization of resources and also served the purpose of recording vehicle earnings, etc. Each week a summary of operations, income only, and OPS 24 included actual labour costs and estimates of other costs, so every Monday the branch managers had revenue and mileage figures for the previous week and on Thursday estimated costs which gave a trading out-turn figure. (Interview, BRS company finance director.)

Len Payne, who had originally joined the organization as finance director, brought a style to BRS that emphasized management through financial control. He also introduced an important change to the financial control system at the head office level of the organization by instituting corporate planning. In doing that, Len Payne implemented a policy that was being applied throughout the NFC, and throughout most of the nationalized industries:

> Since the late 1960s some UK nationalized industries have undertaken corporate planning as a means of exercising control. In the early 1970s, the UK government, on the advice from one of its select committees, required that all UK nationalized industries undertake corporate planning. This requirement has been reinforced through the White Paper in 1978, in which the government reiterated that it saw corporate planning as a major instrument of control both for the nationalized industries themselves, and also for government in its relationships with the industries (Harris and Davies 1981:15).

The 1971 NFC Annual Report made specific reference to corporate planning under the heading Planning for Profit:

> During 1971 attention has been concentrated on key issues, outlined in a document called 'Planning for Profit' approved by the Board and issued by the Chairman in February 1971. It aimed at providing 'a comprehensive corporate framework of manoeuvre' designed to make a 'forceful impact on current urgent challenges' to 'sustain the momentum of initiative'. It laid down the basis on which 1971 'profit improvement and cost reduction were to be firmly planned and positively pursued. Expansion by volume must give way to expansion by profit and the more effective utilization of essential resources'. The Corporation's approach must be 'to improve substantially on budgeted profitability in 1971'.

> In setting the stage the Board decided that 'the purpose of the NFC HQ was to define the parameters, define targets and monitor progress — Company Managing Directors and their senior colleagues would then carry the essential responsibilities for operating efficiently and profitably against the objective set and agreed' (NFC Annual Report 1971:29).

The first report of the Select Committee on Nationalized Industries (1973:15) had recommended that the system of planning devised for the British Steel Corporation become the model to be used by all nationalized industries for corporate planning. The British Steel Corporate system, later called the Benson Brochure model, suggested an annual three-tier system of planning and specified the information and proforma to be used for each plan. The suggested three-tier system of planning is shown in Figure 4.3.

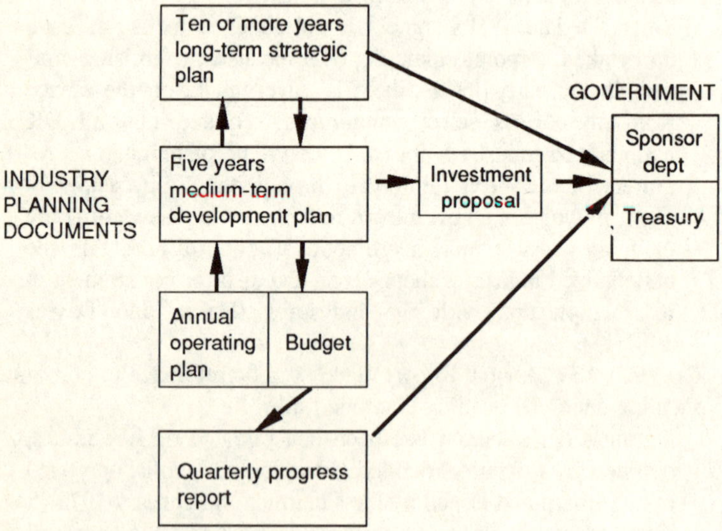

The annual planning cycle involved not only the Annual Operating Plan but further, two other planning documents, a 'strategic' plan (10 years or more) and a 'development' plan (5 years) with the latter being the vehicle for investment decisions (Harris and Davies 1981:15).

Figure 4.3: The nationalized industries planning model

As a part of the major move towards decentralization, the Transport Holding Company, in 1963, attempted to replace the bureaucratic system of central control with a holding company. Four key decision-making areas were identified over which the THC continued to exercise control:

> The influence of the Holding Company over controlled companies is exerted in four main ways. First, the Holding Company lays down the general structure of the organization. Secondly, the Holding Company determines the appointments to the boards of the subsidiary companies and of the senior managers and officers. Thirdly, the Holding Company exercises a financial control through the medium of capital and revenue budgets and returns, and the approval of individual projects above a certain size. Borrowing money and raising capital are also controlled. And finally, the Holding Company receives, examines and discusses periodical progress reports. (THC Annual Report 1963:11).

Peter Thompson adopted a similar philosophy on the relationship between BRS group and the newly established regional companies. Although Thompson, and for that matter the NFC, retained the right of approval of senior management appointments and company structures, he allowed the managing directors a great deal of flexibility and discretion. The individual BRS company structures varied greatly — some managing directors opted for area structures; others chose to have all of their branch managers reporting directly to them. Similarly, the composition of the company boards was not fixed along specific functional lines, but rather, was determined by the managing directors selecting those senior managers best suited or most worthy of the position. Some managing directors appointed senior branch managers to the Board; others restricted it to the company functional managers.

One of the most important changes instituted by Thompson took the form of a modification to the management decision-making and control system, changes consistent with his stated policy of company autonomy. Previously, the activities of the BRS districts had been coordinated primarily through policies initiated by the head office team and controlled using the financial reporting system and quarterly review meetings with each of the district managers. District Management conferences had also been held, where ostensibly the District Managers were given the opportunity of contributing to, or commenting on, central policy issues. The style of these 'conferences', however, was perceived to be autocratic, as is illustrated by the following comments on a quarterly district manager's conference:

> it was held in a hotel in the Midlands. He was completely autocratic. There was no participation at all. There was no revolt because they were all scared of him; it was an organization based upon mutual fear, very finely balanced.
>
> The district managers were lectured to at the conference; he would put up an issue knowing there would be no consensus, so he would step in and make the decision; he formed the executive board at head office, executive directors and heads of departments. (Interview with a BRS managing director.)

One of the instruments Thompson used to implement the changes was corporate planning. Thompson had previously been employed by the British Steel Corporation, and he brought to BRS a young British Steel corporate planner, Clive Beattie. In July 1973, Beattie published a document entitled 'Notes on Long-Term Corporate Planning 1974-78'. The first few paragraphs of the document made it clear that Thompson intended to change the planning process within BRS:

> It is the intention that the planning process will in future broaden in scope, and that there will be a fundamental change in method. In the past, planning has in general started from the present and looked one year forward, with the longer-term being an extension of the trends shown in the first year of the plan. Last year, for example, the Long-Term Plans were in reality an extension of the Budget for the year. The proposed method will be to look into the future to see how the company should look and be operating at that time, and by a series of steps, year-by-year. Hence, it's intended that the Budget will be derived from the Long-Term Plan.
>
> The planning process then will be split into two parts: firstly, the production of a Long-Term Plan, the elements of which will be described later in this note: and secondly, a Budget which will essentially be a forecast of the next years' performance, based on the first year's operation of the Long-Term Plan. This planning method is in harmony with the latest procedure emanating from the N.F.C. They are proposing that the long-term corporate plans and the short-term budgets should be made at a separate times — the Long-Term Plans in March/April and the budgets in September/October. In following this procedure there is a problem this year of not having current Long-Term Plans on which to base the Budgets. The N.F.C. have decided that the October budgets will be based on

> the plans for 1974 made in last year's planning process, but with modifications where required. Next year, the full change in procedure will be adopted and long-range plans will be made in March/April. (Notes on Long-Term Corporate Planning 1974-78:1.)

This document summarized many of the features of the new management philosophy. Profitability based upon an assessment of the longer term industry attractiveness and competitive position was an important feature of the new philosophy outlined in the document:

> The basic aim in producing the Long-Term Plan will be to produce a long-term broad plan of action to meet the objectives of the Company in terms of market development and the location and operation of resources to meet the market plan. In practice, the main objective will be concerned with making money, and the plan will be concerned with how in the future the financial objectives will be met. The key will be to find profitable markets and so define the markets and types of business in which the Company sees its future, with plans and targets for penetration.
>
> This market plan should derive from fundamental consideration of competition, profitability, the nature of the Company, and hence future role. The resources referred to are the men, machines, vehicles and premises of the Company, and the second step of the Plan will be to form a Long-Term Plan for the development, disposition and operation of these resources, to meet the market plan.
>
> The presence of a properly thought-out Long-Term Plan will allow individual project evaluation and policy decisions to be made against a coherent backcloth, and will enable the total effects on the Group activities to be properly measured. (Notes on Long-Term Corporate Planning 1974-78:1, 2.)

One of the fundamental changes made to the planning process was the introduction of a strong 'bottom-up' orientation. This was in sharp contrast with the earlier approach:

> The organization of the planning process should be both 'bottom-up' and 'top-down' in order that a balance is obtained of the views of both the policy makers and those closest to the operational conditions. Hence, it is thought the planning process should be as follows:
>
> a. The Group long-term objectives and policies will be considered in broad terms and transmitted to the companies.
>
> b. Each Company will consider its own objectives and

policies in the light of those of the Group, local conditions, and fundamental consideration of role.

c. Each branch will submit a Long-Term Plan for market and physical development, based on company policy and local branch conditions.

d. Each Company will form its Long-Term Plan, which may or may not use each branch Plan.

This approach is in line with the Group's management philosophy that each level of management has a part to play in the formation of the plans of the Group. The Group objectives and broad policies are included as part of this note. (Notes on Long-Term Corporate Planning 1974-78:2.)

These changes were fundamental to the new management philosophy in BRS, and although some of the features outlined in the July 1973 document were never fully implemented, some five years later the planning process was still substantially intact. During a presentation to the Eastern BRS Company Joint Committee,[1] Beattie outlined the planning process using the diagrams shown in Figure 4.4.

The first year of this 'bottom-up' approach to planning involved all the branch managers who developed detailed plans for their branches. Extensive market surveys were carried out, and a careful review of existing and potential activities was undertaken. In subsequent years, the detailed planning at branch level was gradually abandoned and replaced by a more broad brush approach, usually based on discussions between the branch managers and their managing directors assisted by their finance or planning managers. The initial exercise, however, provided a valuable base of knowledge about the business and the market on which planning could be based. It also reinforced the philosophy of decentralization and company autonomy that Thompson was establishing throughout the group. The new planning procedure allowed each of the managing directors, for the first time, to develop a five-year plan for his company based upon the characteristics of the region and his aspirations for the company. Within the broad financial guidelines provided by the group, the managing directors were free to plan the development of their companies and this gave substance to Thompson's philosophy of company autonomy because it gave the managing directors an analytically supported view for their positions on policy issues.

The group policy committee

Thompson, in keeping with this philosophy and as part of the

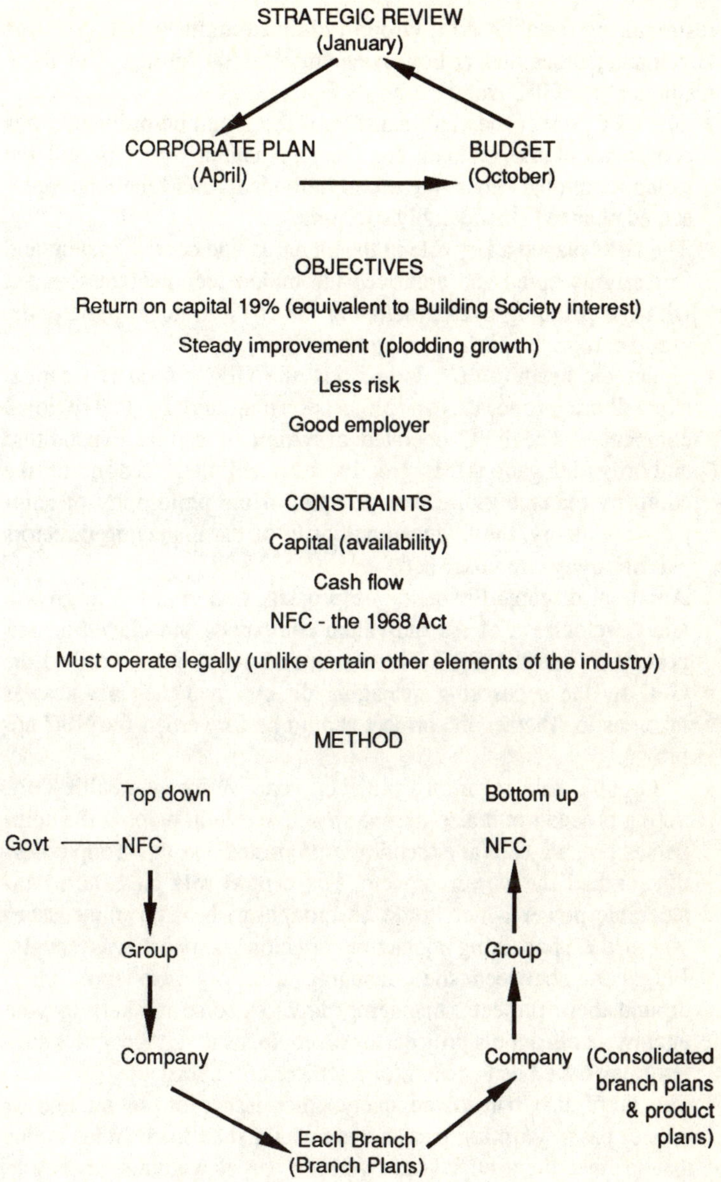
STRATEGIC REVIEW
(January)
CORPORATE PLAN
(April)
BUDGET
(October)
OBJECTIVES
Return on capital 19% (equivalent to Building Society interest)
Steady improvement (plodding growth)
Less risk
Good employer
CONSTRAINTS
Capital (availability)
Cash flow
NFC - the 1968 Act
Must operate legally (unlike certain other elements of the industry)
METHOD
Top down
Govt
NFC
Group
Company
Bottom up
NFC
Group
Company
(Consolidated branch plans & product plans)
Each Branch
(Branch Plans)

Figure 4.4: The features of BRS planning

restructuring, established a Group Policy Committee (GPC) as the key management and policy mechanism of the group. The basic features of the GPC were:

- The GPC, under the chairmanship of the group co-ordinator, was composed of the regional company managing directors and the group functional heads (the actual individuals and functions represented changed considerably over time).
- The GPC played a key role in the planning and control system and formally accepted and approved the major documents associated with the planning cycle, including the BRS strategic review, the group corporate plan and budget.
- Under the heading of 'submissions' the GPC considered capital expenditure proposals, or 'projects', submitted by the regional companies. The NFC operated a system of capital expenditure authority delegation that greatly restricted the freedom of the company managing directors. In spite of the philosophy of company autonomy, the financial authority of the managing directors was narrowly circumscribed.

  Approval of capital expenditure projects was vital to the growth and development of the individual companies and played an important role in the GPC. These proposals were introduced to the GPC by the sponsoring managing director and then a vote was taken as to whether the project should be forwarded for NFC approval.

  Group's role regarding projects went well beyond this GPC voting procedure: it also played an active role in helping the companies prepare capital expenditure proposals and the group co-ordinator had the power of veto. His central role gave him considerable power which could be brought to bear on other issues where the sponsoring managing director's support was sought. Bargaining between the managing directors also took place around these projects: managing directors were unlikely to vote against a colleague's project, for example, as that colleague's support may have been needed for a project of his own.
- The GPC also considered many other issues on an ad hoc or project basis. Working parties were established to consider issues that spanned the group. These working parties were responsible to the GPC, which reviewed progress and considered the recommendations submitted.
- The GPC was at the centre of the decision-making structure of the organization: virtually all major decisions were either made, or formally ratified, by the committee. Minutes of the meetings con-

stituted the formal statement of group policy. The decision-making process formally employed was that of voting, each member, in principle, having an equal vote.

The organizational planning and control structure is summarized in Figure 4.5.

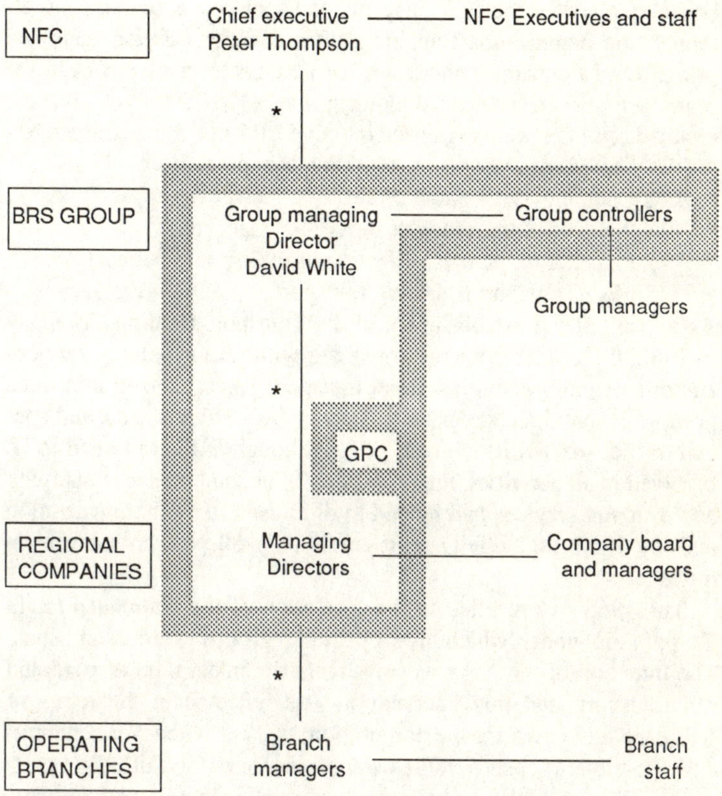

*Authority and reporting relationships plus integrating mechanisms - financial reporting, quarterly review meetings, the planning cycle (Strategic Review, Corporate Plans, Budgets), and capital expenditure projects.

Figure 4.5: The planning and control structure of BRS

A strategy of diversification

To this point in the history of the organization one fundamental element remained unchanged, namely the central thrust of its product-market strategy. BRS was originally established as the operating company responsible for the long-distance road haulage sector of the nationalized transport industry. This sector was composed of a wide range of activities, and soon after its establishment, BRS also became involved in specialized activities such as contract hire, tipper trucks, parcels and meat transport. Until 1953, this monopoly resulted in BRS being involved in the full range of road transport activities, and although the organization remaining after denationalization consisted primarily of the parcels and trunk services, some involvement in the other activities remained. Following the 1956 Transport Act the retained activities were organized into five BRS operating companies:

- BRS Ltd: general activities (trunking, tramping, etc.);
- BRS Contracts Ltd: contract hire;
- BRS Pickfords Ltd: removals, heavy haulage, etc.;
- BRS Parcels Ltd: parcels collection, trunking, and delivery;
- BRS Meat Transport Ltd: meat transport.

As a result of the establishment of the Transport Holding Company in 1962, these interests were combined with provincial bus services and other sundry activities. Road transport was organized into three groups: general haulage, parcels (largely BRS Parcels Ltd), and special traffics (ex BRS Pickfords Ltd). Although BRS continued to be involved in all activities, the proportion of general haulage, tramping and trunking services had tended to diminish after denationalization and, by 1968, the activity represented only 50 per cent of vehicle mileage.

The 1968 Act resulted in the formation of the National Freight Corporation under which five operating groups were established. The intention of the Act was once again the integration of road and rail transport, and this intervention was reflected in the terms of reference laid down for the corporation, that is, 'whenever economically possible to ensure traffics were transported by rail'. Two parts of the railways, both of which involved road collection and delivery, were transferred to the NFC, and these activities were established as separate operating groups. The activities of the NFC were distributed between the operating groups as shown in Figure 4.6.

As a result of the 1968 Transport Act, BRS reverted to its original role of being predominantly a general haulier, although the proportion of contract hire was significant.

By the late 1960s, the poor profit performance of general haulage was no longer acceptable, particularly in the light of the strong emphasis on profitability, which the 1962 Act had confirmed as central to the organization. Until this time, the decline of general haulage

National Freight Corporation

- **BRS Group**
  * general haulage
  * contract hire
  * warehousing (largely integrated with the general haulage activity)
  * distribution (limited)
- **Freightliner** (ex Railways)
  * rail trunking service with road collection and delivery
- **National Carriers** (ex Railway Sundries Division)
  * collection, trunking and delivery of items less than 3 cwt
- **Roadline** (previously BRS Parcels)
  * collection, trunking and delivery of parcels
- **Special Traffics** (previously BRS Pickfords)
  * heavy haulage
  * household removals
  * car transport
  * bulk liquids and powders

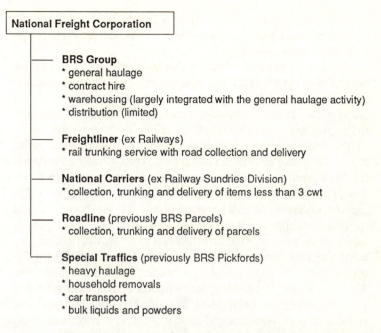

Figure 4.6: NFC operating groups and activities

had been by default, almost as an inevitable response to organizational changes and to industry problems, rather than as part of the strategy implicit in the Conservative government's policy as expressed in the 1953, 1956 and 1962 Acts. The stated policy of BRS until the late 1960s included general haulage as the raison d'etre of the organization, and BRS was perceived by the industry, and saw itself, primarily as a general haulier. The planned decline of general haulage in the late 1960s was the first step towards a conscious change in general haulage strategy and a fundamental rethinking of BRS's role in the industry.

The programme of general haulage decline was associated with the rationalization of the organization structure. The number of BRS districts were cut from twenty-one to ten and there was a substantial reduction in the number of branches. Although this planned decline continued through into the early 1970s, BRS's main reason for being unquestionably remained general haulage.

Contract hire continued to grow during this period in terms of both revenue and profit. Although the separate operating companies formed in 1956 (BRS Ltd and BRS Contracts Ltd) were merged after the establishment of the Transport Holding Company, contract hire continued to develop as a separate activity, and almost as a separate organization within BRS.

Although the existing managers were generally unified in a strong orientation to profitability and to a decentralized style of management, in terms of business activities they fell broadly into two categories — those committed to general haulage as the mainstay of the organization, and those whose affiliations lay with contract hire.

The division between the two was long-standing, and at times during the history of BRS the two activities had actually been operated by separately constituted companies. Separate accounting systems, management structures and operating organizations had led to different attitudes and at times open hostility. It was not unheard of for contracts branches to refuse fuel and other services to general haulage vehicles, and vice versa. As late as 1971, the London contracts activities were operated as a separate district with its own district manager and nine operating branches in the South East area. Similarly, in the North West, the contracts activity was separated from the rest of the organization, and although not constituted as a separate district, was managed as if it were. This continued in the North West beyond the transition to the regional company structure, until the retirement of the managing director and the death of the contracts director in 1978. A coherent contract hire culture became well established and could be clearly distinguished from the traditional, and still predominant, general haulage culture.

In spite of the planned general haulage decline being symptomatic of a tentative reformulation of strategy, BRS was still perceived by the market as being primarily in general haulage, and most of the management and operating staff continued to identify with this activity. Many of those still committed to general haulage attributed its lack of profitability to the constraints of the large organization (for example, lack of labour flexibility and high overheads) and argued that to be successful BRS had to become more like the private hauliers.

The Transport Development Group, which many BRS managers considered to be a paragon of private enterprise road haulage, recognized the same profitability patterns as BRS and were also moving away from general haulage in favour of specialized activities: 'Developments in the haulage field continue to underline the wisdom of the group of companies in concentrating on specialist traffics and on contract hire' (Transport Holding Company Annual Report 1967).

Although a few general hauliers did achieve good levels of profitability, the general success of private hauliers was a myth in BRS. Much of the claimed success of small hauliers reflected their lack of financial sophistication, which resulted in their overlooking, or inadequately providing for, the servicing of capital and the replacement of vehicles. Some BRS branches were operating general haulage profitably, either because they were in an area where profitable traffic was abundant or because of astute management and operating practices.

The poor profitability of general haulage in BRS could be attributed to three factors:

- *The economic structure of the general haulage sector.* The highly fragmented nature of the sector (largely as a result of the ease of entrance associated with low capital costs and the limited operating and management skills required) made the activity extremely competitive and susceptible to oversupply with relatively small fluctuations in the general economy.
- *The general haulage management philosophy.* Fragmented ownership and small-scale operation was associated with an entrepreneurial rather than a professional management philosophy. Little management information was available to operating staff who therefore quoted rates on the basis of experience, or what was thought necessary to obtain or hold the traffic. Loads were often chosen on the basis of past associations or convenience. Backloading at uneconomic rates was rife and tended to depress the overall rate structure. Hauliers were often unwilling to pass on cost increases to their customers, and even when the Road Haulage Association recommended specific increases in rates, many hauliers maintained their old rates rather than risk losing traffic.
- *Decentralization of the BRS management and operating structure.* The increasing autonomy of management and the emphasis on branches as profit centres was contrary to the operational requirements of co-ordination and control across regional boundaries and between branches. By the mid-1960s the performances of branch managers were being assessed in terms of the profitability of their individual branches. Branch managers were expected to optimize the profitability of their individual organizational unit regardless of the impact on overall general haulage performance. Any advantages BRS could have gained through inter-branch co-operation were largely lost because of this emphasis on decentralization and profit-centre management.

Peter Thompson's transport expertise had been substantially in the area of distribution, and hence he was free from the emotional attachment to BRS's traditional business activities that some of the long serving managers felt. He considered that BRS would never be able to compete profitably with the myriad of small hauliers who had lower overheads, greater flexibility, frequently applied unsound financial criteria, and often operated on the edge of legal constraints. Thompson quickly grasped that the profitability of general haulage was also inevitably poor and that its continued decline within BRS was inevitable. The difficulties inherent in the general haulage area had been discussed openly within the industry for many years. As early as 1963, comments in Transport Holding Company Annual Reports indicated a growing realization of the inherent lack of profitability of general haulage.

From the recognition of these factors, Thompson developed a strategy that involved concentrating the resources and management of the organization on activities, new and existing, that offered reasonable levels of profitability but would offset the declining general haulage activity. He concluded that BRS had to diversify away from its dependence on general haulage. Thompson argued that the risk of the business had to be reduced by developing contractually based activities or 'products' similar to the long-established BRS contracts activity. This new product strategy was formalized by the group planning and development controller, Clive Beattie.

The diversification strategy initially involved the application of marketing concepts such as segmentation and product management to existing business activities rather than product innovation itself. Until this time, the only product differentiation applied was that between 'contracts' and the various types of general haulage, for example, trunking, tramping and round-trip. Warehousing and distribution income was treated under the accounting heading of 'general activities'. The newly identified products were distribution, ware-housing, property, and truck rental. An important change in the management structure associated with this strategy of diversification was the appointment of product managers at group, company and, in some cases, branch level.

Of the four new products identified, truck rental had the greatest impact. The other new products were considered as part of the existing management's area of expertise, but truck rental was perceived as requiring skills and knowledge not held by the existing management. Almost all of the newly created truck rental management positions were filled initially by people from the car and truck hire industry. The impact of this influx of managers from an industry, the management philosophy and style of which were different from that of BRS, was dramatic.

The new strategy directly confronted the well-entrenched attitudes and was met with a good deal of resistance, at both company and branch level. This was particularly true in the case of truck rental, which was resented generally because of the influx of the rental industry people and the somewhat ostentatious marketing style they brought with them. It also resulted in branch managers having to give up their spares fleets. When support vehicles were required, branch managers had to hire vehicles from the truck rental activity at what they considered exorbitant cost.

The difference in attitude between the existing managers and the new truck rental managers was exemplified by an anecdote about the livery for the new truck rental product. The truck rental people argued that the livery should be red and blue on a white background because of the marketing benefits that would flow from the visual impact. Some of the traditional managers argued that such a livery was unsuitable because it would 'show the dirt', to which the truck rental managers retorted, 'Yes, you will have to wash the bloody things, won't you.'

In spite of the rapid growth of the new products, particularly truck rental, general haulage still represented over half the group's revenue, and many branches were still largely dependent on it. Most of the branch managers, however, were now eager to adopt the role of general manager of a broadly based autonomous business unit, and they understood that general haulage was unlikely to provide the profits necessary for success and growth. The dramatic financial success of Truck Rental played an important part in bringing about its acceptance and in influencing the management attitude to the new strategy in general.

By the end of 1977, only three years after its launch, truck rental represented over 5 per cent of BRS's total revenue and almost 30 per cent of trading profit. Its impressive profit performance even forced the most reluctant managers to accept the financial validity of the diversification strategy. The profitability, image, and panache that this activity brought to the organization had a crucial influence on the acceptance of the new product strategy, and ultimately on the predominant philosophy and style of the management of BRS.

A coherent organizational culture

A coherent organizational culture was finally being forged out of the wide range of factors which had influenced the organization since its inception. At the core of the culture was a management philosophy or collective cognitive structure — a set of beliefs and values which were predominantly shared by the managers of BRS. This collective cognitive structure was reflected in, and reaffirmed by, a fabric of behaviour patterns and artefacts.

The major changes introduced by Thompson brought about much greater internal consistency between the strategy, structure, and management style of BRS. The substantial management changes that had accompanied the restructuring, and Thompson's persuasive interpersonal style, resulted in a growing commitment to the philosophy underlying the changes. A coherent BRS culture had now emerged with the following set of beliefs being predominantly shared within the management population:

- A strategy of diversified transport activities which could be nationally co-ordinated and directed through broad policies while allowing a high degree of operating autonomy.
- A structure of regionally based autonomous companies composed of operating branches that were managed and judged as profit centres.
- A style of management which allowed for direct operational responsibility, using a formal, but highly interpersonal planning and control system to communicate and co-ordinate between operating units and organizational levels. The management style involved patterns of behaviour which were essentially open, encouraged innovation and change, and emphasized direct interpersonal contact rather than formalized and impersonal interaction.

The culture towards which BRS was rapidly moving in 1972 is compared with the original, general haulage culture in Table 4.1.

Diverse perceptions of general haulage

The key elements of the BRS culture were internally consistent and appropriate for the environment in which the company was operating. The organization was moving towards a state of equilibrium with a high level of internal and external consistency.

Major incongruities, however, remained that were primarily centred around BRS's traditional activity, general haulage. Many managers, including those at the most senior levels, clung to a set of beliefs that put general haulage at the heart of the organization's strategy and maintained patterns of behaviour more appropriate to small-scale, independent haulage operations than to managing within a large, complex organization.

Although an internally consistent culture had been created, the extent to which the management philosophy and style were shared,

General Haulage Culture

- Owning and operating lorries
- Regional structure/local autonomy
- 'Operating' — wheeling and dealing
- Business style
  - — short-term
  - — uncertainty
  - — intuitive

  } 'deals'
- Management Style
  - — individualistic
  - — informal
  - — 'amateur'
- Power base
  - — personal/structural

A 'bureaucratic' organizational culture was overlaid on this general haulage culture as a result of nationalization of the industry in 1948.

This culture was characterized by a dominant belief in central management control through a bureaucratic structure. It was believed that road transport could be provided most efficiently through central planning and control.

Management performance was appraised on the basis of conformity to the 'Management Manual'.

Operating managers were expected to facilitate national co-ordination of road transport and forego any advantage of their organizational unit for the good of the whole.

Transport Services Culture

- Offering a range of transport services
- Regional structure with a strong national product overlay
- Product policies
- Business style
  - — longer term
  - — risk
  - — analytical

  } 'contracts'
- Management Style
  - — corporate
  - — formal
  - — 'professional'
- Power base
  - — expertise/performance

The formal planning and control system was a central feature of the culture. Beliefs were strongly held regarding organizational processes:

- — decision making
- — control mechanisms
- — planning processes
- — resource allocation processes
- — performance evaluation
- — conflict resolution

Table 4.1: The key elements of the BRS culture in 1947 and 1972

even at senior levels, remained limited. The coherence of the culture, although much greater than it had been at any time in the past, was still only partial. A high degree of consensus about the management structure existed, and general support for the new strategy and style were growing, but a wide range of perceptions about the general haulage strategy and the most appropriate style of managing that activity remained.

Each of the regional company managing directors held certain views on the management of general haulage, but very few of them shared Thompson's belief that the activity could be pared down to a profitable core. Some managing directors believed that just the opposite was true: increasing volume was the only way to make the general haulage activity profitable. Others recognized that the effectiveness of operational management could often be the difference between business being 'good' or 'bad', and they believed this to be the secret of success in general haulage. Some branch managers consistently operated general haulage profitably, although these managers were unable to attribute their success to factors other than a commonsense approach to the activity: the careful selection of traffic, a thorough knowledge of costs and an awareness of the need to review prices in order to maintain profits, and the economic use of resources. Several managing directors believed none of these approaches was valid, because the small haulier would always have a competitive advantage over BRS.

The differing perceptions of the regional company managing directors on diversification and the role of general haulage were reflected in the manner in which they managed their companies. Given these differences it is not surprising that significant variations existed in the mix of business activities between the regional companies (see Table 4.2).

The different responses, which constituted company or regional 'strategies', could be explained in terms of the influence of a number of forces. In spite of the fact that the companies operated in the same industry, used the same technology, and had the same basic structural configuration, from the inception of BRS each of the regions displayed different characteristics.

- *The history and tradition of the region.* Even in 1948 the newly formed divisions and districts exhibited differences because the small private hauliers from which the organization was formed brought with them traditions reflecting regional differences. These traditions continued to be built upon over the years.
- *The business environment of the region.* Differences existed between the regions in terms of geography, demography, and the type and intensity of industrial and commercial activity. The regions, however, were difficult to characterize in overall terms because a great diversity existed within them. This diversity was reflected in the heterogeneity of the branches within any region. Essentially

ACTIVITY	SRS *	NEBRS	NWBRS	EBRS	MBRS	WBRS	SBRS	MORTONS
General haulage	58	42	52	44	40	42	32	55
Contract hire	28	35	32	26	20	29	37	4
Distribution	4	6	8	17	15	15	16	27
Truck rental	5	5	5	5	5	6	9	3
Warehousing	2	2	1	3	2	2	1	8
Property	1	1	-	1	3	2	2	2
Eng. services	2	9	3	4	15	4	3	1
TOTAL	100	100	100	100	100	100	100	100

(Source: BRS Group Financial Budget 1978: Appendix 5)

* SRS - Scottish Road Services Ltd
NEBRS - North Eastern BRS Ltd
NWBRS - North Western BRS Ltd
EBRS - Eastern BRS Ltd
MBRS - Midlands BRS Ltd
WBRS - Western BRS Ltd
SBRS - Southern BRS Ltd
MORTONS - Mortons BRS Ltd

Table 4.2: BRS budgeted revenue 1978 (in percentages)

the companies were characterized by the nature of the branches comprising them.

- *The dominant management philosophy and style.* The original management population of BRS was drawn almost exclusively from the acquired haulage firms, and these people brought with them a traditional haulage philosophy — a set of beliefs concerning the nature of the industry and how BRS could and should operate within it — and a particular, essentially entrepreneurial, management style. Over time, as management and circumstances changed, different philosophies developed and a more formal style of management began to emerge. The role of the managing director was central in determining the management philosophy and style of the region, and as different individuals assumed this position the philosophy and style changed.
- *The policies imposed by group.* The policies imposed had a greater impact on some regions than on others, depending on the

nature of the region and the skill exercised by the managing director in managing the boundary relationship between his company and group.

In spite of the diversity of these influences, in 1973 all of the regional companies were in broadly the same position in terms of the range and mix of their activities, although variation between individual branches continued to exist. There was a natural tendency for each of the operating locations to respond to the local demand for transport services. This was particularly true after branches were given greater autonomy and branch managers were judged on the basis of short-term profit performance. For some branches, few alternatives were available. Some were exclusively, and many more almost exclusively, tied to a single major customer or industry: Consett, Corby, Sheffield, Scunthorpe were dependent on the steel industry; Grimsby depended on the fishing industry; many branches in the Midlands were dependent upon the motor industry; the whisky industry was the life blood of some of the Scottish branches; the potteries in the North West; agriculture in East Anglia; and so on, right around the country. The requirements of some of these industries, and the attitudes within certain industries to transport, led to BRS being involved in purely ad hoc general haulage tramping; in other locations BRS became involved in a much broader range of activities, some of which were of a contractual nature. With the exception of certain areas, where an aggressive contract hire culture had developed, it is probably true to say that BRS simply responded to the demands of the market.

Notes

1. Company Joint Committees, in which management and union representatives met to discuss various issues, were an important element of the BRS industrial relations system.

5
THE EMERGENCE OF A STRATEGIC DILEMMA

In 1976 Peter Thompson was promoted to the position of chief executive of the NFC. He was replaced by David White, the managing director of one of the BRS regional companies.

After several years of barely acceptable financial results, the performance of the general haulage activity slumped. In 1977, declining general haulage gross margins became the focus of disagreement about general haulage strategy. Underlying Thompson's strategy was the belief that a profitable core of general haulage business existed. The rate of general haulage decline was a contentious issue. If it were too slow, the financial objectives of the NFC would not be met; if it were too fast, the result would be a significant contraction of the organization. The general haulage activity demanded a management structure and style very different from that appropriate for the new products. Decentralized ownership and control was not feasible with general haulage.

White, the recently appointed BRS group co-ordinator, was confronted with a dilemma. The pressure from the NFC to improve the financial performance of general haulage meant that the incompatibility between the decentralized structure and the existing general haulage strategy could not be maintained. It was the catalyst for the search for a new strategy, which would improve the profitability of general haulage while maintaining the decentralized management structure. The dilemma arose because the managerial collective cognitive structure failed, it no longer provided workable solutions. A new strategy required a shift in the collective cognitive structure of the decision makers.

A new group co-ordinator

In January 1976 an important change was made to the management structure of BRS. Peter Thompson was made chief executive of the NFC and was replaced as group co-ordinator by David White.[1] This was a significant change in both the structure of the organization and the personalities involved. As group co-ordinator Thompson had reported directly to the chairman of the NFC, and his promotion to chief executive effectively introduced another organizational level (Figure 5.1).

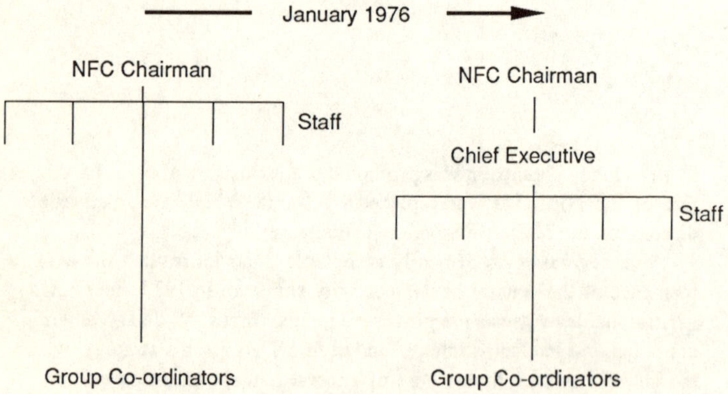

Figure 5.1: Change to the management structure of the NFC

Thompson's replacement, David White, had previously been managing director of Eastern BRS. When Thompson formed the regional companies in 1973, White had been one of the five district managers to be appointed as a company managing director. White's background, however, was not in the haulage industry; he joined BRS some years earlier after serving as a master mariner with a large oil company.

In assuming the role of group co-ordinator, David White inherited an organization the performance of which had steadily improved following the changes in structure and strategy three years earlier. The inheritance had within, it, however, the seeds of a strategic dilemma that he would inevitably have to confront.

The issues facing David White

At the end of 1976, almost five years after the implementation of the new product-market strategy, BRS's rapidly declining general haulage fleet was still losing money. As a senior NFC executive quipped to White: 'Soon you will have one vehicle losing half a million pounds.'

White had inherited a paradoxical situation. The structure and style introduced by Thompson had given the regional company managing directors a central role in the policy-making process, particularly through the GPC, but a significant number of BRS managers had not wholeheartedly adopted the new strategy. The new structure, which had been eagerly embraced by the company managing directors, combined with their now central role in the policy-making process, gave the senior management group the power to resist change. The culture was in danger of becoming trapped between the new structure and the management philosophy and style that underlay the old general haulage strategy.

Thompson's 1972 strategy assumed that the decline of general haulage would be offset by the growth of new products and that as the general haulage activity shrank a 'profitable core' would be revealed. For a number of years the strategy was successful and BRS's financial performance improved significantly. By 1976, however, it was becoming clear to BRS management that the rate at which the new activities would continue to grow was no longer sufficient to compensate for the planned decline in general haulage. There was a growing awareness that the opportunity for the development of major new products was limited and the profitability of the rapidly declining general haulage activities continued to be extremely marginal — the putative profitable core of the business was proving to be very elusive. This became a major issue in 1976 because in order to sustain a moderate rate of general haulage decline during the preceding three years, substantial capital investment had been required to renew dilapidated vehicles. During this period, the average capital employed and fleet size declined some 15 per cent despite a cumulative capital investment of more than £10 million. The problem of the capital demands of general haulage had been exacerbated by rapid inflation of vehicle prices during the early 1970s — the price of a large truck had increased from about £8,000 in 1971 to £22,000 in 1977.

The situation was further aggravated by NFC cash-flow difficulties, which resulted in increasing demands for profit and more constrained capital availability. This was manifested in a number of different ways. In the case of BRS, the result was that Thompson exerted greater pressure for the accelerated decline of general haulage. The intention was to reduce capital requirements and improve profitability. The rate of the decline became the basis of a fundamental strategic disagreement between Thompson and BRS and a contentious issue in strategic planning meetings. In the 1977 Strategic Review document submitted by the BRS group to the NFC, the perceived problems associated with the accelerated decline of general haulage were clearly spelled out:

> In the past the broad philosophy of the Group has been to reduce the general haulage activity, given that the general haulage product is not profitable, and replace it with other, more profitable products. A headlong flight from general haulage was considered unwise, as it would lead either to heavy redundancies and poorer results, linked to a reduction in the selling outlets for the growth products. Hence, the plan has been the steady substitution of new products to mop up the resulting redundant overheads and branch facilities. These new products have been more profitable and less risky than general haulage.
>
> As a result of this action, the Group is now far more robust and better able to weather economic storms.
>
> This philosophy is a reflection of the basic strengths and weaknesses of the Group. The Group is too dependent upon the general haulage product from which it is unlikely it would ever be able to produce adequate returns. Other smaller hauliers are able to operate much more effectively and sail much closer to the wind than BRS, whose large national structure is a disadvantage in this keen market. On the other hand, many products depend on and need a national presence to be effectively sold and it is these products which the Group is pushing as hard as it can, for example, Contract Hire, Truck Rental, BRS Rescue, and National Distribution Schemes. This philosophy leans upon the major strength of BRS — that it has a national network of branches.
>
> Given that the Group has this national structure, plus the supporting management expertise, it has been able to develop new products which need a national presence, very cheaply and effectively [e.g. Truck Rental]. In the future similar developments are likely to become a major feature of the Group's progress (BRS Strategic Review 1977-1980:4).

The Strategic Review argued that the maximum rate of decline that could be sustained would be achieved by adopting a policy of no general haulage investment or replacement of vehicles. The effect of this policy, it was suggested, would be to cause a 'rapid run down' in the size of the organization, which would in turn jeopardize the Group's ability to market and operate new products on a national basis. The Strategic Review therefore stressed that because general haulage would still be a substantial proportion of BRS turnover in 1980, and would have a major impact on overall profits, the activities 'must still be diligently managed and supported with capital to supply the correct equipment'.

It was the question of the capital required to sustain a moderate decline of general haulage that was the nub of this emerging disagreement. During 1976 general haulage had in fact performed well above budget, and although the return on capital was unacceptable, the higher profitability of the other activities meant that the overall position was not untenable or demanding urgent action. However, as a result of financial pressures within the National Freight Corporation, an additional objective had been imposed upon the BRS group: 'To generate over the planning period sufficient funds from profit and asset realization to enable the replacement of resources, the finance of minor developments and expansion and still allow adequate returns on capital (BRS Strategic Review 1977-80:1).

BRS expressed objections to this additional objective on the grounds of both philosophy and practicability. At the time of preparation of the 1976 Corporate Plan the Group had looked at several ways of attempting to meet this requirement of a balanced cash flow, but as the Strategic Review pointed out it was not possible while maintaining either the profitability or the fabric of the business: 'Instead, a policy of no investment . . . led to lost profits of over £3 million per annum by 1980, high redundancy payments, and a continued negative cash flow . . . at least 20 major branches would have to be closed. The Group considered such a strategy quite unacceptable (BRS Strategic Review 1977-80:7).

Finally a compromise was reached between the NFC and BRS and the 1976 Corporate Plan figures were agreed upon. The compromise had in fact been achieved largely by considering truck rental capital as financed by two-year rental deals, and therefore outside the NFC capital constraints.

It is probable that Clive Beattie, group planning and development controller, had a major influence on the philosophy espoused in the 1977 Strategic Review, and on David White's general attitude and approach to the issue at this time. White had been group co-ordinator for only eighteen months and was a little unsure in his dealings with Peter Thompson, particularly with regard to areas of strategy where Thompson had been such an obvious success. Preparation of the Strategic Review was within Beattie's area of responsibility and reflected his ideas.

As the issue developed, David White's philosophy on general haulage became clearer, and was much closer to Thompson's strategy than to that presented in the 1977 Strategic Review. White's main concern at that time appeared to have been with immediate results, and success in these terms was clearly being threatened by general haulage. To White, the accelerated decline of general haulage was a necessary element of what he described as the 'stop-the-bleeding' strategy, that is, to shed identified 'bad bits'. Underlying this strategy was a belief that the profitability of general haulage could be improved by selectively shedding or retaining certain business. This policy had been successfully applied by David White as managing director of Eastern BRS, but it was essentially a tactical measure within Thompson's overall strategy of product substitution.

Although Beattie had helped Thompson to develop the strategy of product diversification, their views now appeared to be diverging. Beattie explained this in terms of Thompson's underlying management philosophy: Thompson believed that it was essential to show a steady improvement in financial performance in order to gain the confidence of those around him, and Thompson was ruthless in the pursuit of this trend. It is doubtful whether he would have been concerned had the price of improved performance been a substantial reduction in the size of BRS. The 'marketing outlets' argument was of doubtful validity anyway. BRS had continually shrunk in size since 1948 and had continued, at least in recent years, to improve in terms of profitability. Thompson's view of the structure of the organization was not constrained by traditional boundaries and arrangements. He later said that he envisaged that, at some time in the future, the various NFC groups could be rationalized along product lines. The 'marketing outlets' argument had little validity within this broader view of the organization. The NFC had a very large number of branches and many of the branches, belonging to other groups were better located to market BRS products than the closest BRS branch.

The problem of structure — strategy alignment

The changes made by Peter Thompson had, to a large extent, brought about the alignment of the strategy and structure of the organization. The strategy of diversification resulted in an emphasis on activities that were suited to branch ownership of assets and local management control, and these were compatible with the regional company structure and branch autonomy. General haulage remained unaligned, but as the strategy assumed the continued decline of this activity, this too was consistent.

The issue of the incompatibility between the decentralized structure and general haulage was well understood in BRS. The most obvious solution involved changing the structure to make it compatible with the requirements of general haulage. The difficulty was that structural changes would have involved co-ordination and control across regional company boundaries. This was unacceptable to the managing directors who jealously guarded their 'right' to run their own companies, and it ran counter to a central element of the culture — a decentralized regional structure with substantial local autonomy, at least on operational matters. BRS had attempted to control and co-ordinate general haulage by means of central policies and control systems. Each attempt had failed dismally, and there was consensus that general haulage could only be operated successfully if BRS managed the activity like the private haulier sector, that is, on a totally decentralized basis.

Profitable operation of general haulage depended upon the effectiveness of a number of people, including the drivers and traffic operators. In many industries, operators at this level are responsible for largely routine activities that can be programmed and easily monitored. In the general haulage industry, although much of the work was routine, drivers and traffic operators often had to use their initiative to respond to the many unanticipated circumstances that arose. The geographically dispersed nature of the activity compounded this reliance upon autonomy: for much of the time supervisors were not able to contact those they supervised. Clearly managerial direction and control was much more constrained than in more routine and physically proximate situations. The successful management of general haulage required the constant, detailed monitoring of performance by the manager rather than the establishment of broad guidelines, policies or systems. Each of the constantly emerging non-routine situations required the attention of the drivers and traffic operators, and the competence of the branch manager in monitoring their performance, and continually developing their knowledge and skills determined the ultimate success of general haulage.

Hence, the inherent nature of the activity meant that central policies were hard to define and harder to enforce. Exceptions to a policy could always be argued on the basis of peculiar area or customer requirements. This same difficulty also existed between regional companies and their branches, and even between branch managers and drivers. The story of the branch manager, whose insistence that his directives on vehicle routing be strictly adhered to, resulting in a vehicle becoming stuck under a low bridge, had taken on the status of a legend in the industry. The belief that the individual should be left free of constraints to operate in the way he saw best fit was a key element of the general haulage culture of the industry and applied at all levels — drivers, traffic operators and managers.

General haulage was therefore notoriously difficult to manage, and difficulties experienced at group level were shared by the managing directors within their own companies. General haulage could not be managed by the managing director establishing broad policies or comprehensive management systems. The activity had to be managed on a branch by branch, customer by customer basis. Company management meetings inevitably took the form of reviewing the performance of the company on a branch by branch basis, but the action that company management could take if a branch failed to perform satisfactorily in general haulage was limited. They could seek price increases, or instruct the branch manager to seek price increases, withdraw the vehicles from the branch and make the drivers redundant at great cost and at the risk of industrial relations problems, or sack the manager who was usually a scarce resource.

The diversification strategy resulted in the development of activities (contract hire, truck rental, warehousing, etc.), which were compatible with the philosophy of decentralized regional management, but at the same time allowed a high degree of central control in key policy areas. The regional companies were left free to own, operate, and market the various activities within a policy framework that provided central control over investment, pricing, product characteristics and quality, and key management appointments.

Hence the company managing directors tended to have a detailed involvement with general haulage on a branch by branch basis, and much greater authority to act in this area because they were free of the group policy constraints that applied to the other activities. For many of the managing directors, general haulage gave them most problems, but also most challenge, interest, and job satisfaction. In this area they were truly autonomous within the capital constraints placed upon them.

An implication of Thompson's strategy was that a product structure would inevitably tend to emerge alongside the regional structure. Although Thompson reduced the senior head office staff substantially, thereby confirming his intention to give greater autonomy to the regional companies, the director responsible for contract hire was retained and later a truck rental controller was appointed. Shortly after White became group co-ordinator, a distinct product structure began to develop with contract hire and distribution product managers reporting to the marketing controller. A product structure was also emerging at the regional company level, and its continued development was strongly encouraged by White. The idea that the co-ordination of activities at both the national and regional levels should be through a product structure was gradually established.

White certainly felt that the structure of BRS would change, and he apparently saw strong product management at group as a key factor. The view of the managing directors was that product management should be limited to the company level, with only the essential functions (for example, finance) being represented at group. This attitude was rather difficult to justify, however, given that the strategy of diversification was based upon national products. Contract hire, truck rental, distribution, and warehousing were all developed using national policies on pricing, product characteristics and quality, advertising, corporate image, and the servicing of national customers. These policies were agreed on at the GPC, but there remained an obvious need for national product management. The development and co-ordination of national product policies across the regional companies required group product management.

White's inclination to strengthen group product management was interpreted by the managing directors as a tendency to centralization. In a sense this was true, because there was inevitably a political aspect of the issue, namely the balance of power between the regional company managing directors and group. Thompson relied heavily on the planning and control system as an integrating mechanism, and in particular used the GPC to co-ordinate activities on a national scale. His personality and power as the founder of the regional company structure and the GPC were important elements of the co-ordination process. Although Thompson wielded significant formal power, he had relied heavily on direct personal contact with the managing directors through the GPC and quarterly review meetings. David White's personality and style were very different from Thompson's. The position to which he was promoted was different from that previously occupied by Thompson, who had reported directly to the chairman of the NFC. Further, White was not the author of the regional company structure and the GPC, and he had been promoted from among the other managing directors. White made no attempt to mimic Thompson's style in running the Group but determinedly set about establishing a role based upon his own style.

The general haulage dilemma

During 1977 the performance of general haulage became substantially worse than it had been in the previous year. Instead of being more profitable than budget and making a small net profit, general haulage sank into a net loss position in spite of revenue being ahead of budget. The problem was one of falling gross margin, and it was this issue around which the disagreement over general haulage strategy came to a head.

At the 1977 Corporate Plan review meeting with the NFC, BRS management came under severe pressure about the general haulage financial results and, in particular, the declining gross margin. Thompson insisted that action be taken throughout the group to improve the situation. As a result, White agreed to embark upon a course of action involving two elements:

- A general pricing policy of approaching general haulage customers and attempting to obtain an across-the-board price increase of 15 per cent.
- A specific pricing policy aimed at ensuring that the 1978 budget did not show any branches achieving less than 6 per cent margin[2] on general haulage. At branches where 6 per cent gross margin was not achieved, general haulage was to be discontinued and, if necessary, the drivers made redundant.

Thompson and White had struck a deal whereby the BRS 1978 general haulage capital investment budget was approved on the understanding that the general haulage gross margin and pricing policies would be implemented. In agreeing to these policies, White placed himself in a difficult situation, however, which demanded that he satisfy the conflicting demands of Thompson and the regional company managing directors. The policies were clearly an instrument for implementing Thompson's strategy of accelerated general haulage decline, and that this would be obvious to the regional company managing directors was a matter of concern to David White. He expressed this concern at the controllers meeting on the day following the Corporate Plan meeting: 'We'll get resistance to this ... we want the policy to flow from us, not from on high (NFC). We got the Corporate Plan agreed which gives us £2.7 million (capital) for general haulage. The price is the 6 per cent gross margin policy.'

Having struck a bargain with Thompson, he was faced with the task of gaining the commitment of the GPC, using the rationale that the quid pro quo for the gross margin and pricing policies was the general haulage capital included in the Corporate Plan.

The manner in which the issue of these general haulage policies developed reflected White's style and his role within BRS. White was still relatively new to the position and was struggling to establish his role vis-à-vis Thompson, whom he replaced, and the regional company managing directors, from among whom he had been promoted. Clearly White was concerned to establish a group role independent of Thompson and not to be seen simply as the 'NFC Post Office' (a term used within the regional companies when criticizing Group). He was therefore understandably concerned that the policies should appear to be emanating from BRS group and not from Thompson.

David White's approach to gaining the commitment of the GPC was to send out two policy papers before the GPC discussion. Although identified as discussion papers, the documents read very much like policy statements for ratification. The papers made no attempt to present an analysis of the problem but rather stated a proposed solution. White's tactic of circulating the policy papers as discussion documents probably created additional difficulties for him in the GPC meeting. By declaring his hand in a very open and direct way, he was inevitably faced with a situation in which he either had to accept the managing director's views, (and fail to achieve agreement to the policies), or obtain agreement by imposing his views on the GPC. The first alternative would have put White, who had agreed to implement these policies as a quid pro quo for approval for general haulage capital, in an impossible situation vis-à-vis Thompson. The second course risked damaging his already delicate relationship with the GPC. This would have created a situation in which it would been even more difficult to assure implementation of the policies.

A second difficulty with the discussion paper tactic was that it gave the managing directors an opportunity to collude on a united response to the policies. Although all the members of the GPC claimed such collusion and lobbying did not occur, there was clear evidence that a good deal of communication took place between GPC members on important issues before meetings.

The policy papers represented a threat to the managing directors on two accounts: implicit in the policies was the accelerated decline of general haulage and hence the possibility of shrinkage or even disappearance of their companies; and the policies threatened the autonomy and traditional freedom to act in the general haulage area by applying policy constraints rather than purely financial performance demands. It appeared that White was attempting to draw general haulage into the group policy arena. The GPC debate that followed the tabling of the papers was based upon fundamentally different philosophies about both the nature of general haulage and the BRS management structure.

The Group Policy Committee debate

White introduced the papers to the GPC meeting in the context of reporting the Corporate Plan discussions held with the NFC: 'The Corporate Plan in total was accepted by the NFC, but the soft spot of the Plan is whether BRS will be able to achieve the gross margin of 12 per cent in general haulage (upon which the Plan is based).'

The pricing policy immediately met with vehement opposition from the managing directors to which David White responded: 'By and large the companies must set their own pricing strategies, but 12 per cent gross (margin) must be achieved or suffer loss of capital.'

With this statement, White made his position quite clear. He had accepted the general haulage policies in exchange for an assurance of capital from the NFC, and he was determined that the same exchange would apply between group and the regional companies. By introducing the threat to cut capital, White committed himself to achieving agreement to the policies or acting on the threat; he had left himself with little room to manoeuvre and few opportunities for compromise.

The managing directors responded by offering counter-arguments:

Wilf Bates: 'The 12 per cent margin could be achieved by suitable cost saving action . . . pre-1948 the business ran with loss-leading trucks.'

Clive Beattie: 'We are not in that business now.'

Wilf Bates (and several other managing directors): 'Oh yes, we are!'

Wilf Bates: 'When the companies were set up we were told only the bottom line was of concern.'

Ron Fortune: 'What do we get to invest in general haulage anyway? We all think we should get out of general haulage, but it's a decision for the individual companies.'

This exchange captures quite clearly the two strategic issues in dispute: the role of general haulage in BRS's strategy, and the way in which the organization was to be managed — on the basis of autonomous regional companies with overall profit responsibility, or on the basis of central policy direction and control.

Fortune's claim that the issue should be handled by the individual companies free from group policy reflects his strong feelings about company autonomy. He was one of several of the managing directors (in particular, Wilf Bates and Ron Irons, but to some extent all the managing directors) who were inclined to protect their area of autonomy by agreeing in principle to group policies but then failing to fully implement the policies in their own company. This developed into what could be described as a 'catch me if you can' game between the managing directors and White. The game was played with all the activities but focused upon general haulage or other specific issues where White was attempting to exercise increased control. The game was elaborate and was played within the planning and control system using the financial reporting documents as a focus.

Many of the managing directors were by this time obviously upset, and there was some sense of them coming together to form a united opposition to the proposed policies. Wilf Bates's reference to the founding of the companies was particularly pointed. He was in effect claiming that the position being adopted by White was illegitimate in terms of the way that Thompson had established and operated the group. White was by nature sensitive to any suggestion of improper or unreasonable action, and the remarks would certainly have had some effect.

White's attempts to focus solely on the immediate aspects of the policies and avoid the more far-reaching implications met initially with some resistance. The debate fairly quickly became entrenched around the detail of general haulage, and other managing directors took Bates's lead of suggesting alternative methods of improving the general haulage gross margin.

Three alternatives were put forward by the managing directors were:

- *The appointment of a general haulage group product manager.* This was suggested by Eric Shortland (managing director of Mortons BRS) and was interesting because it implied that there should be a major element of central control over general haulage. This was diametrically opposed to the position being taken by the other managing directors. The concept of group product managers had been introduced as part of the diversification strategy, and although the effectiveness of the position was largely dependent upon the personality and credibility of the person in the position, it was an important element of group control formally incorporated in the structure.

The suggestion was also interesting because it was an issue that was shortly after taken up openly by White, who pursued the matter persistently for two years until such a position was finally accepted by the GPC. It was not however taken up by the GPC on this occasion as an issue for debate.

- *A 'stop-the-bleeding' strategy.* This approach, suggested by Bill Atkinson (managing director of Eastern BRS), was similar to the 6 per cent gross margin policy. It was the description given by White and Atkinson to the Eastern BRS approach to general haulage and gave support for the policies proposed by White.

  As time went on, there was growing evidence to support the contention that Atkinson collaborated with White on many issues. Bill Atkinson had been marketing director of Eastern BRS when White was managing director of that company, and his promotion to managing director probably owed a considerable amount to the support given by White.
- *Encourage the exchange of trailers to more fully utilize the branch network.* In raising this approach, Wilf Bates (managing director of North Western BRS) made reference to the basic conflict between the decentralized structure of profit centre branches and major elements of general haulage. He also said that the process of general haulage decline was aggravating this problem: 'A lot of branch managers know general haulage is a dying product and are demoralized — that's part of the problem — obviously each company looks after its own interest.'

White then directed the discussion specifically to the 6 per cent gross margin policy:

David White: 'How does 5(e) (the agenda item for the 6 per cent gross margin policy) grab you? We are talking about Western and Scottish substantially (these are the companies most affected) in 5(e), Eastern and North Eastern a bit.'

Douglas Leithead (representing Scottish Road Services): 'If we had no 5(e)'s (branches with general haulage gross margin less than 6 per cent), our gross margin would be 17 per cent.'

A number of key managing directors (John Copland, Steve Abel, and Ron Irons) were not present at this GPC meeting, and their deputies could play only a limited role. White was able to brush aside such opposing comments partly because the managing directors of the two companies most affected by this policy were not present. While in theory the company representatives deputizing for their managing directors formally represented the views and interests of the company on the Managing Director's behalf, in practice their authority and credibility in policy issues were very limited. The opposition David White met on the general policy issues would probably have been much greater had all the managing directors been present.

All three of the absent managing directors played important roles within the GPC and could have provided strong opposition to the proposed policies — John Copland and Ron Irons because the policies certainly would have had a major effect on their businesses, which had a number of weak branches with a heavy general haulage commitment, and Steve Abel was philosophically committed to general haulage and also would have felt that the policies were an unnecessary intrusion into the normal running of the business. This objection would have been shared by all the managing directors, and this issue of company autonomy versus group control underlay the whole debate. Further, Abel would have offered particular support to Copland because of personal loyalty and respect, and because of allegiance to his native Scotland. This support would have been telling in the debate because of the credibility of his company and his conspicuous success in operating general haulage. Abel was young, had a record of proven success, and was an advocate of general haulage.

As the debate proceeded none of the alternatives suggested was seriously examined or developed; they were used as counter-arguments to the policies proposed. White did not respond to the alternatives or the issues raised, but continued to refer the discussion back to the specific policies. On several occasions he referred to the possibility that general haulage capital restrictions would be imposed in subsequent years if gross margins were not improved: 'The stark facts are that as a group, we are below survival level in general haulage. Take the issue of the 6 per cent gross margin: is anyone finding that philosophy impossible to live with? Can we take it as a policy? There is not the slightest doubt that if the 1978 budget does not have 12 per cent gross margin on general haulage that we will not get a capital allocation (for general haulage).'

Following a break for lunch, White sought agreement to the policies but moderated slightly the demands he was making. The managing directors eventually agreed to accept the gross margin policy 'in principle' and agreed to 'soften the customers up' and to apply price increases selectively on an individual company basis.

It appeared that White realized he was not going to obtain agreement to the pricing policy, and he quickly moved the meeting on to the next item on the agenda. After announcing the (upward) revision to the overall company capital budgets, the managing directors were all instructed to cancel varying amounts of their general haulage capital expenditure. The managing directors reacted angrily to this sudden, unexplained cut in general haulage capital but accepted the instruction after only a brief discussion. They seemed to understand the situation, and to accept White's apparently blatant use of his authority:

David White: 'I ask you to cancel the following general haulage capital expenditure.' (He specifies amounts for each company.)

Wilf Bates: 'Why has mine been reduced when my (general haulage) gross margin is good?'

David White: 'Because the group margin is falling.'

Wilf Bates: 'We won't be able to meet the available business.'

David White: 'Then put your prices up!'

Wilf Bates: 'And put us out . . . (of business).'

David White: 'Look at the figures.'

Wilf Bates: 'Well, figures don't run a haulage business, David.'

David White: 'I want this general haulage thing faced up to. Shall we move onto the next subject?'

The following day David White explained that he had taken this action 'because the managing directors didn't accept the pricing and branch closure policy and so the capital allocation had to be cut'. One of the group controllers described the situation in terms of David White 'pulling one of the many levers available to him'. In his controllers meeting, White expressed dissatisfaction with the GPC meeting: 'Yesterday was a long day, I suppose I lost control of it. I'm not sure when it was . . . the substitutes were part of it of course.'

White had not been successful in achieving what he had intended from the meeting. This was only partly because of the nature of the actual policies. The gross margin policy was probably acceptable and similar in effect to the management action already being taken in most of the companies; the pricing policy was more difficult, but that could easily have been modified to allow for more discriminant application by each company — but rather because of the underlying differences in philosophy on strategic and organizational issues. Instead of seeking compromise, White tried to force the issue using his control of capital as a source of power, and this had the effect of generating resentment rather than commitment.

He was successful, however, in bringing general haulage policy and pricing within the arena of group policy. This was a major step towards the group being able to establish central policy control of general haulage legitimately, and was manifested in a number of ways. A norm was established whereby general haulage price increases were reviewed regularly in GPC meetings, thus bringing this activity in line with most of the other products where central control of pricing was accepted practice.

A catalyst for strategic change

The strategic dilemma arose because of the incompatibility between the organization structure and general haulage. The most obvious solution involved changing the structure to make it compatible with general haulage by providing co-ordination and control across regional company boundaries. But this ran counter to the strongly held philosophy of decentralization.

When general haulage emerged as a major strategic issue in 1977, White argued that a group general haulage product manager was the most viable solution. In the case of the other products, the regional company managing directors may have resented the group product managers, but they accepted reluctantly the legitimacy of the product management role. In the case of general haulage, however, the implications of a Group product manager were quite different. The newer activities were compatible with the decentralized structure because they lent themselves to national product management within a structure of local asset ownership and operational management. Traditional general haulage was incompatible with a decentralized structure because national product management was not viable unless direct managerial control was exerted as had been attempted earlier in BRS's history. Local ownership and operational control within national policy co-ordination did not appear to be feasible with traditional general haulage.

The regional company managing directors' refusal to accept White's proposal of a group general haulage product manager must be considered within this context. The managing directors strongly resisted the proposal for two reasons.

First, they believed that because of its inherent nature general haulage was not suited to central product management, and they argued that the problems of general haulage were specific to a region, industry, branch, and even a single customer. 'Universal' solutions or policies were inappropriate. This was true for most of the general haulage activity, although some parts of it would have been amenable to national policies.

Secondly, a group general haulage product management implied that group would gradually assume direct authority over almost half of the regional company operations. It was most unlikely that this is what White intended, but equally the longer term implications must have been obvious to the regional company managing directors. They naturally opposed these threats to their autonomy and were able to do so because of the central role Peter Thompson had given them in the decision-making process. In a sense, they had not only been given autonomy but had collectively been given the authority to maintain that autonomy. Their position was further strengthened by Thompson's consistently refusing to approve policies proposed by group that cut across the regional company structure.

Each regional company managing director held certain views regarding the management of general haulage (refer to Appendix II), but very few of them shared Thompson's belief that the activity could be pared down to a profitable core. They did, however, share the perception that the continued decline of the activity would result in a significant organizational contraction. Organizational shrinkage could have been considered by the NFC as an unfortunate expedient necessary to achieve their financial objectives, but to the management of BRS it was a direct threat to their careers.

Implicit in the strategic dilemma confronting BRS were fundamental organizational changes. The BRS case demonstrates clearly that the formulation of a new strategy involves more than the adaptation of the organization to a changing environment. In BRS a dilemma arose because certain beliefs and values regarding key aspects of the organization, the environment, and the nature of the relationship between the two, constrained incremental adaptation. The managerial collective cognitive structure failed, no longer providing workable solutions. The dilemma was the manifestation of the dissonance between the organizationally defined reality and the environment. A new strategy required a shift in the cognitive structure of the decision makers: the core shared beliefs and values failed to adequately deal with the circumstances facing the organization.

Earlier studies of the strategy process have lacked a coherent theoretical framework. Much of the work has focused on incremental, routine decision making and change. Little attention seems to have been paid to the processes associated with what was defined in

Chapter 1 as 'second order' or strategic change. The cognitive theory based model of the strategy process presented here indicates that two quite different patterns of decision-making behaviour exist; one being the outcome of a sharing or substantial overlapping of the cognitive structures of the decision-makers; and the other resulting from the mismatch, or differences that occur when the established collective cognitive structures fails (Figure 5.2).

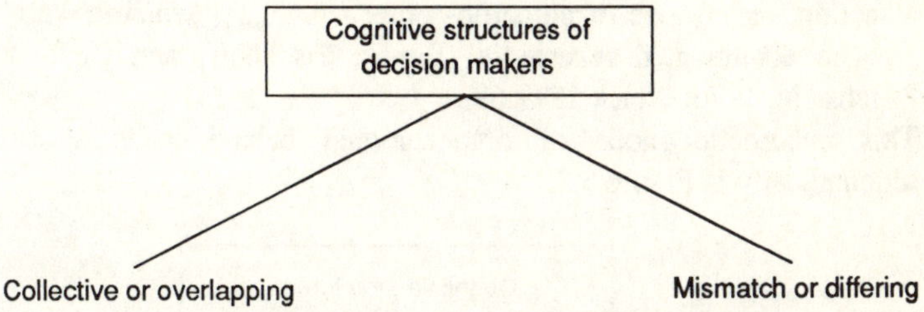

Figure 5.2: Collective or differing cognitive structures

The more strongly the cognitive structures of top management, or organizational elite, are shared, the more coherent and pervasive will be the organizational culture. A consistent set of organizational behaviours and processes will be in action that will determine the variables influencing internal and external functioning (Schein, 1984) — consensus on mission or primary task, the means to accomplish goals, ways of defining and managing authority and influence, the people selected and promoted, socialization practices, which behaviours are rewarded or punished and how: in short, the strategy, structure, and style of the organization.

These behaviours and processes will act to reinforce the established collective cognitive structure and thus re-affirm, as well as reflect the culture of the organization.

When in this processual mode the organization is operating cybernetically (Steinbruner 1974):

- monitoring a small number of critical variables and relying on limited information coming from established feedback channels;
- keeping goals separate and dealing with them sequentially until crisis forces some fundamental change;
- keeping the problem narrowly focused and fragmented;
- employing a repertoire of routines, or standard operating procedures, to deal with marginal variation in the environment.

This mode of operation can be logically explained as the outcome of human cognitive processes. As Weick has pointed out, organizational members simplify and vulgarize the information to which they are exposed:

> Organizational members try to manage uncertainty by imposing categorical inferences rather than probabilistic judgments (Steinbruner 1974:110), they operate under the constraint of consistency to introduce cognitive economies, they manage inconsistent information by collapsing or stretching time, by wishful thinking, by inferring the impossibility of implied action, or any one of numerous other techniques which have been documented repeatedly (Slovic, Fischhoff, and Lichtenstein, 1976; Weick 1979:68).

This cybernetic mode of organizational behaviour is shown schematically in Figure 5.3.

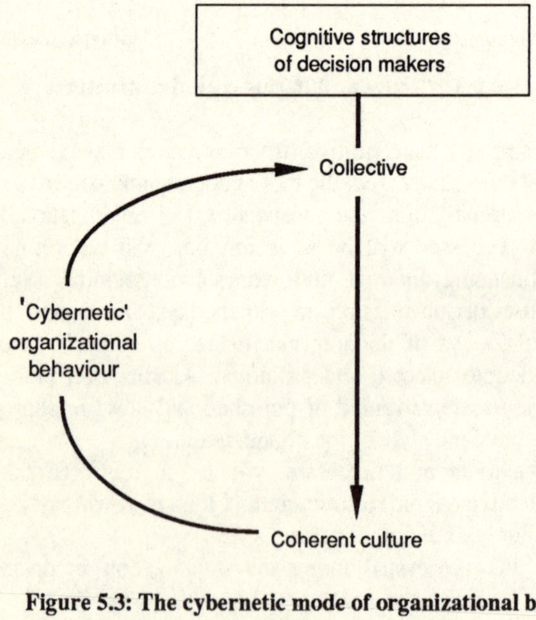

Figure 5.3: The cybernetic mode of organizational behaviour

The organizational behaviours and processes associated with a coherent culture, maintain stability and continuity, but can only cause the existing collective cognitive structures to be further shared and refined. They can enhance the coherence of an existing culture and play an important role in incremental, non-strategic change. The metamorphic change dependent on a transformation of the cognitive structures of management can only come about, however, through a strategic decision process being triggered.

There is considerable evidence that organizations maintain this cybernetic mode of operating long after it fails to be effective in successfully adapting the organization to its environment (Metcalfe 1979). Beyer (1981), in her review of ideologies and decision making in organizations, draws on a number of sources in making this point. Organizations use cybernetic processes of attending to issues separately and sequentially and creating solutions incrementally with established routines to simplify environmental complexity. This process might make the analysis too simple to deal effectively with the environmental complexity, with a consequent failure in organizational adaptation. McCall (1977) observed that incongruities critical to adaptation may be missed or misinterpreted because they do not fit within existing collective cognitive structures.

Organizations, by using cybernetic processes to deal with uncertainty and complexity, may be warding off the very inputs they need to survive (Pondy and Mitroff 1979). Thus, as Weick (1979) has pointed out, organizations need to develop ways of enriching as well as simplifying their environments. This is the paradox of the cybernetic mode of organizational decision making — the essential processes of simplifying in order to cope with complexity and uncertainty filter out the information necessary to survival in changing circumstances.

The catalyst for change in BRS, the thing that broke the management of the organization out of the cybernetic pattern of behaviour, was a strategic dilemma. BRS managers were forced, through external economic and internal financial performance pressures, to deal with a problem that did not have an acceptable solution within the existing collective cognitive structure. The system was 'shocked' by these pressures to confront an issue for which the existing frame of reference was inadequate. This 'shock' provided the catalyst for the organizational behaviour and processes to shift from one pattern to another, from cybernetic to strategic behaviour.

Notes

1. Refer to Appendix I for details on the senior managers of BRS.

2. When Peter Thompson had been group co-ordinator of BRS, the group planning and development controller, Clive Beattie, had undertaken an economic analysis that indicated that the branches needed a minimum of 6 per cent gross margin on general haulage business in order to avoid a net loss. Peter Thompson used this analysis to argue that branches earning less than 6 per cent gross margin on general haulage should be closed.

6
DIVERSITY AND A DISPERSED POWER STRUCTURE

A great deal of diversity remained within the coherent culture that was being forged within BRS. Each of the regional companies had its own traditions and operated in a business environment with different types and intensities of industrial and commercial activity (see Appendix 2). Similarly, the managing directors and management teams of the regional companies came from a range of backgrounds and experiences, which resulted in some variations in management philosophy and style. It was inevitable therefore that a diversity of perceptions would be brought to bear on policy issues and that the responses of the regional companies to Peter Thompson's strategy of diversification and the contraction of general haulage would vary.

These differences in perceptions and preferences acted on the decision-making process through the organization's power structure. In BRS this was relatively dispersed. The structures and processes established by Thompson had given the regional company managing directors considerable power.

This diversity of beliefs and preferences, combined with the dispersed power structure resulted in political processes which were a key feature of the strategic decision-making process.

Culture as a constraint on strategic change

The culture of the organization — the shared beliefs and values, and the behaviour patterns and artefacts that reflected and reaffirmed them — was a key factor in the dilemma facing BRS. The cognitive structures of the senior management contained certain beliefs and values about strategic and structural issues. These cognitive structures placed high utility on certain things, for example a decentralized operating structure, and involved strongly held beliefs about certain causal relationships. The beliefs and values that constituted these cognitive structures reflected the experience of the individual managers (Appendix 2) and tended to have the effect of precluding new approaches to these issues. The environmental pressures were such, however, that the strategy-structure mismatch had to be confronted, and management was eventually forced to initiate a strategic decision-making process in search of innovative solutions.

The decision-making process was initiated by group management's seeking approval for a series of policy proposals. The development and approval of the proposals, however, were constrained by the culture. First, the decision-making process had to account for both the strategic and structural issues; the effect of a strategic change on the structure of the organization became a major criterion in the decision-making process. Certain structural requirements had to be satisfied for any strategic proposal to be generally acceptable.

Secondly, the culture of the organization regarding certain substantive and processual issues tended to exclude innovation. The decision-making process essential to the development and approval of innovative approaches to both strategy and structure required a framework of thinking and action outside the boundaries of the existing collective cognitive structure.

These constraints applied to important substantive issues, particularly those concerning management's perception of the industry, BRS's role in it, and the most appropriate structure for effective operation. The major business activity of the organization was to a large extent bound by tradition, and the managers responsible for the activity tended, understandably, to be constrained by their previous experience. Those, usually more junior managers, who were not constrained by the enculturation effects of a long experience of BRS, lacked the expertise and credibility to readily develop convincing alternatives.

An equally powerful and pervasive constraint on the decision-making process were the shared beliefs and values concerning processual issues. The formal decision-making structure had a powerful influence on the strategy process primarily because it defined these processual constraints. The planning and control system was a central element of the culture, and a great deal of time was devoted to activities, the prime purpose of which was apparently to re-affirm key aspects of the underlying cognitive structure.

A crucial processual aspect of the culture was that which defined the boundaries of legitimate 'political' behaviour. An intuitive response to the concept of a coherent culture, and the collective cognitive structure that underlies it, is that it is inconsistent with the frequently observed political behaviour that arises out of diversity among the interests of individual organizational members. Even within a collective cognitive structure, however, a genuine diversity of interests might exist, and processes and behaviours essentially political in nature will emerge. Pettigrew (1985:44) discusses this overlap between organizational politics and culture and suggests that 'a central concept linking political and cultural analysis is legitimacy'.

In BRS certain forms of behaviour and argument were acceptable within the forums and processes that were central elements of the culture; others were not. For the regional company managing directors to resist group policy initiatives by arguing in the GPC that the policies cut across 'regional company autonomy' was acceptable (and almost mandatory), but to argue the case on the basis of the diminution of the power or career prospects of the managing directors was unacceptable, even though the underlying issue was essentially the same.

Perhaps the most comprehensive treatment of this issue has been undertaken by Pfeffer (1981), who argues that the effect of diversity of interests will be mediated through processes of legitimization and rationalization in organizations with a coherent culture. The impact of diverse interests on the organization will be mediated by processual constraints of the culture. Certain decisions, policies, and behaviour will be rationalized and legitimized, while behaviour perceived to be outside the norms of the organization will be sanctioned.

Hence, the culture of BRS placed powerful constraints on management's response to the dilemma, and the development of a new strategic thrust required careful management of these issues, particularly concerning organizational processes — innovation in substantive strategic terms presupposed innovation in processual, decision-making terms.

Cultural coherence in BRS was essential to stability, continuity, and unified, concerted action, but it also acted as a constraint on innovation. Earlier in its history, strategic change in BRS had almost entirely resulted from imposed government policy, or through the influence of a new chief executive coming from outside the organization. Innovative responses to the 1977 dilemma, however, were generated because of the dispersion, rather than the coherence, of the culture. The culture tended to have a stabilizing or damping influence on the impetus for change through the substantive and processual constraints it imposed. These constraints could be shifted, however, using analytical, political, and other processes that acted on the cognitive structures of the organization's managers. Major strategic initiatives implied a change in the culture of the organization, and a crucial aspect of managing the strategy process involved influencing the cognitive structures of those participating in the decision-making process, that is, managing cultural change.

The role of diversity and power in the decision-making process

Several writers (Burns 1961; Pettigrew 1973; Salancik and Pfeffer 1977) have stressed the functional role that political processes can play in organizations. Burns suggests that political processes are mechanisms through which organizations adapt to their environment: 'Political action is the necessary instrument for the accomplishment of internal change which to an outsider is the inevitable consequence of a new situation' (Burns 1961:266).

Salancik and Pfeffer make the same point more forcefully: 'Political power far from being a dirty business, is, in its most naked form, one of the few mechanisms available for aligning an organization with its own reality' (Salancik and Pfeffer 1977:3).

These observations were confirmed by the BRS research. Political behaviour was a key mechanism for bringing about fundamental change. For a new general haulage strategy to be adopted within BRS, certain fundamental changes had to take place. The new strategy had implicit in it a different view of BRS and its role in the industry from that traditionally held. The cognitive structures of the organization's decision makers had to change, and a crucial aspect of the decision-making process was the way the cognitive structures of individuals gradually underwent change.

Differences in preferences and perceptions on essential substantive and processual issues existed within a senior management group, the power structure of which was sufficiently dispersed so that policies could not simply be imposed. These differences became sharply focused within the arena of the GPC, where individuals and subgroups championed their own solutions to the dilemma. None of the championed solutions was viable in its original form, but each provided the seeds for innovative approaches to the problem.

Even when a new view of the world developed, it was shared to a varying extent by the members of the top management group. Some senior managers embraced the new strategy totally; others clung steadfastly to the traditional view. Hence there were continuing elements of resistance and, for some people, the new strategy had to be driven through the organization. This required changes in the power structure.

The central issue of concern here is how these changes were influenced and managed by David White who, as group managing director had prime responsibility for the strategic direction of BRS. What could White do to manage this complex, strategic situation? He, like all managers, could act only within the set boundaries. Essentially the avenues of influence were limited to certain mechanisms, most of which were specified by formal organizational considerations or by established precedent and practice. The most important mechanisms available to David White were:

- *The Group Policy Committee*, which was central to the strategy process because virtually all major decisions were made (or at least endorsed) by the committee. The GPC was the focus of policy within BRS and it was primarily through the management of this mechanism that the group managing director exercised influence over the organization.
- *Quarterly Review meetings* between group and the regional companies; they were the focus of the relationship between these two levels of the organization. These meetings were the formal mechanism through which the financial planning and control system operated. Regional company five-year corporate plans and annual budgets were agreed on and monitored through these quarterly review meetings. In dealing with individual companies, White was able to exercise more direct control than was the case in GPC meetings where the regional company managing directors, were able to present a united front.
- *The appraisal, promotion, and reward systems*: these gave White a certain, although fairly narrowly circumscribed, avenue of influence over the regional company managing directors. The promotion of individuals to senior management positions within the regional companies required White's approval, and future appointments to the position of managing director were dependent upon White's recommendations to Thompson. The present standing, and future promotion, of the incumbent regional company managing directors, however, was also strongly influenced by their companies' performance and their personal relationship with Thompson.
- *Personal contact* between White and the senior management of BRS played a central role in the management process. Data about interpersonal relationships and contacts were more difficult to ob-

tain and interpret than about the more formal aspects of the management process. However, as will be discussed later in this chapter, certain aspects of this dimension of the strategy process were central to the management of change in BRS.

The changing power structure within BRS

In effect White had two roles within the organization. The first role, that of group managing director, was defined in terms of direct reporting relationships. In this capacity, White dealt with each of the managing directors on a one-to-one basis. His relationship with each of them revolved around a wide range of formal and informal managerial contacts, including the quarterly review meetings, which provided the primary formal framework of the relationship. The requirements of this first role were largely defined by the planning and control system — agreeing on company corporate plans and budgets, and then reviewing and controlling the actions of the managing directors within the agreed plans. David White's style was well suited to this role, and after a 'settling-in' period he managed these relationships in a relaxed, confident manner.

White's second formal role was that of chairman of the GPC. It was largely his growing influence in this role that allowed him to exert control over the strategic direction of the group. At the time of the emergence of general haulage as a strategic issue, White was still consolidating his role in the GPC. The other members naturally made comparisons between White's approach and that of his predecessor. Thompson had developed a GPC role that involved a delicate balance of true participation by its members in some important issues and accepted direction on others. This role reflected Thompson's natural style and the personal influence he held as author of the GPC. His position was further strengthened by his having appointed the managing directors. White recognized that he could not adopt the same role as Thompson because of both personal and structural factors. Not only had he been promoted from among the other managing directors but, as group managing director he still reported to Thompson. His authority was therefore more circumscribed than Thompson's had been as GPC chairman.

White attempted to establish a role based upon his own style. Thompson was gregarious and socially skilful (variously described by BRS managers as charismatic and silver tongued). His style was to develop personal relationships with his business colleagues. White's position in the GPC was made more difficult by Thompson's continued personal association with most of the BRS regional company managing directors. This contact went beyond normal business dealings. There can be little doubt that the situation made it difficult for White to establish an independent, credible role in the GPC.

The attitude of White towards the general haulage activity was, at least initially, very similar to that of Thompson. White's approach to general haulage as managing director of Eastern BRS had been something of a model of how Thompson's strategy should have been implemented. The so-called stop-the-bleeding strategy revolved around the selective shedding, often through the process of unilateral application of price increases, of unprofitable business. White's identification with this approach did nothing to strengthen his role in the GPC. The managing directors did not share his view of the best way to manage general haulage.

Perhaps an even more crucial point of disagreement was White's philosophy on the management structure. During the second half of 1977, the managing directors became increasingly anxious over what they perceived as a tendency by White to impose group control over areas within the established management authority of the regional companies. The managing directors described this as a move towards centralization. The issue of group product management of general haulage became a major point of contention between White and the managing directors who felt threatened by what they saw as a trend towards increasing group control; they considered it outside the mandate given to White by Thompson.

For all of these reasons White's role in the GPC was initially very difficult. Within a short period of time, however, he was able to establish a strong role independent of Thompson, and he began to exert an increasing amount of influence over the committee. The strengthening of White's role in the GPC and the emergence of a coherent general haulage strategy were closely linked. As White worked determinedly around the obstacles and opposition to proposals for a new approach to general haulage, he progressively assumed greater control of the strategic decision-making process within the group. It was through this that a clear, coherent strategy was gradually conceived at group level. The group's rapidly growing knowledge of the analytical aspects of the general haulage problem and the development of the innovative approaches to the problem greatly enhanced White's influence.

This process itself was facilitated, however, by David White's increasing power within the organization — within the group, the GPC, and also the National Freight Corporation. This changing power position was brought about by a number of interrelated factors. First, there was a natural process of settling in to the new role. The GPC had to go through the natural group process of sorting out roles and become comfortable with a new style of operating. Secondly, the continuing good financial performance of the BRS group. In spite of difficult economic conditions, in 1979 BRS achieved its profit budget for the fourth consecutive year, its third under White, who was proving to be an extremely capable group managing director. Had the group failed to meet its financial targets, it is doubtful whether he would have had sufficient credibility and influence to continue with the implementation of Thompson's 1972 strategy. Thirdly, important changes in the membership of the GPC occurred, some of which were instigated by White, while others were the result of a natural process of demographic change. In both cases the changes had a significant effect on the power structure of the organization.

Changes in the BRS management structure

Just before White's appointment (January 1976) to group, the senior management structure was as shown in Figure 6.1. Twelve months after White's appointment, the senior management structure was as shown in Figure 6.2.

Although the formal structure of the GPC had not changed, the individuals occupying the roles had changed considerably. White had begun to build his own team. The only appointment in the group management team over which he had not had some influence was that of Clive Beattie. This growing sense of patronage was clearly an important factor in White's increasing power as GPC chairman.

In October 1977, White made further changes to the group management structure. The changes had been planned for some time, but the opportunity to implement them occurred when the marketing manager of Eastern BRS accepted the position of finance director of Southern BRS. White arranged for Clive Beattie to be appointed assistant managing director of that company, with special responsibility for marketing. David White then offered the planning and development controller's position to Kieren Fielding, and Gerry Simmons was appointed marketing controller.

During 1978 further changes occurred. In June the group personnel manager, Harry Osborne, retired and was replaced by the Scottish Road Services personnel manager, Charlie Williams. In September David Cutler left BRS to take up a position with British

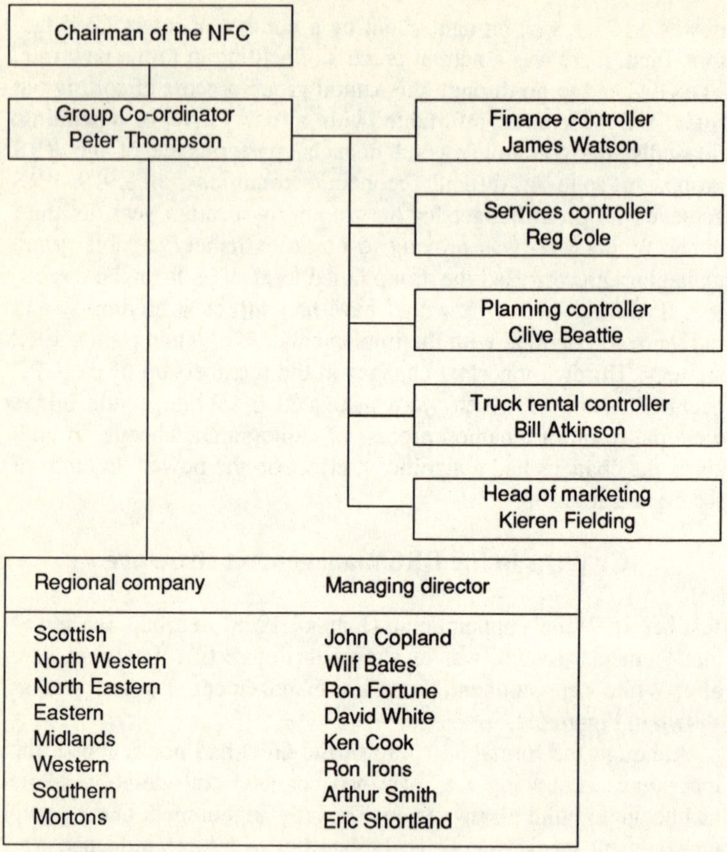

Figure 6.1: The BRS senior management structure in late 1975

Leyland, and White appointed the finance director of Tempco (another NFC company), Hugh Mellor, as his replacement. The group management team was then as shown in Figure 6.3.

The apparent effect of these changes was to weaken the group representation on the GPC because the controllers, who had equal 'voting rights' with the managing directors, were now one less in number. The numerical strength of group's representation on the GPC was not restored until July 1979 when Mark Bedeman was appointed membership products controller. In practice, however, these changes increased group's influence in the GPC. The influence of individual controllers in the GPC depended very much on the credibility they had with the managing directors. This in turn

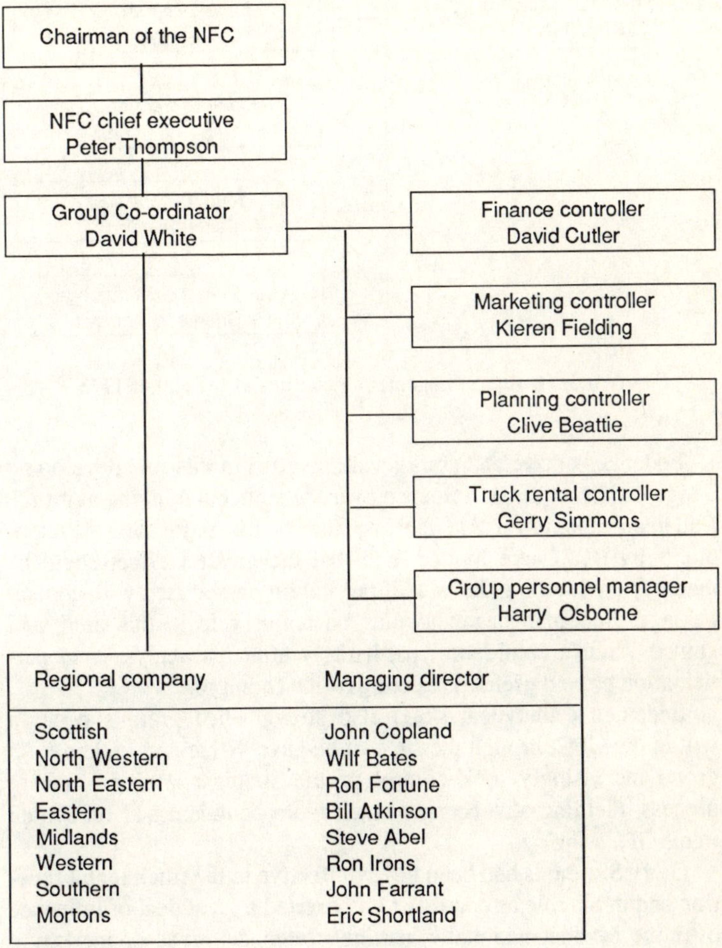

Figure 6.2: The BRS senior management structure in late 1976

depended upon the personal style of the individual and the perceived competence he had in the area for which he was responsible. In these terms, the changes significantly strengthened the group team.

Kieren Fielding was more suited, in terms of abilities and temperament, to the planning and development function which was more analytical and 'backroom' in character. The corporate planning function was further enhanced by the appointment of Mark Bedeman as group corporate planner in January 1978.

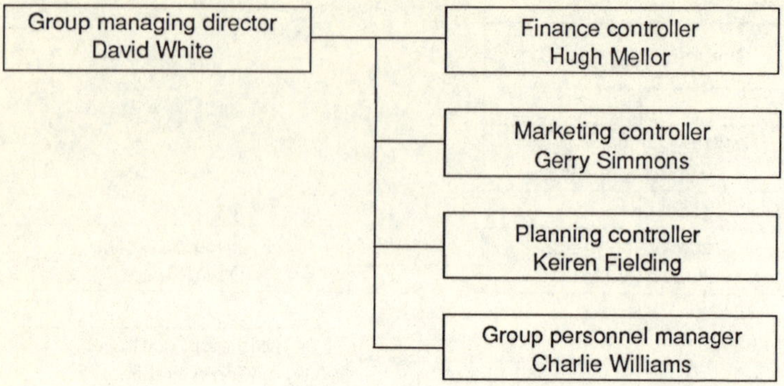

Figure 6.3: Group management structure at the end of 1978

Bedeman's drive and ability soon resulted in this role developing a high degree of direct influence over the strategic thinking at group. Bedeman recognized that the opportunity for major new developments by BRS were limited, and that the greatest effect could be made by overcoming the lack of profitability associated with general haulage. Bedeman began to play an active role in this area, and gained White's confidence, particularly after his analysis and participation proved useful in meetings with Thompson.

Bedeman's analytical skills also strengthened group's position within the GPC through the support he gave White and Fielding. As group increasingly took control of the strategic decision-making process, Fielding also became much more confident and influential in his GPC role.

Gerry Simmons had been highly effective in the truck rental function and in his role as controller had exerted a great deal of influence over the product nationally, particularly in the areas of marketing and vehicle acquisition. Under the financing arrangements BRS adopted, central purchasing of truck rental vehicles proved cost effective, and Simmons developed a reputation for 'doing good deals'. Central purchasing of vehicles, in conjunction with other controls, allowed Simmons to exercise considerable control over the regional companies' truck rental fleets. Central control of truck rental advertising and pricing was also exercised. The truck rental product operated on the basis of a published national tariff schedule, which was established in principle on the basis of GPC approval of the recommendations made by the truck rental managers committee, chaired by Simmons. In practice, the initiative on pricing was taken by group. This was possible largely because of the credibility Simmons had in the truck rental area, based on his experience and proven record. Although his credibility as truck rental expert was not transferred automatically to the marketing function, he attempted to establish a high level of influence in the GPC in this new role. He met initially with a great deal of resistance and criticism from the managing directors but was gradually able to establish much more influence over the marketing function throughout the group than had previously existed.

Similarly, Harry Osborne was succeeded by a man more determined to exercise influence throughout the group. Charlie Williams was not without credibility with the managing directors, because he had been held in high regard within the group when in the role of personnel manager of Scottish Road Services. He was keen to establish an influential role in the GPC in the personnel function. He also met with a considerable amount of resistance from the managing directors. David White gave both Williams and Simmons the opportunity, encouragement, and support necessary to succeed in establishing these more influential roles.

David Cutler's resignation came as a disappointment to White. Cutler, of all the controllers, had established a strong, credible presence in the GPC and had also developed good personal relationships with the managing directors. Cutler shared David White's understanding of the sensitive balance between company autonomy and group control, and this allowed him to exercise considerable control through the financial reporting system without generating resentment among the managing directors. This subtle understanding of his role, and his obvious competence in the function greatly assisted White, particularly during his initial period in the role of group managing director. Cutler's successor, Hugh Mellor, had the technical competence but had yet to develop an appreciation of the subtleties of the group role. He tended to adopt a less flexible or accommodating role than Cutler. By this time, however, White's position in the GPC was well established, and Mellor's straightforward technical competence was sufficient for him to be effective.

The decreasing influence of the managing directors

During this period the roles of the individual managing directors also underwent considerable change. The increasing power of group was mirrored in the decreasing power of the managing directors. This general trend of declining power was the result of a number of events, perhaps the most significant of which was the change of one managing director, which this otherwise extremely stable group underwent.

Early in 1978 Wilf Bates, the managing director of North Western BRS retired, and White appointed the company engineer, Ian Blundell, as his successor. This greatly strengthened White's position in the GPC because, of the relationships he had with the managing directors, that with Bates was the least satisfactory. Within GPC meetings Bates could be least relied upon by White to provide support on important issues. Further, the perceptions of the two men on general haulage were dramatically different. Thompson had been unsuccessful in convincing Bates to conform to the strategy of diversification and general haulage decline. White continued to force this issue with Bates and this resulted in conflict in quarterly review meetings and the GPC.

As Bates's retirement approached, his strong position in the GPC weakened, and his opinions began to carry less weight with both the controllers and the managing directors. The fact that Bates's influence declined rapidly, however, did little to strengthen White's position, because Bates still had the power to vote against proposals, and his presence continued to be unsettling.

The opposite dependency relationship existed between White and Bates's successor. Ian Blundell was conscious that he owed his promotion to White. An earlier incident involving the expenditure of general haulage capital in North Western BRS had threatened to cloud Blundell's future. In spite of this, White decided to promote him after interviewing a number of other candidates. Blundell articulated the need for the company to diversify and move away from general haulage, and this was clearly the mandate White attached to the appointment.

As Blundell confronted the problems of comprehensively implementing the strategy of diversification long after the other companies, and within severe capital and time constraints, a new perception of general haulage began to develop in North Western BRS. Blundell concluded that Southern BRS's clearfreight strategy of retaining general haulage traffic through subcontracting while reducing the fleet of vehicles was the only viable option for the North Western BRS. Thus, White and Blundell shared a vested interest in a new general haulage strategy. For Blundell, a new approach to general haulage was a means of achieving the transition to a diversified product base upon which his success depended. This single change in the membership of the GPC had a considerable influence on the balance of power and the balance of perceptions and preferences on general haulage strategy.

Before this change, White could rely on the following GPC voting pattern on most controversial issues where group and company interests were perceived as being divided (Table 6.1):

In support of group	*In support of the companies*	*Uncommitted*
David White	John Copland	Bill Atkinson
David Cutler	Steve Abel	Eric Shortland
Kieren Fielding	Ron Irons	
Gerry Simmons	Ron Fortune	
Harry Osborne	John Farrant	
	Wilf Bates	

Table 6.1 The Group Policy Committee voting pattern

The position of Bill Atkinson and Eric Shortland fluctuated according to the issue under discussion and other circumstances. Shortland was in the difficult position of trying to sustain a company with deep family traditions with which he was personally closely associated, but which was something of an anomaly within the BRS structure. Mortons was much smaller than the other BRS companies, and perhaps would have been absorbed into the contiguous regional companies if it had not been for the personal involvement of Shortland. In Thompson's desire to make manifest his philosophy of company autonomy, Mortons had played an important role. Once established as a BRS company, the situation was hard to reverse, in spite of the logical arguments that existed for absorbing Mortons into the regional companies. Shortland's role in the GPC was therefore circumscribed, and he relied on the goodwill and patronage of the more powerful managing directors and White. Shortland's attitude to the notion of a new general haulage strategy was hard to assess. In many ways it would have had little effect on Mortons compared with the other companies and, for that matter, compared with the more general business and industrial circumstances threatening the survival of his company.

Atkinson's position was stronger than that of Shortland. Aspects of his relationship with White were similar to those that existed between Blundell and White. Atkinson was an ex-driver and shop steward, who by dint of his commonsense, personality, and diligence had achieved a senior position within the management of BRS. Atkinson's background and lack of formal education would not have helped him in his rise through the hierarchy of the organization. He clearly appreciated the support White had given him in the past, particular in his appointment as managing director of Eastern BRS. There was considerable evidence that Atkinson frequently helped White in obtaining GPC agreement to controversial proposals. Although in his frequently-adopted role as GPC humorist, storyteller and wit Atkinson criticized the group management team, he lent support to White on numerous issues in important, and often crucial ways.

White, however, was never assured of Shortland's or Atkinson's support because they could, and often did, side with the other six managing directors; and White needed the support of both of them in order to gain a majority in the GPC. This balance was altered when Blundell replaced Bates as managing director of North Western BRS. The balance within the GPC then became as shown in Table 6.2:

In support of group	*In support of the companies*	*Uncommitted*
David White	John Copland	Bill Atkinson
David Cutler	Steve Abel	Eric Shortland
Kieren Fielding	Ron Irons	Ian Blundell
Gerry Simmons	Ron Fortune	
Charlie Williams	John Farrant	

Table 6.2 The Group Policy Committee voting pattern

The new balance made it much easier to get a majority vote in the GPC. The three 'uncommitted' managing directors were probably more susceptible to lobbying by White than the others, but this varied with the issue and the circumstances applying at the time.

The positions of the other managing directors

The positions adopted by the managing directors listed in Table 6.2 as typically 'voting with the companies' were the outcome of a complex set of factors. The history and circumstances of their companies, and personal factors were crucial in influencing the attitude they adopted to particular issues.

At the time that the general haulage dilemma arose, Scottish Road Services was going through a difficult period. The two organizations from which it had been formed, Scottish Road Services and Tayforth, were still undergoing considerable change and were certainly not fully integrated into the BRS group. The old Tayforth philosophy and attitudes were continuing to have an influence, and some lingering resentment remained following the action taken by the NFC in rationalizing its Scottish interests. The continuing poor financial performance of the company placed its managing director, John Copland, in a weak position vis-à-vis group. The difficulties associated with the restructuring and poor financial performance of the company also had an important impact on the role that John Copland was able, or perhaps prepared, to play in the GPC.

The high regard in which Copland was held in the organization, and the industry, created expectations about the role he might adopt in the GPC. Copland made it very clear, however, that his primary concern was to rebuild the Scottish Company, rather than to take a leading role in the GPC or the strategic direction of the group as a whole. As time went on, expectations changed, and Copland appeared to settle into a quiet role with limited influence. His role in the GPC and the background and the continuing difficulties of his company cannot be divorced, however: the man's personal qualities and reputation meant that a sense of potential influence remained, even though he he chose to use it rarely in the GPC.

Further, largely because of its unique history, Scottish Road Services was less concerned about the possibility of a fundamentally new general haulage strategy. The company was still struggling with the implementation of the 1972 strategy, and to come to terms, on an individual and organizational level, with the changes implicit in it. Had a new general haulage strategy been of more immediate significance to Scottish Road Services, Copland could have been expected to adopt a more active and influential role in the strategy process of the group.

The organization had been through a period of upheaval, and Copland realized that the company was now dependent on BRS group for the capital necessary to consolidate and, he hoped, rebuild the company. As Scottish Road Services was now not a strong profit generator, and was not likely to be in the near future, Copland was to some extent dependent upon the goodwill of White for the required capital injection. Thus, Copland had much to lose and little to gain by opposing White's strategic initiatives.

Ron Fortune, and the entire North Eastern Company, was something of an enigma. His apparent indecisiveness, particularly in the GPC; the repeated references to 'closing branches and shrinking the company' when the opposite was happening; the mixture of traditional general haulage managers nearing retirement and young graduate managers who had been rapidly promoted by way of truck rental; his strong opposition to change and his success in obtaining group approval for development projects requiring substantial investment — all within the framework of a company that had gone from failure to success under his management.

The role played by Fortune in the GPC was generally not especially influential. As a result of repeatedly displaying a marked reticence to commit himself on controversial issues, he developed a reputation for 'sitting on the fence'. In spite of this, however, reputation and a generally weak role in the GPC, Fortune took a strong stand on a number of important issues. This was the case with all the proposals associated with White's new general haulage strategy. Fortune opposed the idea of a new product, trailer rental, and his was the only company (with the exception of Scottish Road Services) which did not implement this new product, in spite of considerable pressure from White and the advice of his own truck rental manager.

Fortune's opposition to a new general haulage strategy seemed to be based, very largely, on a concern about the erosion of company autonomy. It appeared that Fortune was possibly more attached to the structure and philosophy created by Thompson in 1972 than he was to traditional general haulage. He was more concerned about the change in this philosophy than the decline of general haulage: far better that the decline of general haulage should continue than to adopt a new strategy, which in halting the decline of general haulage, threatened the regional company structure. If Fortune had once been reluctant to adopt Thompson's strategy of diversification because of a natural disinclination to change, this attitude combined with a very strong attachment to company autonomy made him vehemently opposed to White's strategy proposals.

Steve Abel had considerable effect on the decision-making process with the new general haulage strategy. His influence stemmed partly from the high regard in which he was held throughout the organization, and partly from the success of his company, Midlands BRS. The fact that the most profitable company in BRS was still heavily dependent on general haulage, and was run by a well-respected managing director who proclaimed that general haulage could be profitable, if properly managed, was a powerful argument against a completely new strategic approach. Many of Steve Abel's attempts to influence the GPC were unsuccessful however, because of the direct and open style he brought to bear. The nature of the GPC was such that directness and openness were often outflanked by the more subtle attempts at influence by others.

The philosophy and general haulage strategy that Ron Irons

applied within Western BRS was inevitably reflected in the attitude he displayed towards the general haulage initiatives proposed by group. While Irons was prepared to test new ideas cautiously, an inherent conservatism resulted in a reluctance to support any proposal that would have committed his company to something radically different. This resulted in his often trying to maintain an uncommitted position on important issues being debated in the GPC. Further, his influence in the GPC was greatly weakened by the relatively poor financial performance of his company at this time. This made him more dependent upon White than would have been the case had his company been producing good profits and cash flow. Within the results-oriented BRS culture, company financial performance and the standing of the managing directors, including their influence in the GPC, were closely linked. A company's position on the group profit 'league table' was an important indication of the influence its managing director had in the decision-making process.

Farrant's strongly held views on the proper role of group in the organization shaped his approach to the GPC. These views derived from a broad concern about the organization structure of BRS. Farrant felt that White intended to move the organization towards a structure with a much stronger product orientation. He was by far the most outspoken member of the GPC on the issue of the changing structural philosophy and what was described as the trend to centralization. He became associated with a consistent 'anti-centralization' stand in the GPC and was frequently in conflict with White over matters that implied some move in this direction. The appointment of additional group staff, for example, and in particular product managers. For Farrant this was an important issue: tampering with the allocation of power and authority in the organization was a direct threat to the philosophy of company autonomy established by Thompson.

Farrant was one of the most politically astute members of the GPC. He was acutely conscious of the implications of issues for the power and authority structure of BRS, even when these issues were being presented and discussed purely in terms of substantive strategy. He was also extremely articulate, and was therefore able, through the clever use of language, to expose subtlely the political aspects of an issue, and to bring to the surface the deeper philosophical and structural implications of strategy proposals.

These attitudes and skills resulted in Farrant's frequently being the focus of opposition to group proposals in the GPC. This role was enhanced by the dramatic improvement in the financial performance of Southern BRS about this time. Further, Farrant's earlier experience as headquarters operations manager had naturally shaped his perceptions of general haulage and the nature of the strategic problem BRS was confronting. It also allowed him to speak with authority on matters such as the national co-ordination of general haulage. The fact that a key element of the new strategy proposals was a derivative of Southern BRS's general haulage strategy placed him in the awkward position of supporting the strategy in principle, while being strongly opposed to the organizational implications of implementing the strategy nationally.

The role of politics in the strategy process

Analysis of the BRS data indicates that political behaviour can take two forms (see Figure 6.4):

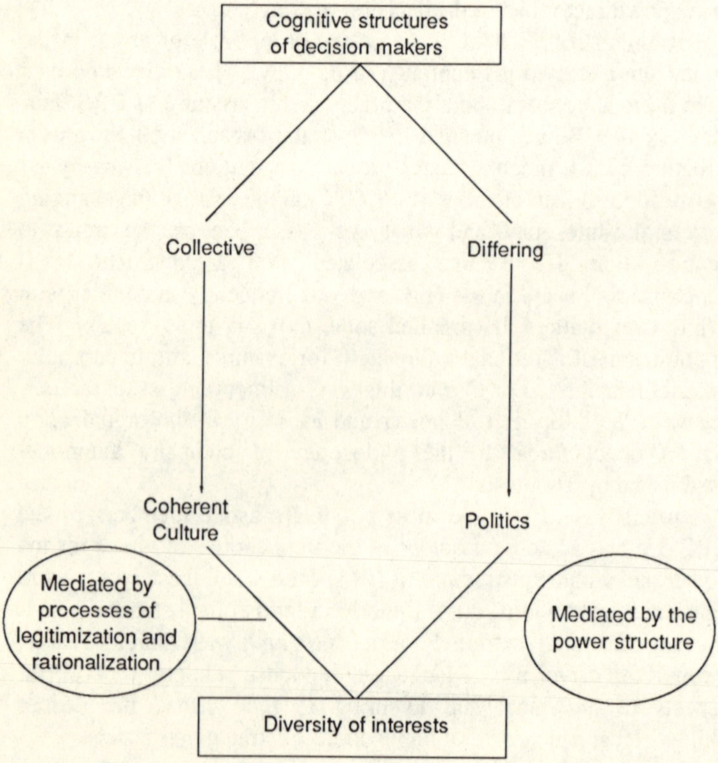

Figure 6.4: The impact of diversity on the strategy process

- Rationalization and legitimization of decisions, policies, and behaviour to mediate diversity of interests in organizations dominated by a collective cognitive structure. This form of political behaviour has been discussed in detail earlier in the chapter.
- Where the collective cognitive structure has broken down, political behaviour is a key mechanism through which strategic change can be effected. In these circumstances, the political behaviour will be mediated by the power structure of the organization.

In organizations with highly concentrated power structures, a new cognitive structure can be imposed and will become internalized by organizational members with time. The processes associated with this internalization of new beliefs and values is discussed in Chapter 8. Where the power structure is dispersed, political behaviour is a key element of the processes through which new cognitive structures develop.

The analysis of the role of organizational culture and politics in the strategy process can be further explicated by drawing on Grinyer and Spender's (1979) concept of a 'feasible solution space'. This feasible solution space is defined in terms of what Grinyer and Spender called a 'recipe', or in terms of the model presented here, a collective cognitive structure. Management is confronted with a 'dilemma' when a solution to a problem can not be found in the feasible solution space, that is, the established collective cognitive structure.

The situation is more complex in multilevel organizations with dispersed power structures like BRS. Within BRS the strategic dilemma had to be resolved between three levels of management: the chief executive of the NFC, the group managing director and the managing directors of the regionally based, autonomous operating companies. Acceptable 'solutions' existed within the cognitive structures of one level of management, but these solutions lay outside the cognitive structure of the other levels (see Figure 6.5).

The Chief Executive's solution of progressively contracting the traditional business activity was outside the managing directors' feasible solution space and, further, was unacceptable politically because of its career implications. Within the managing directors' cognitive structure, a solution did not exist that would meet the chief executive's demands in terms of financial performance.

The task facing the group managing director (whose position in the structure and strategy process placed him in the role of mediator between the chief executive and the company managing directors) in managing the strategy process was to create a new collective cogni-

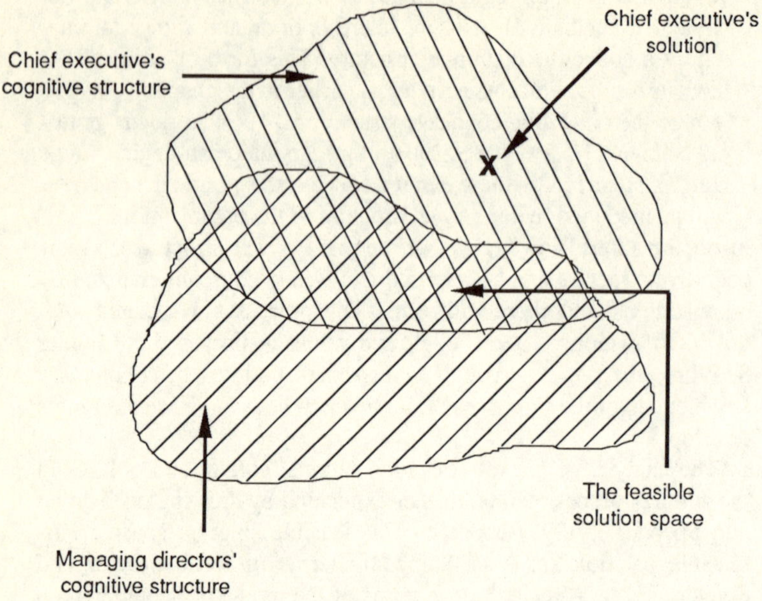

Figure 6.5: The feasible solution space

tive structure that encompassed an acceptable solution (see Figure 6.6).

The catalyst for change, the thing that broke the management of the organization out of one pattern of behaviour and into another, was a dilemma. BRS managers were forced, through external economic and internal financial performance pressures, to deal with a problem that did not have an acceptable solution within the existing collective cognitive structure. The system was 'shocked' by these pressures to confront an issue for which the existing collective cognitive structure was inadequate.

The dispersed power structure meant that the implementation of the proposals made by the chief executive depended on the active support of the company managing directors. If it had not been for the dispersed power and the consequent political behaviour, this 'solution' would simply have been imposed on the organization. This solution would have come from the existing cognitive structure and therefore would not have constituted strategic change within the metamorphic model of strategy developed in Chapter 2. The combination of a strategic issue that did not have a solution within the overlap of the

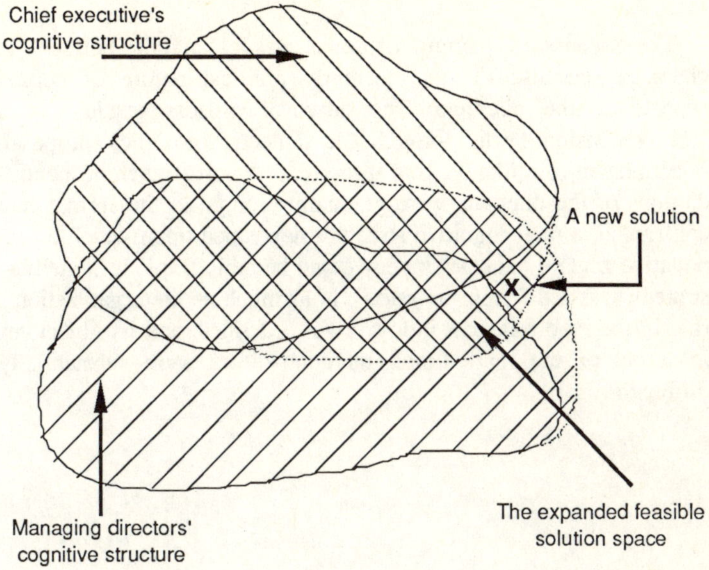

Figure 6.6: The expanded feasible solution space

feasible solution spaces of the various decision makers and a dispersed power structure resulted in political behaviour that was a crucial aspect of the strategic decision-making process.

White initially attempted to obtain approval for his preferred solution, which was naturally based upon his own cognitive structure. This cognitive structure was derived largely from his experience as a successful regional company managing director who had developed ways of dealing effectively with the problem of general haulage. When these attempts were frustrated by BRS's dispersed power structure, he used the authority of his formal position and various political tactics to change the decision-making structure. This moved the strategic dilemma temporarily outside the existing substantive and processual constraints, and allowed a more analytical approach to be applied.

The issue then came within the sphere of direct group control, and so the group managing director obtained powerful political resources in the form of information, new insights into the problem, and analysis that could be used to argue a case in the GPC. The analysis that was undertaken also provided the group managing director with a set of loosely connected policy proposals. These policies did not, however, constitute a new strategy, and they did not deal effectively with the dilemma confronting the organization.

The process of gaining approval was essentially political in character, because of the inherently political nature of certain aspects of the dilemma. The approval process resulted in a 'comprehension cycle' through the dialectic of policy proposal, rejection, re-formulation and proposal. As the inherent contradictions of the dilemma were gradually brought to the surface and confronted, a new cognitive structure developed upon which an innovative general haulage strategy could be built. Implicit in the new strategy was a different 'mission', in as much as the organization's role in the road transport industry was redefined, and its objectives in terms of the market and its competitors were substantially different.

7
THE PROCESS OF STRATEGIC CHOICE

A complex array of perceptions and preferences, within the pressures of NFC cash constraints and general haulage profitability problems, had created a dilemma. After five years, Thompson's 1972 strategy had run its course, and a new strategic initiative that satisfied the conflicting demands of improved financial performance and the avoidance of organizational contraction had to be found. The incompatibility between the decentralized structure and the existing general haulage strategy could no longer be sustained.

Contextual pressures in the form of NFC financial and product policies seemed to make significant organizational contraction inevitable. This was unacceptable to the management of BRS, however, because it jeopardized their careers and, they believed, the future viability of the organization.

David White found himself in a situation where the chief executive of the NFC was insisting that he apply certain general haulage policies within the BRS Group, and the regional company managing directors were refusing to accept them. This could not continue. Some resolution had to be found, but it depended upon a solution to the problems underlying the dilemma. A general haulage strategy needed to be developed that would significantly improve the profitability of the activity with limited capital investment, and be compatible with the decentralized management structure. The incompatibility between the strategy and structure within environmental and contextual constraints generated a dilemma that acted as a catalyst for the strategic decision-making process.

The process of strategic change

The dilemma that confronted the management of BRS acted as a catalyst for strategic change. BRS managers were forced, through external economic and internal financial performance pressures, to deal with a problem that did not have an acceptable solution within the existing collective cognitive structure. The system was 'shocked' by these pressures to confront an issue for which the existing common cognitive structure was inadequate. This 'shock' provided the catalyst for the organizational behaviour and processes to shift from one pattern to another.

Political processes and behaviours were constrained by the culture of the organization and were amplified or moderated according to the power structure. These political processes played a key role in bringing about change by means of a 'failure recycle' (Mintzberg et al. 1976) — see Figure 7.1. Political processes resulted in policy proposals being rejected and this forced BRS group management to 'recast the strategy'. This cycle of policy proposal → rejection → reformulation and resubmission for approval → rejection → reformulation, and so on, constituted a 'comprehension cycle' that resulted eventually in a coherent strategy based on a new collective cognitive structure.

'Inherent in it (strategic decision making) are factors causing the decision process to cycle back to earlier phases . . . the decision maker gradually comes to comprehend a complex issue' (Mintzberg et al. 1976:265). This comprehension cycle was a crucial aspect of the decision-making process at group level. The failure to gain approval, which was essential to the comprehension cycle, only occurred because the power structure made possible political activity that was manifested in the rejection of policy proposals. Mintzberg et al. refer to political activity and suggests it 'generally manifests itself in the use of the bargaining routines among those who have some control over choices' (1976:262). What Mintzberg et al. fail to identify is that this political activity is one of the major 'inherent factors causing the decision process to cycle back to earlier phases' (1976:265), that is, political activity plays a crucial role in generating the comprehension cycles essential to a decision-making process that moves outside the constraints of the prevailing cognitive structure (see Figure 7.1).

The comprehension cycle that developed within the strategy process observed in BRS is a clear demonstration of the role that political behaviour plays in the transformation in the cognitive structures of managers, and therefore in the strategy process. This transformation in the cognitive structures of decision makers is at the heart of the

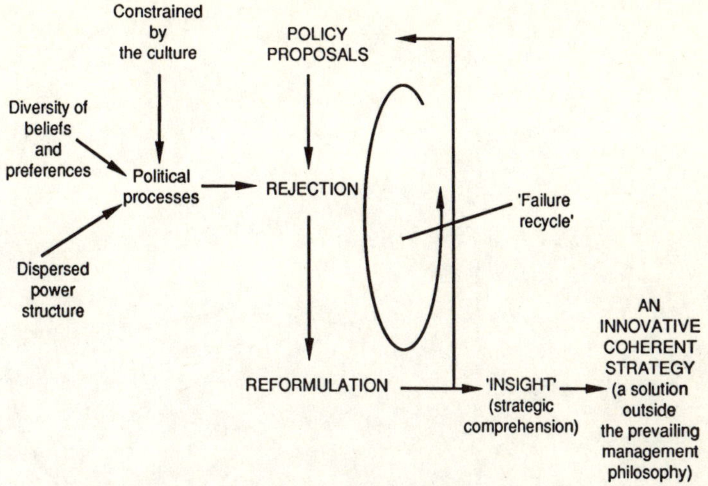

Figure 7.1: The comprehension cycle

strategy process; a process involving a shift from one pattern of organizational processes that provide continuity and stability to a different set of processes that drives strategic change (see Figure 7.2).

Initiating the strategic decision-making process

The strategic decision-making process initially took the form of a range of policy proposals from the key individuals:

- Chief executive (Peter Thompson) — accelerated decline of general haulage.
- Group managing director (David White) — product management of general haulage at group level.
- Regional company managing directors — management action at the individual company level.

The discussions in the NFC and GPC meetings made it clear that the onus for resolving the general haulage dilemma rested primarily with White. Thompson was committed to the 1972 strategy and the continued decline of general haulage, in spite of the organizational implications. The regional company managing directors were not prepared to implement a policy of accelerated decline of general haulage and resisted any attempts by group to resolve the problem by means which threatened their autonomy.

With pressure from above and resistance from below, White was left to find a solution to the problem within a complex set of

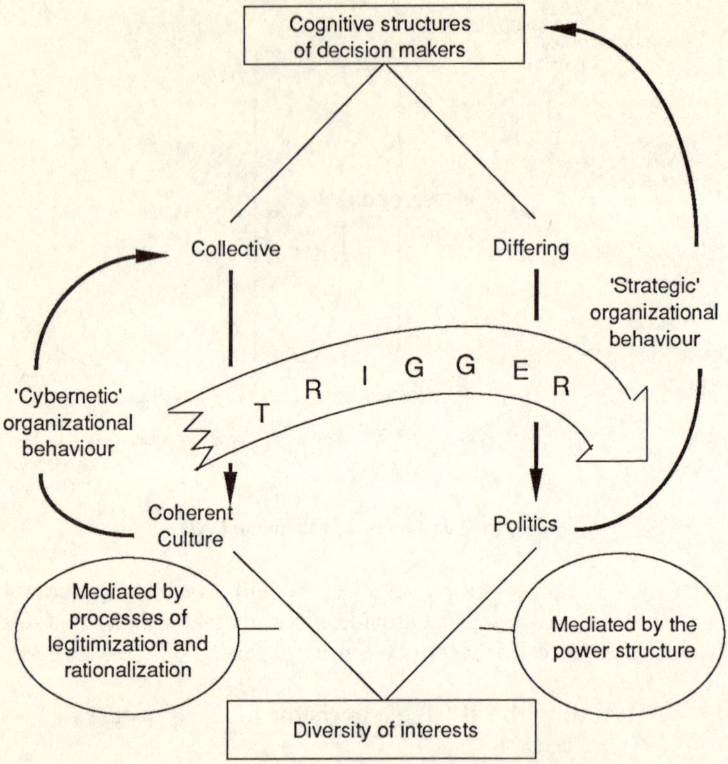

Figure 7.2: Schematic representation of strategic change processes

contradictory perceptions of the nature of the problem and diverse preferences regarding outcomes. Finding a solution involved managing a complex process of organization decision making and change. It required recognition of the fundamental issues underlying the dilemma, and insightful analysis of those elements that were fixed constraints and those that were amenable to change. In addition, sensitivity to the various perceptions and preferences, and the power structure of the organization was required.

White was faced with an extremely complex and difficult situation. He was in effect in the role of mediator between two fundamentally different views of general haulage. To act as mediator in this strategic issue he had to rely on the formal channels available to him, namely the planning and control system links with the chief executive and the individual managing directors, and the GPC link with the managing directors as a group. Of course, a great deal of informal activity was associated with the decision-making process, but ultimately the outcomes of these activities were reflected within the formal decision-making structure.

Stages in the decision-making process

Central to the earliest theories of decision making (Dewey 1910) is the idea that the process involves a series of phases, stages or steps. A considerable amount of research has attempted to verify that decision-making processes in organizations do conform to this stage theory. Witte (1972) tested the hypothesis empirically that 'In order to arrive at a complex innovative decision in a microeconomic unit, a process takes place which consists of a number of different operations that occur at different points in time' (1972:166). This hypothesis was accepted, but a second hypothesis, that the operations follow a specific sequence, was rejected. Witte found that the decision-making process consisted of a plurality of decisions, and when he tested the phase theorem in terms of the subdecisions, he again found no support for a specific sequence. Mintzberg, Raisinghani, and Theoret studied twenty-five different strategic decision-making processes and concluded that a basic 'structure' underlay the process, but agreed with Witte (1972) that a simple sequential relationship did not exist between the process elements of which the structure was composed (1976:252). They did argue, however, that in spite of the immense complexity and dynamic nature of strategic decision-making processes 'they are amenable to conceptual structuring' (1976:274).

Quinn's (1980) study of the processes used in ten major corporations for achieving significant strategic changes has also resulted in an integrative model of the strategic decision-making process. He argues that the discrepancy between normative models and actual behaviour in organizations on strategic decision making should not be a matter of surprise or concern. Quinn presents a purely descriptive model that encompasses analytical and political processes within the corporate culture of the organization:

> . . . large organizations should not — and do not — follow highly formalized textbook approaches in long-range planning, goal generation, and strategy formulation. Instead, they artfully blend formal analysis, behavioural techniques, and power politics to bring about cohesive, step-by-step movement toward ends which initially are broadly conceived, but which are then constantly refined and reshaped as new information

> appears. Their integrating methodology can best be described as 'logical incrementalism' (Quinn 1980:3).

Quinn also describes the process in terms of stages or steps. Unlike Mintzberg et al. (1976) and Horvath and McMillan (1979), Quinn argues that these steps are neither sequential nor discrete. He does argue, however, that certain patterns are associated with the successful management of strategic change and that 'executives do consciously manage individual steps proactively' (1980:4). Quinn offers some valuable insights into the various processes involved in strategic decision making but does not attempt to develop a framework of sufficient formality to be tested against new data. The 'steps' in Quinn's 'logical incrementalism' are actually actions that top managers undertake as part of the decision-making process and in effect constitute tactics in the management of the decision-making process. No attempt is made to structure these steps. As Quinn points out: 'While these process steps occur generally in the order presented, stages are by no means orderly or discrete' (1980:4).

The decision-making process in BRS concerning the strategic issue of general haulage involved a number of stages as shown in Table 7.1.

As indicated by the research discussed earlier (Witte 1972; Mintzberg et al. 1976; and Quinn 1980), these stages were not discrete, and the process was extremely complex with a great deal of overlap, cycling between various stages, and ambiguity.

The initial strategic response

White's initial response to the general haulage dilemma had a critical influence on the way the decision-making process subsequently developed. His response took four forms.

First, he insisted that the managing directors submit reports on the action they intended to take on branches earning less than 6 per cent general haulage gross margin. The lack of success of this approach was illustrated by White's comments a few weeks later in a group controllers' meeting: 'There's not much point in talking about the reports — they're a waste of time. I'll tell them at the next GPC that it will be dealt with in-house (at the quarterly review meetings). Let's face it, we are flying a hell of a kite here.'

At the next GPC meeting, White again pressed the company managing directors for a commitment to raising general haulage prices and expressed his disappointment about the managing directors' plans regarding the 6 per cent gross margin policy. Once again

Stage	Key Events
Problem Recognition Feb 1977 - Mar 1978	General haulage becomes a strategic dilemma.
Initial Strategic Response July 1977	David White attempts to impose general haulage policies but meets resistance in the GPC.
Modification of the Decision-Making Structure December 1977	GPC commitment to a working party.
Search for New Alternatives Dec 1977 - July 1978	The working party generate and evaluate policy proposals.
Managing the Approval Process July 1978 - July 1978	Policies proposed by group are rejected by the GPC or the NFC. The policies are modified and re-presented. Out of this cycle a coherent strategy emerges and is approved.
Formal Articulation July 1979	Formal articulation of a new strategy based upon the provision of a wide range of services to the transport industry, using a computer-based information system linking BRS's national network of operating branches and management expertise.

Table 7.1: Stages in the decision process

he introduced the threat of withholding general haulage capital, but could still not obtain agreement to an across-the-board price increase:

David White: 'I have received your responses to the less than 6 per cent gross margin and price increase strategy and can only express my considerable disappointment. I think you are making unwise business decisions. I will take it up with each company in the budgets and quarterly reviews. There will be no investment in branches making less than 6 per cent gross margin in general haulage.

Wilf Bates: 'I spoke to other hauliers. They are not increasing prices.'

David White: 'You are putting the capital for general haulage at risk next year.'
Wilf Bates: 'But if we make the outturn (budgeted profit)!'
David White: 'But we are not, we are £500,000 adrift already! I can say no more. We didn't grasp the nettle, and I think that we will have trouble.'

White transferred the 6 per cent gross margin issue to the quarterly review forum where the policy could be monitored on a company-by-company basis within the planning and control system. The managing directors co-operated with him on this issue during the quarterly review meetings and over time became committed to the policy. Some accounting manipulations undoubtedly were used to ease the pressure, but a number of specific actions were taken in the worst areas, and general haulage was abandoned in a number of major branches. Thus Thompson's demands about general haulage activities earning less than 6 per cent gross margin were substantially satisfied.

Secondly, general haulage pricing became a regular GPC agenda item, and White continued to press the managing directors to apply price increases. The action taken by the companies became subject to a formal monitoring system. The issue of price increases remained controversial, however, and was a constant source of conflict in GPC meetings. This was the case with the pricing policies of the other activities also, especially truck rental. It was the underlying issue of the central control that remained the basic source of conflict.

Thirdly, White proposed, and continued to argue, that a group general haulage product manager should be appointed. This was resisted strongly by the managing directors and remained a constant source of conflict. Again the underlying issue was the managing directors' concern about a 'tendency towards centralization'.

Finally, he contrived GPC agreement to an inter-company working party. This effectively constituted a major change to the decision-making structure and was a key step in the process of strategic choice.

A crucial modification to the decision-making structure

At the September 1977 GPC meeting, White suggested that an overnight GPC be held and they 'could spend the time discussing life in general'. This suggestion received strong support from the managing directors, and it was agreed than an overnight GPC should be held in Scotland in November.

Over dinner at the GPC meeting in Scotland, a wide range of subjects was discussed and a number of decisions were made about peripheral issues. White suggested that the idea of a general haulage product manager should be considered, but the managing directors did not respond, and the broader organizational issue of the 'tendency to centralization' was not broached. The following morning the formal meeting reconvened, and White summarized the dinner discussion, primarily for the purpose of having the agreed items minuted. The subject of general haulage was raised and during the ensuing discussion Bill Atkinson suggested that an inter-company committee should be formed to examine the problem of co-operation between companies in general haulage.

Although the discussion was inconclusive, it did lead to the broader issues associated with the general haulage strategy being formally placed on the GPC agenda. This was a vital step of significant symbolic and substantive value. The question of general haulage strategy had now become a legitimate issue of discussion; it was on the agenda. Until this time, the companies, and to a large extent the group, had operated within a given strategic framework, namely the 1972 strategy of diversification away from general haulage. Southern BRS and Eastern BRS had taken some strategic initiatives, and all the companies had responded differently in terms of the degree to which they actually implemented the strategy (see Appendix 2), but generally they were responding within an accepted strategic framework.

When the general haulage agenda item was raised at the GPC meeting in December, an extended debate followed, and out of this debate came a commitment to establish what subsequently became known as the general haulage working party. Although the GPC formally agreed to only a single ad hoc, inter-company meeting, it was clear that White and Kieren Fielding (group planning and development controller), intended that a continuing working party should be established.

This GPC discussion was interesting from several points of view. First, it was apparent that the group people had a very firm idea of the outcome they wanted. It was a question of gaining support for an idea rather than generating alternative courses of action. Secondly, there was a strong sense of 'orchestration', of White having gained the support of certain of the managing directors before the meeting. Thirdly, agreement was gained partly because the proposal was presented as the least of three evils — central co-ordination/control of general haulage through national operating procedures; central co-ordination/control of general haulage through a group product manager; or an inter-company committee to study the problems. Once White had established general haulage as a GPC agenda item, and thereby legitimized group's initiative in a fundamental re-evaluation of the strategic framework within which the companies were operating general haulage, by carefully managing the decision process he was able to exercise a high degree of control over the outcome. The skill and sensitivity that David White applied in managing this complex process was crucial to the development of an innovative strategy.

The formation of the general haulage working party involved two crucial changes. First, a new attitude to the implications of the existing strategy began to emerge. Before this two views had prevailed. Thompson (and to a large extent White) considered the continued decline of general haulage to be inevitable, and perhaps even desirable. Most of the managing directors resisted this view because of the unacceptable organizational implications and clung to a traditional view of general haulage. Now a new view was emerging, namely that innovative solutions to general haulage had to be sought. Thompson's view continued to be pursued through the gross margin policies, while the new approach was reflected in the general haulage working party.

The second crucial change was that the decision-making structure itself had changed. A group forum for the examination of general haulage had been established outside the GPC. This was a key step in the decision-making process because it effectively moved the general haulage dilemma out of the established decision-making structure and brought it more directly under group control (see Figure 7.3).

The working party was composed of representatives of each of the regional companies. Some companies nominated senior branch managers, others nominated a member of the company management team. Group was represented by three members of the planning and development department, including Kieren Fielding, group planning and development controller, who was appointed chairman of the working party.

The designated reporting relationship of the working party was through the GPC, but it was managed in such a way that it was remote from it. The managing directors received some information from their representatives on the working party, but this varied from company to company, and appeared to be limited in all cases. Control of the working party was exercised by the group planning

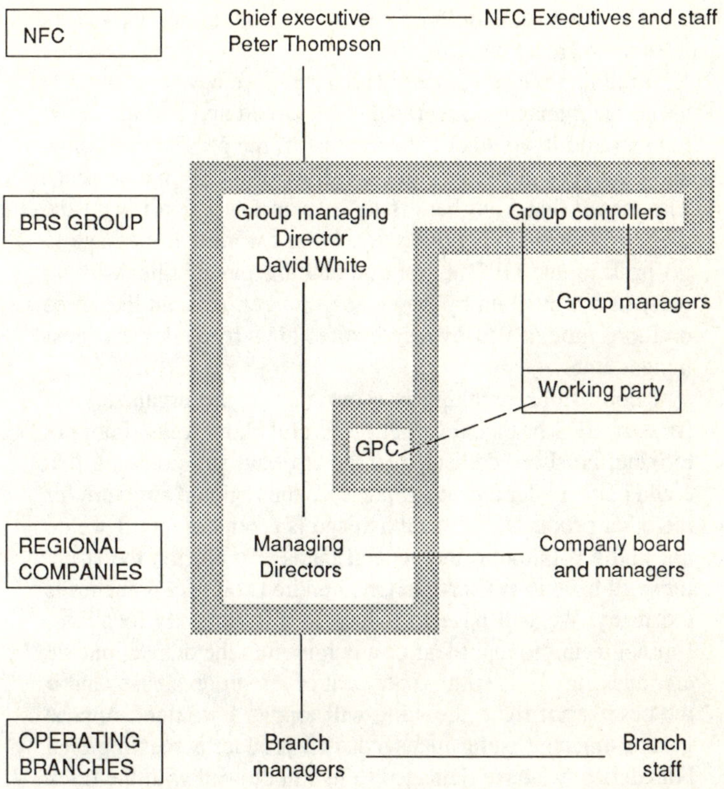

Figure 7.3: Modification to the formal decision-making structure

managers, who assumed a managerial function within the working party, as well as making a significant contribution to the process of analysis.

The search for strategic alternatives

The working party was initially concerned with reaching agreement about objectives and the approach to be adopted. The focus of their activities then changed to identification and evaluation of a range of alternative solutions.

The first meeting of the working party involved a general discussion about the terms of reference, and the identification of a number of central issues. White arrived midway through the meeting and listened to the discussion for some time before taking the chair and addressing the meeting:

> 'I'm running out of mañana. The truth is we have a problem. I asked the managing directors if they would agree to the meeting and said it would only be as good as the people who come, and I am very pleased (with the calibre of the people present). The reason that I am here is to tell you that I don't want the message that there is no answer, I don't want that message to go back to the GPC. I want something out of this working party or it wound up by the end of summer. I would like three or four strategies to evaluate, something ready for the next budget time.
>
> I don't think anything is sacrosanct in the organizational sense in BRS or the NFC, but be careful about leaks. I am not looking, no, I am dedicated to the regional structure and that could come under attack . . . preserve the regional structure for the other products if general haulage is taken out, but if we do not find a solution to the general haulage problems the structure will have to get smaller. One hundred and fifty branches is too many. We will have to reduce by fifty or sixty locations. I'm not trying to input fear or anything into the debate, but we are mucking about with 50 per cent of the group's base, and if the base is not right, the thing will topple. I wouldn't oppose general haulage being managed as a product across regional boundaries; we have managed to live quite well with the truck rental syndrome (a centrally managed product).'

During the wide-ranging discussion that followed White's departure from the meeting, a number of issues that individuals felt contributed to the general haulage problem were identified:

- Eastern BRS's stop-the-bleeding strategy;
- Southern BRS's clearfreight (subcontracting) strategy;
- lack of traffic operator expertise and knowledge of costs;
- lack of co-operation between BRS companies/branches;
- incompatibility between general haulage as an activity inherently requiring co-ordination between branches, and the decentralized structure of autonomous companies and branches;
- the possibility of establishing separate companies to cater for specific traffic flows or commodities;
- a national information system to improve backloading;
- new wage package for traffic operators;
- a national clearing house linked to the Freefone service and a radio network.

The meeting concluded with Kieren Fielding saying the working party would 'look at ways of salvaging the general haulage product, then look at the information needed to evaluate the alternatives. If we get the green light, we will find ways to get the information. We will then get together and decide and present a paper to the GPC.'

Although the meeting did not reach any specific conclusions regarding general haulage strategy, a forum was established in which the existing approaches and established ideas about the business could be openly examined. The dilemma of the incompatibility between general haulage, an activity requiring national co-ordination, and an organization structure based on regional, autonomous companies, had been openly confronted. Certain strategic alternatives had also been raised and the process of evaluating alternatives had been set in motion.

The following day Kieren Fielding reported back to the GPC: 'As the meeting progressed all the delegates were of the opinion that the decline of general haulage needed to be arrested . . . and that we should consider radical ways of carrying on what is called general haulage . . . The next step, having exhausted ideas, the meeting would like approval to get together in a few weeks during which time I would sketch out a scheme for putting the numbers together.'

The ensuing discussion followed the well-established pattern of the managing directors expressing their own views on the management of general haulage, and finally resulted in approval being given for the working party to continue.

Kieren Fielding and Mark Bedeman (group corporate planning manager) started to formalize the activities of the working party. In a letter circulated to the members of the working party, Fielding suggested that certain members take responsibility for the evaluation of specific topics:

- central/regional clearing house;
- gross margin (examination of reasons for Scottish Road Service's relatively high general haulage gross margins in some areas);
- specialist companies;
- pricing;
- commodity companies (e.g. steel, chemicals, paper products);
- pre-policy statement number 7 (centralized ownership of trailers);
- pulling out (complete withdrawal from the general haulage activity);
- traffic management (improving the quality of the branch operating staff).

Subsequent meetings of the working party over the following

months resulted in the evaluation focusing on five areas that were to form the basis of recommendations to the GPC:

- *A clearing house*. The working party concluded that the best alternative was probably a national system, operated at branch level on the basis of a central information system.
- *Commodity companies.* The working party considered companies specializing in the brewing industry, containers, chemicals, but finally agreed that a steel carrying company was the most promising.
- *A trunking company.* The special needs of trunking operations in terms of management structure were again discussed.
- *Policy statement number 7*. The essence of 'policy statement number 7' was concerned with the transfer of assets from central control to branch control. The working party agreed that they were concerned with the control of trailers only, and not assets in general. The form that the trailer control system should take was discussed but no conclusions were reached.
- *Wages package and incentives for traffic operators and drivers*. The impact of EEC transport regulations and tachographs[1] were discussed and various productivity and bonus schemes were suggested. The working party agreed that if the GPC supported this as a possible way of improving general haulage, specialist personnel representatives should be co-opted on to the working party.

Mark Bedeman suggested to the working party that smaller subcommittees should be established to concentrate on each of the alternatives. This was agreed and the working party became a group of sub-committees working under the direction and co-ordination of Fielding and Bedeman (both of whom sat on all of the subcommittees).

Managing the approval process

At the quarterly review meeting held in July 1978, BRS Group reported the findings of the working party to Thompson. In his introductory comments White explained:

> We are presenting without the agreement or knowledge of the managing directors, we presuppose we can sell the recommendations at the GPC later this week. Today is a potted version of nine months study, an agreed report by the working party members. The working party was chaired by Kieren and comprised of Bedeman and Marsden plus company people — three branch managers, five functional people, no MDs.

As the formal presentation of the report proceeded, Thompson started to query the recommendations and the analysis on which they were based. He then responded to the recommendations by saying: 'One, I must tick — extend subcontracting; two (product companies) okay, but I'm not sure how it would work; four, trailer fleet rationalization, yes; five yes — employment package. It's the third one which is the big if; a trunking system has been shown not to work.' Trunking is a mode of transport in which vehicles are dedicated to particular routes and are usually operated on a regular schedule.

During the extended debate that followed on the viability of trunking, Thompson expressed two areas of concern. The first was that previous studies and his own knowledge and experience indicated that trunking was not economically viable. The second was that the trunking proposal involved a separate management company cutting across the existing structure of regional companies. He mentioned that he felt the clearfreight concept was 'interesting' and argued that an alternative strategy of building up subcontracting without a backup fleet or marketing support should be evaluated.

Peter Thompson: 'I perhaps shouldn't know this, but Clive Beattie's study was based on Birmingham linked by Motorway. All the other studies showed trunking[2] loses more than tramping.'

David White: 'We may use the railways (for the trunk operation).'

Peter Thompson: I've just been to a Freightliner[3] meeting, nothing makes money under three or four hundred miles.'

* * * *

Peter Thompson: 'You were very keen on the organizational thing, explain that.'

David White: 'It's got to be a separately managed company, with its own employees and a trunking company managing director, et cetera.

Peter Thompson: 'My antennae tell me trunking will be bad news. In organizational terms it's a cuckoo in the nest. The rest (of the organization) is run on a regional company basis.'

* * * *

Peter Thompson: '. . . this is most doubtful, and the way it's set up it's bound to be rogered anyway. It's a question of whether we establish a new product, trunking, or the thrust is to decline the whole business and push it into subcontracting and run the vehicles down as fast as circumstances will allow.'

* * * *

Peter Thompson: 'When do you establish the trunking company then?'

David White: 'If I get agreement in principle today and assuming I can sell it internally get GPC approval, then I'll appoint a senior man to head up the whole general haulage thing, clearfreight, employment package, et cetera. In six to nine months' time, we would maybe start to formalize the trunking organization. We would have to sell it to the unions.'

Peter Thompson: 'An alternative is to keep on pulling out (of general haulage) but building up clearfreight. I haven't seen that evaluated.'

* * * *

Peter Thompson: 'We all understand the subcontracting, that's the gravy train if you can deliver it, 16 per cent margin with just a small fleet to back it up.'

* * * *

Peter Thompson: 'I don't believe it's (the new strategy) deliverable. If you get agreement that it is, I would like to see more on the industrial relations and cash implications. You need to re-present the plan including these two items. The first thing is a closer look at the trunking company, that's at the heart of the credibility of the thing.'

David White: 'Sorry, it still revolves around the trunking company.'

Peter Thompson: 'That's part of it, but there's still a huge industrial relations problem. You've said before you are limited by the speed at which you can run down general haulage because of industrial relations and structural problems, now you've had a look at it and say eureka!, you can run it down faster with subcontracting, et cetera. Why the sudden change in the industrial relations scene?'

Thompson pressed very hard for a modification of the alternatives so that they would form an extension of the existing strategy. The trunking company involved a significant change in both strategy and structure, while the other alternatives could have been grafted onto the existing strategy of continued general haulage decline. Thompson argued that the proposed plan demonstrated that a faster decline of general haulage was possible.

White and his team reconvened immediately after the meeting and discussed the implications for the presentation of the working party reports in the GPC meeting the following day. Group were not entirely clear about their position, but concluded that Thompson approved the working party recommendations with reservations about the cash and industrial relations implications. They agreed that Thompson would never give approval to the trunking company concept. White expressed the view that while he could probably obtain GPC approval for the trunking company, he was unsure whether that was the right thing to do. He finally decided on a different approach, namely, to suggest to the managing directors that they build up trunking commitments between their companies while proceeding with the trailer control system to which Thompson had apparently given approval.

The following morning at a controllers' meeting the group people continued to reflect on Thompson's reaction to the general haulage proposals and to reconsider their position:

David White: 'Yesterday's discussion was all about wrecking the present structure with the trunking company . . . the budget excludes the general haulage strategy but the Strategic Review will build it in: a three year planned progression out of tramping.'

* * * *

David White: 'We'll try to get agreement at the GPC to the trailer control policy, that will be difficult. Also to the clearfreight concept and tramping substantially disappearing over three years. Presently the trunking thing is on the basis that more work is to be done before accepting a national trunking company rather than local arrangements, putting at risk the management structure. I'd be pleased if we could achieve agreement to that . . . Tackle so much in each of 1979, 1980 and 1981. We will reflect the change in the Strategic Review document, for example, 1979 the trailer policy, 1980 interchanges and trunking.'

Gerry Simmons: 'The problem is to overcome Peter Thompson's personal commitment against it (trunking).'

It appeared that by this time White was extremely sensitive to the decision-making process and the influence of his position between Thompson and the regional company managing directors on his role in the process. He recognized that he was seeking the agreement of two parties whose interests and preferences were different, and to some extent in conflict. This discussion indicated not only White's awareness of this but also his flexibility in adopting alternatives for which he felt he could gain the approval of both Thompson and the GPC. White could exercise considerable control over the GPC decision-making process, and the overall decision process had been structured such that he had a central, controlling role.

At the July GPC, the members of the working party presented the following five papers to the managing directors:

- report on clearfreight;
- report by subcommittee on a trunking company;
- report by subcommittee on the status of the BRS trailer fleet and recommendations of alternative methods of trailer ownership and control;
- report by subcommittee on steel carrying product company;
- report by subcommittee on the present responsibilities, remunera-

tion, status, etc. of traffic operating staff within the BRS group. The presentation was followed by an extended debate in which diverse views were expressed by the managing directors. White summarized the recommendations and tried to gain agreement to the idea of implementation on a phased basis — 1979 trailer control, 1980 viewdata (a national subcontracting information system), 1981 the trunking company.

David White was unable to secure the agreement of the managing directors and finally made a strong stand. He said he would have to ask the GPC to ratify the direction he was proposing that the working party take: additional evaluation of the alternatives preparatory to the presentation of specific recommendations and analysis of the phased implementation to the next GPC meeting.

The following morning the GPC reconvened and the general haulage discussion continued for several hours. White opened the discussion by summarizing the position reached the previous day:

David White: 'One, the principle of a trailer company (to provide central ownership and control of trailers) is acceptable. The operation now has to have detailed validation. Two, the employment package for traffic operators will now be handed over to Charlie Williams and the personnel managers for implementation. Three, the concept of viewdata is accepted for implementation for 1980. Four, the trunking company is a question of concern, low-key implementation and further analysis. Put in on the GPC agenda for review. The strategy will be reflected in the 1979 Strategic Review and included in next year's planning cycle. An abbreviated but less volatile presentation at the branch manager's conference in September. Does anyone disagree with that?'

The discussion was started by Steve Abel arguing that the trunking arrangements were required urgently and should not be left until 1981, but he did not receive support from the other managing directors. Eventually White suggested that the matter be discussed further at the next GPC meeting. After several managing directors offered to nominate a company representative to be responsible for liaising on inter-company trunking arrangements as a first step towards co-ordination of trunking, White gave his support to this approach.

The next item discussed was the employment package for traffic operators. After a short debate, White agreed that the wording of the minute on this item should have read: 'The employment package for traffic operators will now be handed over to Charlie Williams and the personnel managers for further examination.'

When the third item, trailer control, was raised, White linked it with the external trailer rental product[4] and suggested that both activities should be under the control of one person, a product manager for trailer rental. He then extended this idea further and suggested: 'I have a feeling we will need some resource to steer us through this, something like a product manager general haulage ... I can't manage this with what I've got.'

This idea was resisted strongly by most of the managing directors, particularly John Farrant. White switched the discussion back to the concept of central ownership and control of trailers and again met with resistance. The managing directors argued that although they agreed 'in principle' the operating details would have to be presented for approval. Some managing directors argued that trailer control could be organized on a regional company basis, and national control was not necessary:

Ron Fortune: 'We are setting up an organization to charge paper money.'

Steve Abel: 'We are talking about control.'

David White and Ron Fortune: 'Ownership!'

John Farrant starts to chuckle. Ian Blundell comments on how it would actually operate in practice. Ron Fortune argues for approval in principle to the trailer proposal but not for implementation. David White and Ron Fortune continue to debate. Now Steve Abel argues against David White.

David White: 'Christ, we are going back to the beginning! We'll have to go to the people waiting outside and continue this during the day. It's crazy to agree at 9.15 and disagree at 9.20.'

Steve Abel: 'Trailer control but not a trailer company.'

Discussion on general haulage resumes at 11.00.

David White: 'It seemed to fall apart at the point where we were talking about appointing people.'

Ron Fortune: 'I thought we had agreed in principle and the operating details were to be presented for approval, but if I'm in the minority, okay.'

David White: 'So you're completely opposed to the concept.'

Ron Fortune: 'No ...'

Steve Abel and Ron Irons comment. Ron Irons is clearly trying to convince Steve Abel and now Ron Fortune. Ron Irons is taking the lead now, David White letting him go, just nodding his head.

Ron Fortune: 'It's the Roadline system.'

Steve Abel: 'I have misgivings. There's trailer rental, I'm all for that, but you can't take the existing fleet to do that.'

Now Steve Abel is arguing strongly against David White. Kieren

Fielding comes back to the principle of trailer control.
John Farrant: 'There's far too many bloody trailers. The branch managers think they stand in the yard at nil cost. They don't. We should put pressure on them to get rid of them.'
Ron Irons: 'Yes, pressure for interchange.'
Steve Abel: 'Kieren is saying central control will reduce the fleet numbers.'
White argues. Ron Irons argues against Steve Abel again. John Farrant states that the Southern BRS fleet reduction was not matched by trailer reduction. Bill Atkinson comments against David White. John Farrant argues strongly for trailer control. Bill Atkinson argues against. The meeting is now very loose. Ron Fortune, Bill Atkinson and Steve Abel are using different arguments against trailer control. They evaluate the savings — 1000 trailers at £500 per annum equals £500,000 per year.
David White: 'For that savings I want to spend £10,000 on a man to control it.'
Bill Atkinson: 'Each company can do it on its own.'
John Farrant: 'The thing that worries me about your man is his job specification and authority. Unless they (trailers) go into a pool, and he has control of it, it won't work.'
David White: 'I haven't thought this through, but I visualize three to four locations in the U.K. where trailers would be held with a person being functionally responsible to the trailer rental man. Then charge for every trailer not in there . . . (he continues to explain how it might operate).'
John Farrant:'I don't go 100 per cent along with that. Have a man at the centre but have it on a company basis (one location in each company). Shown as a separate account in each company. If you take it out of the company structure you've got problems.'
Ron Fortune argues that he already has a trailer pool: 'You can do it in-house without a man at group.' Gerry Simmons argues for a group view of resources.

The debate continues, David White pushes for implementation, the managing directors resisting while 'agreeing in principle'.
David White: 'We need a guy at the centre to think the thing through. What terms of reference should we give this bloke, or do we have another meeting?'
John Farrant: 'No, get the bloke and let him sort it out.'

* * * *

Ron Irons: 'Let's get the guy in. If it doesn't work in trailers, he can go into trunking. We need a company pool but national ownership.'

Bill Atkinson: 'We need someone in the job to think the whole thing out so we can see what to do; we are going round and round.'
Ron Irons: 'Yes, we have agreed.'
John Farrant: 'Appoint someone to look at the problem.'
Charlie Williams: 'We need a man to advise what to do.'
Bill Atkinson: 'That's what we have done with the last two products, why change the pattern.'
David White: 'We've gone past that, we need the detail, enter into the minutes that the principle of a trailer organization is approved, and we need someone to validate the implementation for 1979.'

The structural issues of the role of group and the autonomy of the regional companies, and the substantive strategic elements had once again collided. A new general haulage strategy had organizational implications, and these implications — for example, the loss of authority, status, or even career for the managing directors — meant that the strategic decision-making process was inherently political in nature.

The roles adopted by the managing directors in these discussions were influenced by both of these elements. The substantive or analytical aspects of the general haulage situation, and the political aspects, namely the threat to their autonomy. It appeared that some of the managing directors were more sensitive to these political aspects than others, and further, that some were more adept at influencing the process to suit their position. Certainly none of the managing directors would have welcomed White's proposal for additional group product managers, and yet some of them supported him. John Farrant, perhaps the most politically astute, and also one of the more outspoken managing directors, at the end of the debate lent his support to White. This may have been because John Farrant felt that a trailer organization project manager was preferable to a product manager general haulage. Bill Atkinson's support was more predictable given his typical role in the GPC. Ron Irons had first proposed the trailer rental concept and because of that and other reasons (Western BRS was suffering from the problems of the distribution of trailers amongst the companies[5]) could have been expected to support the proposed trailer policy. It is reasonable to suppose that the support of these managing directors was gained during lobbying on the previous night.

'A Strategy for General Haulage'

In September 1978, a general haulage review meeting was held between Thompson and White, supported by Fielding and Bedeman. A paper entitled 'A Strategy for General Haulage' was presented to Thompson and discussed. The recommendations presented in the paper were as follows:

- the creation of a 'trailer organization' in 1979;
- the launch of a computerized freight brokerage system in 1980;
- the introduction of some form of marketed trunking operation in 1981.

Fielding explained that the paper included the following revisions to the working party recommendations:

- the growth of subcontracting revised downwards to reflect delayed implementation and fear of market reaction to BRS using subcontractors rather than its own vehicles;
- a reduced rate of decline in tramping because of trailer control and the computerized freight brokerage system;
- the proposed level of trunking operations reduced.

Fielding made the following comments about the meeting and the future direction of the strategy:

> Peter Thompson accepted the paper entirely. There was a bit of discussion, but he climbed back a fair way on the trunking organization. We would have had to do more sampling on it anyway before making the decision about implementation. Having raised the subject the companies will now encourage their branches to do more trunking, and the companies will want to look good knowing that Group will check all the information to see what could be trunked.
>
> In the long term, restrictions placed on long distance movements will mean we either lose it or do as Corey (a private transport company) do, set up depots at rail sidings and use Speedlink. BRS can only take advantage of this with a special organization, the companies can't get together to do it. Second, the thing losing money now is the backloading problem. The viewdata system[6] will improve backloading and a very small increase in the present 30 per cent backloading will take tramping to breakeven. The other units of general haulage made a profit so the whole thing will be into profit. The managing directors are particularly keen on the freight brokerage system because there is no loss of local control. The managing directors have always been frightened of central direction. We are playing down the profits we could make on this if we opened it to private hauliers. I said to Peter Thompson that BRS freight brokerage would do for the clearing house industry what BRS rescue did for the recovery in-

> dustry, clean it up. People trust BRS: we don't rip people off, and we are safe payers. Trailer control — in spite of the fact of a lot of conversation about how it would work — the managing directors are ready to accept, not direction, but a service which allows them to control their own trailers. We have a bloke available to work the system out. His first job will be the trailer control system, and he will work closely with the trailer rental guy. David White was clever enough to get dates given to each project in the GPC Minutes. Peter Thompson has seen a copy of the minutes. The next step is the branch managers' conference in a few weeks, I'm not sure what to present at that yet. After that the next step is the external trailer rental product manager appointment, which will put pressure on the internal trailer control system. David White would like a 1979 start.

This step in the approval process raises several issues. The title given to the latest group document, which was a progress report, was revealing. 'A Strategy for General Haulage' indicated that BRS group had a growing perception of 'a strategy', or at least the need for a strategy, rather than introducing new policies to 'put general haulage right' within the framework of the existing strategy.

A second issue is that White again took the paper to the NFC for approval before presenting it to the GPC. Further, to this point in the decision-making process, the examination of general haulage had been kept outside the formal planning cycle of BRS. The major planning documents — the Corporate Plan and the Strategic Review — were at this time still based on the 1972 strategy. The dilemma of general haulage decline had been addressed in these documents, but the actual plans were based upon the previously established strategy. One of the key points made in 'A Strategy for General Haulage' was that the new strategy was to be brought within the formal planning cycle: 'The full implications of the general haulage study will now be evaluated at company level, and from the summation of the companies own application of the strategy the group will form its definitive strategy, which will be presented at the 1979 Strategic Review.'

The next step was the presentation of 'A Strategy for General Haulage' to the GPC for approval, and to obtain the managing directors' agreement to evaluating the strategy within the formal planning system at company level. White decided to present these two issues as separate items at the September GPC meeting.

Fielding submitted a paper entitled 'Strategic Review Format 1979-1984' in which he requested the companies to provide detailed information about various aspects of general haulage operations.

The managing directors opposed this on the basis of the amount of work required and the pressure company people were under with the preparation of the planning cycle documents, that is, budget, corporate plan, quarterly review documents, and now a highly quantified strategic review. White and Fielding argued that this Strategic Review was particularly important because it would encompass three important issues: major investments, the effect of the accounting for engineering services as a separate 'product', and the new general haulage strategy. They argued that the importance of these issues, and the need for better data on general haulage operations, made it essential that the regional companies play a role in the preparation of the strategic review document.

After an extended debate during which a number of managing directors expressed strong disagreement, White insisted that the companies provide the general haulage data as requested. This was a very tense meeting. White's influence in the GPC was growing stronger, and the initiative taken by Group on general haulage strategy had put the managing directors under pressure. White's determination to push through what he considered to be crucial strategic issues generated a certain amount of resentment among the managing directors.

The next item on the agenda was the general haulage strategy. The paper submitted to Thompson ('A Strategy for General Haulage') was tabled, and White indicated how he wanted the strategy to be implemented: 'The way I intend to proceed now in general haulage is to make sure we stick to the agreed strategy — 1979 trailers, 1980 VDUs,[7] 1981 trunking — . . . — We will appoint Stan Ward as system manager reporting to Kieren Fielding. His first job will be the trailer control system . . . Does anyone disagree with the strategy?'

Although White received the tacit agreement of the managing directors, it was clear that several of them, particularly John Farrant, were not happy about the appointment of additional group staff.

The appointment of a group systems manager was an important step in the development of the new general haulage strategy. The first two elements of the 'strategy', as it was conceived at this time, were dependent upon the introduction of new information systems. The appointment of a group manager responsible for information systems gave White continued control over the decision-making process, with the GPC relegated to a passive approval role. Their power was restricted to that of veto.

At the group quarterly review meeting held in December 1978, Thompson displayed only passing interest in the new strategy and appeared more interested in reviewing the progress being made under the existing strategy of diversification and the policies aimed at the accelerated general haulage decline. He expressed satisfaction with the manner in which the existing strategy was being realised, although the problem of inadequate general haulage gross margins remained. White stressed that in addition to continuing the 6 per cent gross margin and pricing policies, BRS intended to implement the trailer control and freight brokerage systems in 1979. Thompson appeared to be indifferent, and he once again treated the BRS proposals as an extension to the existing strategy.

Progress on the development of the strategy was reported at the January 1979 GPC. Fielding explained that a survey of terminal equipment was being undertaken to determine the most suitable branch equipment and the preferred communication and central computing systems. White expressed concern that the freight brokerage system may have been falling behind schedule but was assured that the project was on schedule and that a proposal for implementing the trailer control system would be presented to the February GPC meeting.

The development of the 'service products' concept

The 1979 Strategic Review was discussed at the January GPC meeting, and during the discussion, Fielding outlined some of the ideas that would be included in the document:

> BRS Rescue and Freight Brokerage are concepts that only BRS could take on (because of the national network of branches and management resources). We should take on products that have the characteristics of service rather than resources . . . We will be registering a minimum number of products to 1982. Several products will involve resources, trailer rental, vehicle washing, etc., but other products won't require resources — skills only. For example, freight brokerage, leasing, computer services, etc.

This concept of 'service products' rapidly developed to form a major element of the new general haulage strategy. The concept of 'services products' rather than 'resource products' emerged from discussions among the group planning people and can be seen as a natural development from a number of rudiments:

- the existing service oriented products, particularly the recently launched BRS rescue;
- the trend to subcontracting throughout BRS and particularly in Southern BRS where the clearfreight concept was based upon

marketing and operationally managing a service (subcontracting) to consignors and hauliers;

- the continuing constraints on investment in assets resulting from the cash/capital constraints imposed on BRS by the NFC;
- the realization that BRS's greatest strengths were a national network of branches and a unique breadth and depth of transport management skills and experience.

The development of the service products concept was a crucial step in the formulation of the new strategy. A new strategy was being forged out of the realization that general haulage had to be maintained at a certain minimum level if organizational shrinkage were to be avoided. Just how this was to be translated into a strategy was still not understood because of the dissonance between certain fundamental issues. The new strategy had to assure the revitalization of general haulage, but in a way complementary to the strategy of diversification and the structure of autonomous operating units. The strategy also had to involve low risk and not be cash demanding.

The service products concept, to a very large extent, met all of these criteria:

- investment in the information system was limited, the greater part of the investment required (namely management skills and knowledge, and a national branch network) was already made;
- investment in vehicles and direct vehicle operation was not required and therefore at least the downside risk was limited;
- the activity could be managed and operated on a local basis with the system itself providing the co-ordination between the operating units — central management and operations would be kept to a bare minimum;
- there were no assets (vehicles/trailers) about which ownership and control arguments could develop;
- a large volume of revenue could be generated at fairly assured, if small, margins and the existing fleet could be operated at breakeven at worst.

The problem of how to translate the concept into an organizational reality was still unresolved, but there appeared to have been an awareness within group that a significant change in management philosophy on general haulage was required if the new strategy were to be successfully implemented.

GPC rejection of the trailer control proposal

At the February 1979 GPC meeting, a paper entitled 'General Haulage Strategy, Phase 1, Trailer Policy' was presented by group.

This was a crucial step in the decision-making process. For the first time, specific details of how the strategy was to operate were presented to the GPC. Previously proposals discussed by the GPC were largely confined to concepts to which, often under pressure from White, the managing directors agreed 'in principle'. The proposal in the paper presented at the February GPC meeting was a detailed plan for implementation. This placed the Managing Directors in the position of either committing themselves to the implementation of the proposals or rejecting them. Approval 'in principle' was no longer an available option.

The paper included several crucial proposals:

- A national trailer census and vesting day on 13 April 1979, on which day all general haulage trailers would be given a national fleet number for manually controlled tracking.
- Staff would be recruited/seconded for the development and implementation of a computerized trailer tracking and costing system.
- A central service organization be formed under the direction of either a Group controller, a regional company managing director, or a 'non-regional' company managing director.
- Ratification be sought for the systems requirements of a combined trailer control/freight brokerage system, for implementation in October 1979.
- The ownership of general haulage trailers to be transferred from regional companies to the central services function during October 1979.

The presentation was followed by an intense debate in which all but one of the managing directors raised objections to the proposed scheme. These objections were centred around three main issues:

- the complexity and expense of the scheme;
- the difficulty in obtaining the commitment of branch managers to the system; and
- the change was inconsistent with a central element of the BRS management philosophy, a belief in a decentralized management structure.

Although the managing directors were no doubt concerned about the complexity of the proposed scheme, their objections were more fundamentally related to the issue of the control of assets and transfer of ownership from the regional companies and operating branches. The formation of a central services organization that would own assets across regional company boundaries was an unacceptable way of implementing the new strategy. Despite the potential operating benefits available from such a scheme, the managing directors were not prepared to accept a strategy that threatened regional company autonomy. The belief in the decentralized management structure was held too strongly within the organization for such a strategy to receive general approval.

Two days later, in a controllers meeting, the group managers pondered the reasons why the proposal had been rejected. Bedeman suggested that the underlying problem was the change in management philosophy implied in the proposal. He was supported in this contention by Charlie Williams (Group Personnel Manger):

> We didn't get rejection of the objectives; it's a question of how they're reached. The managing directors see it as a reduction of the power of the regional companies. They don't want to hear, they want to hear how we can help them do it, not centralize. Mark's right; they don't want to hear a new management philosophy.

During the discussion, White made the decision to re-cast the strategy once more to focus their attention on freight brokerage rather than on trailer control. Group management decided to let the trailer census proceed and to progress the trunking alternative by instituting a system for regularly monitoring traffic flows suitable for trunking.

A far more important outcome of the meeting, however, was White's understanding of the role that information technology could play in co-ordinating general haulage nationally without the need to impose a centralized structure:

David White: 'In the next fortnight we will have a re-statement of our position. Change the emphasis at the centre to freight brokerage. Freight brokerage is the one we want, I want that badly.'

Mark Bedeman: 'Another GPC decision in July. It's translating the principle into fact that's the problem. It may need some sort of central rescue[8] set up.'

David White: 'Why does it have to be manned? Why can't information be fed from the branch into the machine and out again? People to implement and market it, okay . . . Mark, why can't we have it so that the branch puts information into the machine, get trailer exchange that way, get trailer control without taking ownership into the centre.'

The response of group to the failure to gain the managing directors' agreement to implementation of the trailer control system was to 're-cast the strategy' as they had done before. It was clear, however, that White recognized that the introduction of a system linking all the branches to a central computer provided the opportunity to achieve many elements of the new strategy without centralization of the management structure.

It was now more than six months since the working party had reported its findings to the GPC, and White was still struggling to obtain agreement to a solution to general haulage. The structure of the organization meant that the decision-making process forced White to move back and forth between GPC and the NFC in an attempt to find a solution that was acceptable to both parties. Thompson was tending to stick to his 1972 strategy and to treat any new initiatives from group as variations on this theme. Meanwhile, the managing directors were resisting any suggestions that smacked of central control or in anyway threatened regional company autonomy. A strategy was crystallizing in White's mind, however, the key being a computerized information system that would allow central control and co-ordination without threatening the autonomy of the managing directors. This idea, along with that of services products, was publicly aired and discussed with Thompson at the 1979 Strategic Review meeting a few days later.

The overwhelming rejection of the trailer control policy by the GPC led once again to what Mintzberg et al. (1976) termed a 'failure re-cycle'. Group management reconsidered their position and 're-cast the strategy' as they had done several times before. The underlying issue of the policy proposals challenging the philosophy on the decentralized structure, however, had been confronted more openly than ever before. Perhaps, what was most important, White grasped the significance of information technology as a means of achieving national co-ordination of general haulage operations without having to impose a centralized structure. This aspect of the decision-making process, which has been described as a 'comprehension cycle' (Mintzberg et al. 1976), took the form shown in Figure 7.1 within BRS.

By combining the concept of 'service products' with information technology an innovative, viable general haulage strategy was formulated. The failure to gain approval that was essential to the comprehension cycle only occurred because the power structure made possible political activity that was manifested in the rejection of the trailer control proposal.

BRS group obtain approval to the strategy

At the 1979 group Strategic Review meeting, White outlined to Thompson the group's thinking on freight brokerage:

> With things like rescue, the hub of the service is central. Also with freight brokerage, the information is in the centre. Truck rental is now bedded down into a pattern which is acceptable. Tight central control on purchasing but operational control is decentralized. Some years ago it was a tender bird, but it's well stuffed now. We are aware that several products have a central control issue. Trailer rental is central, but the plan is to go like truck rental. With rescue there was some resistance, but when the money starts to flow in the resistance goes. Now that profits are flowing through, it's starting to bed down. The market research on freight brokerage is very exciting. To get it off the ground will need a lot of central push, but then we will lock it into the regional companies. In the longer term we are flogging that the management organization needs to be kept in line with the product strategy.

Thompson outlined his own views on the future structure of the organization:

> The current structure has served the business well, and I don't like to depart from it, but at the same time if the multi-product depots become such that there's a span of control problem we may have to go to limited product depots till the mid eighties and then . . . split into two groups, say one set with distribution, warehousing, et cetera, and another set with rescue, freight brokerage, et cetera, we can then split them apart. There's a need to identify two types of branch . . . It's not relevant to 1980 trading, but it is relevant to where you put products. Do it at branch level and avoid the emotion of breaking up the regional companies . . . What I am saying is that if by 1980 the size of the organization makes the structure creak, you don't have to say to the companies that you are going to cut them in two, but you can organize the product branch split. Talk about the question of how many products a branch manager can handle and therefore there must be a policy of a limited number of products (per branch) and that products should be of a certain mix. In seven years' time, we will find that the product/branch situation will allow a split of the organization.

The trailer control presentation was an attempt to gain approval for a fundamental change in the structure of the organization, namely the establishment of a central services organization. The proposal was rejected by the managing directors because it conflicted with a central element of BRS's management philosophy. The 1979 Strategic Review document presented the issue in a less controversial form:

> In overall terms we must be prepared to adjust our organizational structure to meet the new challenge. It may be that the formation of a group services unit or function will be required, as has been the case with rescue, which will provide services to the group operating companies, whilst retaining and emphasizing the profit-making philosophy inherent now in our branches and regions.

Thompson wanted to explore the issue further, however, and expressed doubts about the concept of service products on the grounds that it involved risk because of the lack of customer commitment. Group countered this argument by pointing out that because the concept was based upon minimizing capital investment, the question of risk was not relevant. Thompson then gave his endorsement of the strategy:

> The major thrust — you have four or five major products that you will continue to push, perhaps a major distribution strategy in 1980-81. Then there's the membership products[9] where you help the guy run a truck. A whole spectrum of services; that's the area of major thrust in the new products. I can't see any reason against that. It's not cash demanding, which the other products are, and it utilizes the branch network. I'd say we need to get behind it. We need to look at each element as it comes along.

BRS group was extremely pleased with the positive atmosphere of this meeting and felt that there was now a clear understanding, and approval, of the new general haulage strategy by the NFC.

Only a month later, however, Thompson challenged the concept of clearfreight (Southern BRS's freight brokerage product) and suggested that its performance did not justify group's strategy of 'turning back on yourself and making general haulage pay using the clearfreight formula'. Group attempted to convince Thompson that the new strategy involved more than clearfreight, but he insisted that a study be carried out comparing the clearfreight approach with the 'stop-the-bleeding' of Eastern BRS. Thompson's reasons for this were not clear. When the report was tabled at the following quarterly review meeting, Thompson was again supportive of the approach that group were taking, even though the report by an NFC analyst was rather circumspect: 'On the preliminary assessment of a very limited amount of work, there seems to me no reason to believe that the results of clearfreight so far cast any doubts on the group plan for freight brokerage.'

Thompson did insist, however, that the implementation of the strategy would have to continue to be closely monitored. It was possible that Thompson's strong and rather sudden opposition to the new strategy was a manoeuvre to assert 'rights of access' to monitoring the actions of BRS group. Having decided that the new strategy should proceed, Thompson's concern changed from evaluation and approval to control; and in order to exercise control it was necessary to implement systems to monitor progress.

In March 1978, White obtained the tacit approval of the GPC to the concept of membership services. General haulage received only scant attention during the GPC meeting. Fielding reported to the managing directors the progress that had been made on the selection of terminal equipment and explained that this would comprise part of the presentation to the July GPC meeting. White noted that the Strategic Review had been circulated to the managing directors and had been accepted by them: 'That's the way the Group will go over the next three years, particular emphasis on service products.'

The April GPC meeting similarly contained little discussion of the general haulage strategy. Fielding presented the first analysis of the 'national full load census', which had been instituted so that the amount of traffic available for trunking could be established, in the hope that this information would encourage the companies to initiate trunking operations. The traffic flow analysis was discussed only superficially.

White explained to the GPC that the NFC had requested a study on the general haulage operations in Southern and Eastern BRS. This led to a more general discussion of clearfreight and the group freight brokerage scheme. Fielding explained that group would use the name BRS datafreight and that each of the companies could use their own names linked to the group name, for example, 'Clearfreight — a member of BRS Datafreight'. Several of the managing directors asked John Farrant if their companies could use the name clearfreight; he explained he was reticent about other companies using the Southern BRS name: 'No, I'm very reticent. We have spent a lot of money. It's really only relevant to the South East of England; that's how we launched the thing. I'm not happy about people taking it on board while they are in the learning mode.'

At the May GPC meeting, group submitted a draft of the 1979 Corporate Plan for approval. In the subsequent discussion, White sought the commitment of the managing directors to the concept of membership products:

> In the plan, we have developed the membership concept. I want your approval to this, in principle anyway . . . The way forward for BRS in 1979-80 is continuing with contract hire,

truck rental et cetera, but the surge forward is membership, harnessing technology . . . it's a quite exciting concept, and I want to make sure we have 100 per cent commitment to the principle.

After further discussion of branch terminal hardware and the cost of software, White again asked if the concept was acceptable. The managing directors gave their tacit approval. Later in the same meeting Fielding outlined the proposed pilot scheme: 'Most of the companies have been discussing the details of a run for Datafreight. The program is being written now. Ten terminals will be delivered in September, ten in October and ten in November. The trial will last six months.'

At the June GPC meeting, White openly confronted the issue of general haulage being represented by a member of group management: 'We said we want one more chance to put general haulage right. I'm committed to freight brokerage as a method of rescuing general haulage. I seek your understanding that I intend to advertise for a controller membership products.'

After an extended discussion, during which the managing directors expressed opposition to this idea, the subject was dropped. White intended to proceed regardless of the opposition of the managing director. By this time, White's role in the GPC was very strong, and he made it clear that the strategy was to be implemented in spite of the resistance of the managing directors. The appointment of a membership products controller gave White the group general haulage product manager he had advocated for so long, and it finally brought together openly the two issues of strategy and structure.

White's strengthening role in the GPC was important in the strategic decision-making process. A crucial point in the process was the rejection of the trailer control proposal after which White conceptualized the way in which information technology could be used to overcome the centralization issue. After this, White moved ahead quickly and with a great sense of purpose and commitment.

Formal articulation of the strategy

As a result of the working party report in July 1978 a strategy had been developed that contained four[10] major elements:

- a trailer control system;
- a trunking organization;
- freight brokerage; and
- traffic operators' employment package.

The employment package had been referred to Charlie Williams and the company personnel managers to develop. At this time (July 1979) apparently nothing more had been done. Certainly the matter had not been referred back to the GPC for further discussion or decision.

Thompson's strong opposition to trunking, in general, and to the idea of BRS establishing a national trunking organization that would cut across regional company boundaries, in particular, had resulted in group re-casting the strategy. They decided to defer consideration of this element and instead encouraged inter-company co-operation by providing an analysis of traffic suitable for trunking.

The trailer policy, although it was supported in concept, had not been implemented because of the managing directors' strong opposition to the organizational arrangements under which group proposed to implement it.

Out of a second reformulation of the strategy emerged the concept of membership or service products, the cornerstone of which was to be the freight brokerage system. This was a development of Southern BRS's clearfreight, but with the important difference that the system was to be based on a national information network using a central computer and terminals at the operating branches. In addition to freight brokerage, the 'membership products' concept included a wide range of activities from fuel supply to drivers digs. Although freight brokerage was the main element of membership products, it was the underlying concept that constituted the 'strategy'.

Instead of operating vehicles, BRS was going to offer services to other vehicle operators. These services would be based upon a network of operating branches and management resources supported and co-ordinated by a computerized national information system. The national information system, with terminals in each branch, would allow a BRS member to obtain services from any branch, or arrange for services from branch to branch.

With Thompson's assent, and the tacit approval of the GPC, White could now implement the strategy. At the July GPC meeting, White announced that Mark Bedeman had been appointed controller, membership products and was attending his first GPC in that capacity. The first item dealt with at the July meeting was the inspection of terminals for the piloting of the Datafreight system. After a demonstration and discussion, the GPC agreed that they should proceed with the trial of the system as proposed. A project proposal entitled 'BRS Datafreight' outlining in detail how datafreight would operate was approved by the managing directors after only cursory discussion.

The NFC annual reports record the continuing process towards the final implementation of the new general haulage strategy:

> A significant development has been in freight brokerage through the Clearfreight operation in Southern BRS, which has resulted in greater efficiency in general haulage back-loading. (NFC Annual Report 1978:14.)
>
> The Clearfreight brokerage operation developed in Southern BRS has spawned a more sophisticated computer-based BRS service to be launched in 1980. Pilot studies for this new service were started in all regional companies during the last quarter of the year. These studies have already resulted in greater efficiency in general haulage back-loading. (NFC Annual Report 1979:10)
>
> British Road Services Ltd. Group: BRS offers a total physical distribution service, provides a wide range of freight transport and warehousing, and specializes in contract hire and truck and trailer rental. It has been moving increasingly into services to the transport industry, such as BRS Rescue, and in 1980 extended these to include Datafreight. This is a computer-based information system designed to facilitate and reduce empty running, thus making a substantial contribution to fuel-saving. (NFC Annual Report 1980 [to September]:6.)

The annual report might have added that this computer-based information system, in conjunction with a national network of operating branches and transport management expertise, offered the potential for BRS to play, for the first time, a significant integrating role in the industry. Ironically, this was precisely the role originally designated by the government when the organization was established under the Transport Act of 1947.

Notes

1. Devices for recording various aspects of vehicle operations, for example, speed, distance travelled, etc.

2. Tramping is the most basic mode of road transport. The vehicle's destination is determined by traffic availability, so that the driver goes from place to place without knowing what the next load or destination will be.

3. A division of British Rail.

4. BRS was about to extend its truck rental activities to include the rental of trailers.

5. The exchange of trailers between companies when vehicles crossed regional boundaries resulted, over time, in a situation where one company could be operating trailers while the cost of ownership accrued to another company.

6. A national computerized information network.

7. The 'Viewdata' information network around which a national freight brokerage system was planned.

8. The BRS rescue service was based upon a central operations room at Birmingham, which received breakdown calls on the Freefone system and then provided information to the branches who carried out the work.

9. By this time group were using the term 'membership' products or services because the concept of service products had been developed so that it centred around a BRS 'club', which hauliers would join in order to have access to a range of BRS services.

10. The fifth working party recommendation, a steel transport company, was not taken up either by the GPC or group.

8
CONCLUSIONS: MANAGING STRATEGIC CHANGE

A new model of the strategy process has been developed based upon the analysis of the unique empirical study presented in the preceding chapters. Using assumptions outside the analytic paradigm, the strategy process is conceived in terms of fundamental shifts in the cognitive structures of decision makers.

Drawing on the work of Schein (1985), Gagliardi (1986), and others, a conceptual model of the process of change has been developed. The model allows much of the empirical work on the management of strategic decision making and change (Mintzberg et al. 1976; Quinn 1980) to be examined within a new theoretical framework. Implications concerning the mechanisms available to managers to bring about strategic change are considered.

The process of strategic change

The implications of the findings of the BRS research for managing the strategy process are significant. It is argued on the basis of the evidence from the BRS research that the strategy process involves managing organizational change in the broadest sense, rather than simply being an analytical activity that can be considered in isolation from its organizational context.

Strategic change involves a complex mix of analytic, political, and belief based processes (Quinn 1980; Tichy 1983). These processes are essential to the shift in cognitions, which is the essence of strategic change. Schein argues: 'Leaders must have the ability to induce cognitive redefinition' by articulating and selling new visions and concepts' (1985:324), and that 'The leader must recognize that, in the end, cognitive redefinition must occur inside the heads of many members of the organization' (1985:325).

Based on the analysis of empirical research data and in conjunction with theories of change drawn from diverse perspectives, a metamorphic model of strategic change has been developed. Cognitive theory provides a theoretical foundation for the model. The model proposes two fundamentally different forms of change, each with a particular pattern of organizational processes and behaviours associated with it (see Figure 8.1).

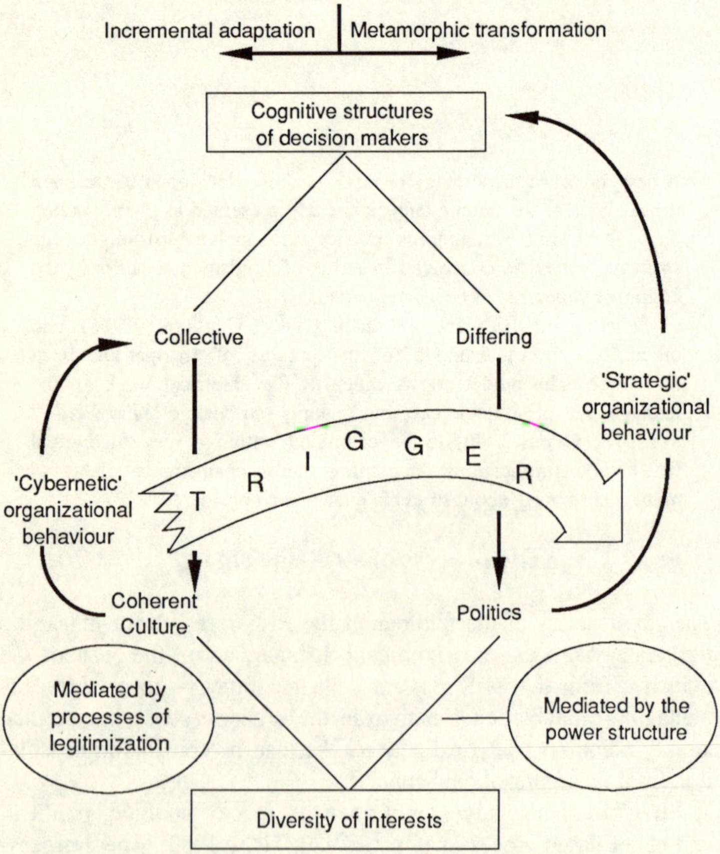

Figure 8.1: Schematic representation of the processes of strategic change

Incremental adaptation involves routine and predictable changes, and has associated with it patterns of organizational behaviour that ensure stability and continuity through constantly re-affirming an established collective cognitive structure. This form of change is based upon inherent cognitive processes and provides an effective and efficient way for an organization to adjust to marginal environmental variations.

The process of incremental growth can be simply explained in terms of cybernetic theory (Steinbruner 1976). When operating in the cybernetic mode an organization:

- monitors a small number of critical variables and relying on limited information coming from established feedback channels;
- keeps the problem narrowly focused and fragmented;
- employs a repertoire of routines, or standard operating procedures to deal with marginal variations in the environment;
- keeps goals separate and deals with them sequentially until crisis forces some fundamental change.

This cybernetic mode breaks down, however, under conditions of 'lethal discontinuity' (Ashby 1952). When environmental uncertainty cannot be controlled, organizational disaggregation (Cyert and March 1963) and the repetition of ineffective standard operating procedures become part of the problem rather than provide the solution. The limited scope of cybernetic behaviour, and the energy required to change established routines, will tend to prevent a dramatic shift in organizational behaviour where it can be avoided, even in the face of continuing failure. Incremental change is the inevitable consequence of cybernetic processes of adaptation based on monitoring a small number of critical variables and reliance on an established repertoire of responses. Successful adaptation in the face of 'lethal' discontinuities requires a range of routines outside the organization's experience and, perhaps, capability.

In circumstances where environmental change threatens to be catastrophic, or where management is determined to effect significant change in the nature of the organization or its strategic positioning, a quite different form of change operates. The predictable and routine collapse and are replaced by organizational behaviours that are unfamiliar and often appear bizarre. Kanter highlights the crucial importance of a catalyst:

> . . . crisis or galvanizing event. If the crisis is defined as insoluble by traditional means, or if traditional solutions quickly exhaust their value, or if the external parties pushing indicate that they will not be satisfied by the same old response — then

> a nontraditional solution may be pushed forward. Organizations with segmentalist approaches to problems will be less 'externally' responsive. The tendency to isolate problems in segmented subunits will result in less ability to perceive earlier crises before they add up to full blown disasters. Perception may be restricted, and so may be action. Integrative approaches may mean that the organization 'sees' more galvanizing events in general and 'sees' them earlier (1983:22).

The notion of metamorphosis captures the nature of this form of change. The biological analogy of the chrysalis, in which the caterpillar enters and from which the butterfly emerges, provides a dramatic image of the process of strategic change. Although the chrysalis is apparently inactive, internally complex processes of breaking down and reforming of bonds that constitute the structure of the organism are occurring. Neither a caterpillar nor a butterfly, the chrysalis is a complex and subtle process through which one becomes the other.

The process of metamorphic change is difficult to understand, for both those involved in it and for outside observers. Cognitive theory provides a conceptual foundation within which these processes can be theoretically framed and analysed.

Metamorphic, or strategic change, involves three overlapping phases:

- the breakdown of an established collective cognitive structure;
- the emergence of a new cognitive structure; and
- reforming — making the new cognitive structure collective.

The processes associated with these phases of strategic change are complex and poorly understood.

In the first phase the established collective cognitive structure that has guided thought and behaviour fails and comes under challenge. This often occurs before a new cognitive structure has been articulated, or even visualized. The breaking down of the old collective cognitive structure, and the supporting cybernetic behaviour, is an integral part of the process of strategic change.

The second phase involves a transformation during which a new cognitive structure emerges. The new cognitive structure enacts (Weick 1979) the organization and its environment in such a way that the demands of the new circumstances are successfully dealt with. The new cognitive structure exists in the minds of the key decision makers but is not shared throughout the organization.

Finally, this new cognitive structure is progressively transmitted so that it becomes shared throughout the organization. The new collective cognitive structure provides the framework within which the organization can again operate cybernetically.

The management of change is an extremely diverse and complex theoretical issue, embracing sociological, organizational, and psychological perspectives. Even in the narrower field of organization development, the literature is extensive. Reviews by Berg (1979), Beer (1980) and Pettigrew (1985) indicate the extent and diversity of the theoretical models and concepts in the area of organizational change. They also demonstrate the lack of a unifying or integrating framework.

The metamorphic model can be used as a framework within which to consider the issue of strategic change from the perspective of the practising manager. The issue then becomes: Where can the manager act to bring about strategic change? What levers, devices, and mechanisms does a manager have available to break down, transform, and re-build the collective cognitive structures underlying an organization's culture?

Two aspects of the process of managing strategic change need to be addressed:

- the techniques available to managers to shift organizational behaviour from the stable, cybernetic mode to the inherently unstable strategic mode; and
- the change processes and mechanisms that can be employed to ensure the development of a new collective cognitive structure once the organization has been triggered out of the cybernetic mode.

Leadership and strategic change

An important issue in the process of strategic change is the origin of the 'shock' that acts as a catalyst to cause a shift from one pattern of organizational behaviour to another. The strategy literature has for some time argued that the strategy process operates at multiple levels within the organization (Burgelman 1983). Similarly, it has been recognized that both external and internal factors play a role in activating strategic change (Pettigrew 1985). The BRS research indicates that a combination of factors operate, and that both the external/internal dimension and the hierarchical dimension need to be included in the analysis.

Presumably, the origin of the catalyst for strategic change could come from any of these dimensions. Normative strategy theory tends to make the assumption that strategic change is driven by top management's reaction to opportunities or threats in the external environment. The BRS research, however, reveals that organizational transformation originates in a complex interaction of factors involving internal as well as external pressures, and that line management, at least in organizations with a dispersed power structure, can play a vital role.

Another important feature of the process is the manner in which it is often actively and consciously managed by a central individual.[1] Although Mintzberg and his co-workers (1976) stress the importance of the 'decision control routines' they do not emphasize the management of the decision process as one of the crucial overriding influences on the structure and effectiveness of the process. This aspect has been considered in detail by Quinn (1980) who describes the steps of the strategy process in terms of tactics employed for proactively moving towards ends that are initially only broadly conceived.

Contemporary management folklore suggests that the strategy of certain firms flows from the 'vision' of a guiding founder or visionary entrepreneurial leader. Thomas J. Watson of IBM, Alfred Sloan of General Motors and, more recently, Dr Armand Hammer of Occidental Petroleum Corporation, Boone Pickens of Mesa Oil, Rupert Murdoch of News Corporation, and John Elliott of Elders-IXL are just a few of the many business leaders cited as not only having driven strategy from the top, but doing so using pressures, usually for growth, generated internally. It would seem that here we have examples of strategic change generated internally and exclusively from the top. Whether this is the way these organizations really operate, and, if they do, the extent to which it simply reflects a concentration of managerial power (or talent) at the top, can only be determined on the basis of further research. It is clear, however, that leadership plays a crucial role in the management of strategic change (Schein 1985).

This formulation of proactively managed strategic change is consistent with Quinn's (1980) 'logical incrementalism'. Based on interview data collected in large, successful organizations, Quinn concludes that the strategy process does not follow the normative theory approach but instead executives 'artfully blend formal analysis, behavioural techniques, and power politics to bring about cohesive, step-by-step movement toward ends which initially are broadly conceived, but which are then constantly refined and reshaped as new information appears' (1980:3).

This model of change fits the notion of 'adaptive' as distinct from 'punctuated' evolution. By proactively and continuously managing a strategic change process that involves constantly evolving new cognitive structures, the inevitable problems associated with the cybernetic mode of organizational behaviour are avoided. In managing these strategic shifts, the chief executive could be seen as having a 'meta frame of reference' (Figure 8.2) — a cognitive structure that encompasses proactively managed changes in the collective cognitive structure of the organization.

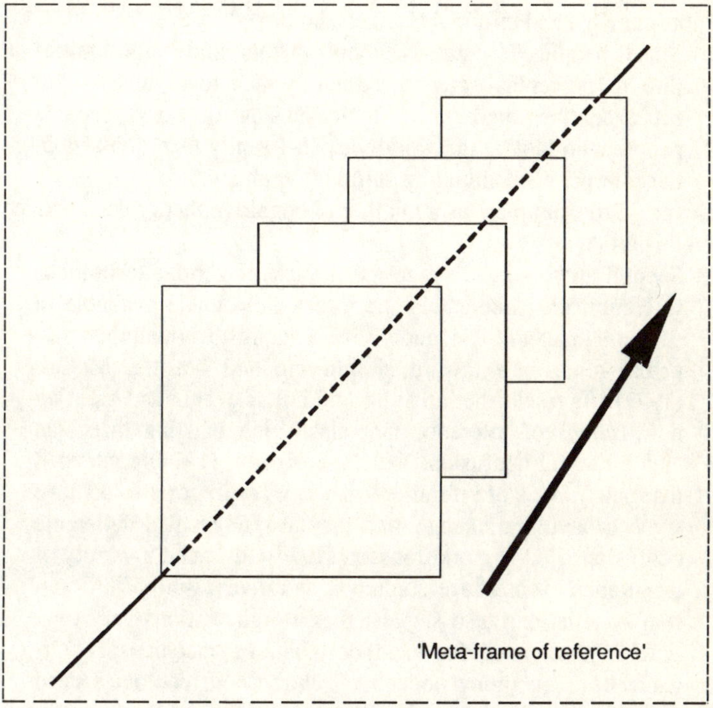

Figure 8.2: Proactive management of the collective cognitive structure

Instead of periods of stability interrupted by short bursts of dramatic change, when the established cognitive structure no longer enables the organization to cope with the changed environment, a constant and gradual transformation is being managed. The executives in Quinn's study refer to strategy 'evolving as a series of incremental steps' (1980:13). It is interesting to note that the various formulations of organizational 'excellence' (Peters and Waterman 1982) embody this idea of adaptability. 'The 'stars' are adept at adapting their business systems to constantly changing conditions' (Gluck 1986:38).

Quinn's (1980) work on logical incrementalism provides a great deal of insight into how, in practice, this is achieved. He describes, under headings such as 'Creating Awareness and Commitment — Incrementally' and 'Continuing the Dynamics by Eroding Consensus', a range of techniques employed by effective executives. These techniques essentially involve avoiding, by-passing, or breaking down the cybernetic processes that are operating. Formal information channels, including elaborate environmental scanning procedures, must be short-circuited and informal channels developed:

> Since people sift signals about threats and opportunities through perceptual screens defined by their own values, careful executives make sure their sensing networks include people who look at the world very differently than do those in the enterprise's dominating culture (Quinn 1980:5).

Beyer (1981) summarizes a number of cognitive theory perspectives on this issue:

> Several authors have suggested the use of various techniques to complicate deliberately the information made available to decision makers. The underlying idea is to counteract perpetual tendencies toward simplifying and biasing. McCall (1977) suggested that creating unfamiliar events and creating new frames of reference that clash with existing ones can create helpful confusion. Watzlawick et al. (1974) contended that new frames of reference are necessary in order to achieve some behavioural change, and they also advocated deliberate confusion. Hedberg and Jonsson (1977) advanced a variety of techniques to introduce confusion and diversity into information systems, but also suggested that organizations vary over time in their need for such destabilizing mechanisms. Organizations operating under well entrenched ideologies need destabilizers, they argue, but other organizations need to consolidate their less established ideologies (Beyer 1981:192).

Paterson (1983) has considered the problem of shifting bureaucratic organizations that have firmly established collective cognitive structures and are well entrenched in the cybernetic mode. Except in the most tranquil circumstances, these organizations are lagging behind environmental changes and need to be managed into the strategic mode of behaviour. Paterson sees the problem of resistance to change largely in terms of self-interest and so concerns himself primarily with the organization's political system. He does recognize, however, that the starting point for 'cultural revolution' is the deliberate destabilization of the system.

In effect, the executives in Quinn's study, and presumably in 'excellent' organizations generally, are managing organizations in a state of 'dynamic instability'. Techniques are employed to constantly shift organizational behaviour out of the cybernetic mode and into the strategic mode. The cybernetic mode is stable, and organizational behaviour therefore tends to drift back into this mode:

> In trying to build commitment to a new concept, individual executives often surround themselves with people who see the world in the same way. Such people can rapidly become systematic screens against other views. Effective executives therefore purposely continue the change process, constantly introducing new faces and stimuli at the top. They consciously begin to erode the very strategic thrusts they may have just created — a very difficult, but essential, psychological task (Quinn 1980:13).

A 'meta-frame of reference' allows top management to prevent the organization from becoming locked into a collective cognitive structure by constantly driving organizational behaviour out of the cybernetic mode. Instead of strategy evolving in a punctuated way, a steady and constant adaptation of the organization to its environment is achieved (see Figure 8.3).

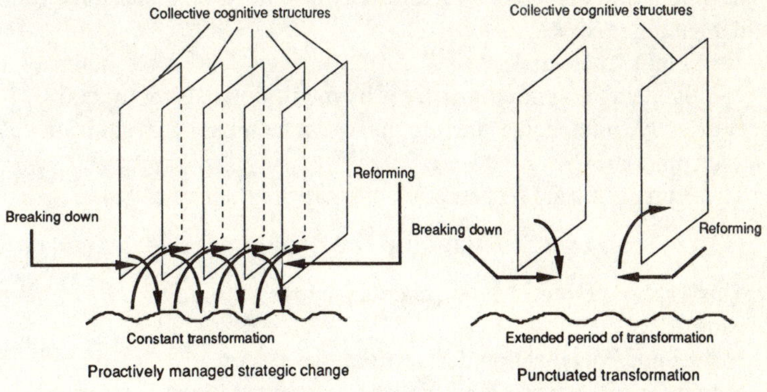

Figure 8.3: Proactively managed strategic changes vs punctuated transformation

Internally the organization is in a perpetual state of dynamic instability, which enables it to remain better adapted to its environment. The metamorphic model predicts that organizations that are managed in this way will be better adapted to turbulent environments and therefore more successful. Miller and Friesen (1982) offer empirical support for this argument. The results of their research indicate that high-performing firms are more inclined to make quick and dramatic changes. Less successful firms rely on gradual adjustments that leave the firm's strategy and structure perpetually lagging in the competitive environment.

Developing new collective cognitive structures

Developing new collective cognitive structures in an organization usually[2] involves change at the individual level. The process of 'reframing' requires individuals to break out of what Watzlawick et al. (1974) have called 'first order' change, and undergo 'second order' change. First order change, which is essentially cybernetic in nature, involves combining different behaviours from a finite, and preestablished, repertory in new sequences. Second order change, which requires a new cognitive structure and behavioural repertoire, is triggered by the processes of a dilemma, confusion, or destabilization, which are discussed in earlier chapters.

The vast array of change techniques that can be used to develop new common cognitive structures can be categorized into three fundamental processes:

- changing the people;
- influencing cognitive structures by modifying behaviour; and
- directly influencing the cognitive structures of organizational members.

These processes are represented schematically in Figure 8.4.

Changing the people

This aspect of the change process involves a number of mechanisms:

- selection/socialization/deselection,
- transfer of key individuals into and out of positions,
- promotion of individuals into key positions.

This approach to organizational change is very powerful, but managers are typically constrained. Dispersed power structures in organizations or ethical, legal, or industrial relations considerations often limit the extent to which these mechanisms can be applied.

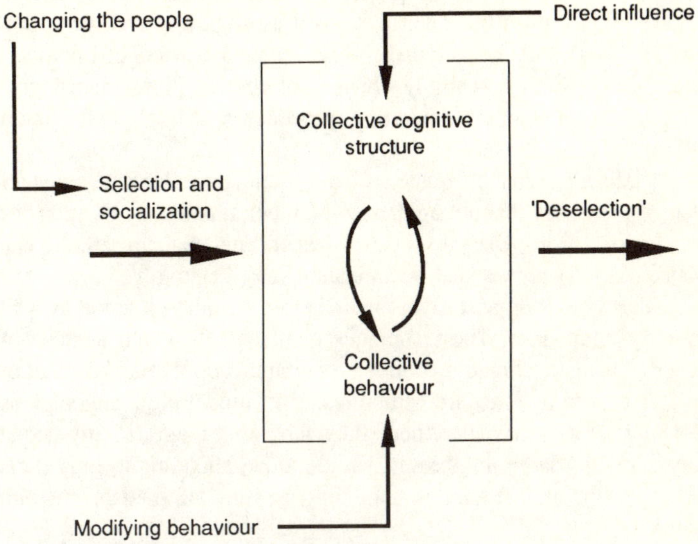

Figure 8.4: The fundamental processes involved in changing cognitive structures

Most of the writers on the management of fundamental organizational change discuss this primary change mechanism (Sathe 1983; Kanter 1983; Pascale 1985; and Pettigrew 1986). Baker claims that 'recruitment is often used as a means of indirectly influencing the culture' and that 'some companies seriously consider cultural issues when making promotion and transfer decisions' (1980:59). Schein points out that 'the replacement of people in key positions by people with different assumptions (cognitive structures) is a powerful way of effecting cultural change. Executive selection and staffing processes are, in this sense, powerful processes of cultural change, but they are also very slow' (1985:290). Tunstall advises that organizations should revise their recruiting aims and methods because recruitment 'is a powerful, if indirect, means of influencing the corporate culture' (1983:24). 'Weeding out', the removal of members who do not fit the culture, is suggested by Sathe, who also argues that 'it is important to avoid irreconcilable mismatches between the person being hired and the intended culture' (1983:21).

Socialization has been identified as a key mechanism for change by a number of researchers. In particular, it has been identified as a key mechanism for changing beliefs (Moore 1969; Schein 1968;

Van Maanen 1978), but the processes of change are poorly understood. Socialization has been described as cognitive reconstruction (Davis 1968) and the acquisition of 'recipe knowledge' of an organization, which essentially consists of routine performance programmes and standard operating procedures (March and Simon 1958).

Socialization can be treated as a generic term for the range of change processes that are applied to new entrants to organizations or occupations. Van Maanen (Van Maanen and Schein 1979, Van Maanen 1978) argues that socialization may be involved whenever individuals cross organizational boundaries, including internal as well as entry boundaries. The techniques involved fall within a range of generic change techniques (training, communication, reinforcement of behaviour through reward structures, role modelling), although as Goffman (1961) has identified, they tend to be applied in special ways: treating large numbers of people alike, attending to only parts of a person, and strictly maintaining systems of punishment and privilege.

Pascale's model of the socialization process is based on evidence that 'strong culture firms that have sustained themselves over several generations of management reveal remarkable consistency across seven key steps' (1985:29):

1. Careful selection of entry-level candidates. The process itself can increase receptivity to change by causing people to question whether they are good enough.
2. Humility inducing experiences. These lead to self-questioning of earlier behaviour, beliefs and values.
3. 'In-the-trenches' training leads to mastery of one of the core disciplines of the organization. Promotion is inescapably tied to a proven track record.
4. Meticulous attention is given to systems measuring operational results and rewarding individual performance. Systems are comprehensive, consistent, and triangulate, particularly on those aspects of the business that are tied to competitive success and corporate values.
5. Careful adherence to the organization's transcendent values. Identification with common values enables employees to reconcile personal sacrifices necessitated by their membership of the organization.
6. Reinforcing folklore provides legends and interpretations of watershed events in the organization's history that validate the firm's culture and its aims.

7. Consistent role models and consistent traits associated with those recognized as in the fast track.

This model of socialization is one of the few integrated, processual models in the literature and represents a more general process by which cognitive structures can be changed. One of the important issues Pascale's model raises is the nature of the relationship between changes in behaviour and cognitive structures.

Influencing cognitive structures by modifying behaviour

Behaviour in organizations can be influenced through a wide range of mechanisms:

- contextual mechanisms
  - technology/workflow/physical settings/authority structures/reporting relationships
  - systems (performance appraisal/rewards/planning and control/resource allocation, etc.)
- interpersonal mechanisms
  - direct (that is, face-to-face) reward/punishment
  - role modelling
  - training/coaching
  - peer-group pressure.

These mechanisms are well covered in the existing management and organizational change literature (Baker 1980; Kanter 1983; Sathe 1983; and Pettigrew 1986) and will not be discussed in detail here. The issue is how this range of mechanisms can be applied to bring about new common cognitive structures through the modification of behaviour. Figure 8.5 is a schematic representation of the processes involved in the behaviour → cognitive structure relationship.

The model in Figure 8.5 contains three rudimentary processes:

- the interdependence, or dynamic equilibrium, which exists between behaviour and cognitive structures;
- the process by which behaviour influences beliefs by way of the experience of success or failure;[3] and
- the process of 'idealization', through which beliefs are transformed into core values.

The interdependence of behaviour and cognitive structure

The relationship between organizational contextual factors (technology/structure/systems), beliefs and behaviour is complex (Beyer

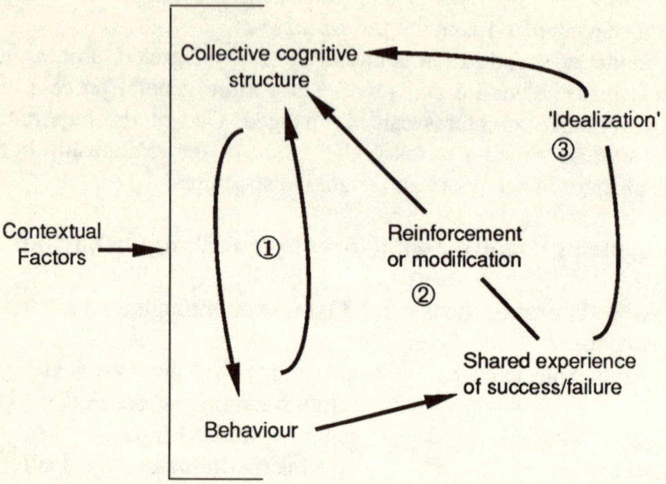

Figure 8.5: The behaviour ⟶ cognitive structure relationship

1981; Sproull 1981). Beyer argues that although it is implicit in many studies of these relationships that people behave as their beliefs dictate, it is also true that behaviours affect beliefs. Sathe suggests that although the 'conventional wisdom' is that beliefs and values influence behaviour, the opposite is also true: 'a considerable body of social science literature indicates that, under certain conditions, one of the most effective ways of changing people's beliefs and values is to first change their behaviour' (1983:18).

Theories based in the analytic paradigm assume that people's beliefs determine their behaviour, including the choices they make (von Neumann and Morgenstern 1947). Although this is a conventionally held view, there is considerable evidence that the relationship between beliefs and behaviour is more complex than this unidirectional model suggests. Recent research confirms the view adopted by learning theorists that under certain circumstances the reverse relationship holds.

Kiesler (1971) showed that inducing people to perform certain actions increased their commitment to beliefs relevant to those actions. For this behaviour → beliefs link to operate powerfully, the action should be explicit, irrevocable, volitional, and public. Salancik and Pfeffer (1977) applied these ideas to organizations, arguing that people may perform the actions initially because they are required to do so by the authority system but, over time, people come to believe the actions themselves are worthwhile. More recently, considerable attention has been paid to the role of ritual, ceremony and symbolic action in organizations (Pym 1975; Pfeffer 1981). Ritual and ceremony are consistent with the characteristics that Kiesler identified as important where behaviour leads to changes in beliefs.

Sathe points out that behaviour change does not necessarily produce changes in beliefs and values, because of the intervening process of justification: 'People were behaving as called for by the new formal systems, but they continued to share the old beliefs and values in common and "explained" their behavior to themselves by noting the external justifications for it' (1983:18). This 'process of justification' is essentially one of the elements of the complex processes of interdependence between behaviour and cognitive structures described in Festinger's theory of cognitive dissonance (1957). If there exist significant inconsistencies, or 'dissonance', between an individual's behaviour and his or her beliefs and values, tension will be generated. This tension, or anxiety, will cause the individual to act in a way that will remove or reduce the dissonance. The options available to remove the dissonance are limited:

- change the beliefs and values;
- change the behaviour; or
- resort to various psychological 'coping mechanisms'.

The coping mechanisms are well documented in the psychological literature (refer to Hilgard et al. 1971 and Sartain et al. 1973) and will not be discussed in detail here. A key concept that is relevant here is that of 'autistic[4] restructuring'. When faced with dissonance between behaviour and beliefs, rather than making changes to either, we may resort to changing the world or ourselves in our own minds. We see what we want to see, we believe what we want to believe. This is not deliberate misrepresentation; we are influenced by our needs to believe something even though the evidence does not support the belief.

While these coping mechanisms are effective in dealing with the transient dissonance we meet in our everyday lives, they tend, however, to be dysfunctional in the long term (Sartain et al. 1973:82). Over time we tend to opt to change either our behaviour or our beliefs.

In organizations in which behaviour is narrowly circumscribed, either because of managerial control or the nature of the work, the only way a member may be able to avoid conforming to certain behaviour may be to withdraw from the organization completely: an option not always perceived to be available for economic or career reasons. Control of behaviour in organizations is thus a powerful mechanism for bringing about change in cognitive structures:

> . . . one can gradually produce change by coercing behavior changes that create dissonance and, over a period of time, put people into the position of realizing that they are no longer acting according to their prior assumptions. If the new behavior has been successful and becomes embedded, it may be easier to change the assumptions to fit the behavior than to undo the behavior to fit one's original assumptions, as the dissonance research has shown (Festinger 1957; Cooper and Croyle 1984). This process may happen silently and without conscious awareness, so that one day the organization's members find that things really are different but they don't know quite how it all happened (Schein 1984:290).

Sathe emphasizes the key role that communication can play in enhancing, or negating, the influence of behaviour on beliefs and values: 'Both explicit and implicit (symbolic) communications must be relied upon to nullify external justifications for the new behavior and persuade people to adopt new cultural beliefs and values' (1983:19).

The experience of success or failure

The second rudimentary change process shown in Figure 8.5 is the reinforcement or modification of cognitive structures by way of the experience of success or failure associated with particular behaviour. Gagliardi's (1986) outstanding conceptualization of the processes by which organizational culture is created and changed provides considerable insight into these rudimentary change processes. He argues that a leader uses 'vision' (a specific set of beliefs) to direct organizational behaviour. The specific set of beliefs that constitutes the 'vision' is made up of ideas of cause-effect relationships based upon experience, education, and knowledge of the environment (1986: 121). Even though organizational members may not share the leader's 'vision', the leader has the power to orient their behaviour, at least in areas where direct control can be exercised. The experience of success that follows from the behaviour results in organizational members adopting the belief set that will guide behaviour, even where direct leadership control cannot be exercised.

In the case of BRS, a clear example was truck rental. This new product was essentially imposed upon the management of BRS by a new leader, Peter Thompson. It was resisted initially, but, over time, managers were successful in applying their transport management skills to the new product. This experience of success resulted in truck rental being embraced by management, and beliefs about this, and other, aspects of the industry and the organization changed.

The process of idealization

The third rudimentary change process shown in Figure 8.5 is 'idealization'. Gagliardi's model of culture creation contends that:

> when members of the organization have been reassured and gratified by the fact that the desired results continue to be achieved, the organization turns its attention away from 'effects' (i.e. evidence of the validity of its belief) and concentrates more on identifying itself with the 'cause'. The 'effects', in fact, go out-of-sight in the life and history of the organization, while the cause remains visible and becomes ideal, i.e. something desirable and important in and of itself and not as a means to an end.
>
> Critics will be treated as heretics and doctrine will be codified and elaborated, so that the ideal becomes part of an organic ideology.
>
> The value now shared unquestioningly by all concerned, is taken more and more for granted, to the point where members of the organization are no longer consciously aware of it. This value automatically orients their behaviour. In terms of Schein's definition (1983), the value now becomes an assumption (Gagliardi 1986:122).

An important issue that needs to be recognized is that the process of idealization is essentially social in nature. It is the shared experience of success over time that results in idealization and a core value becoming embedded in the collective cognitive structure of the members of the organization. Symbolic behaviours and artifacts that reflect and reaffirm these core values become established. It is now the culture of the organization that drives behaviour, both directly, through prescribed behaviour patterns, and indirectly, through the collective cognitive structure (see Figure 8.6).

Gagliardi's (1986) conceptualization of the process focuses primarily on how beliefs and values are created. The basic principles apply equally well, however, to the processes of change. The metamorphic model of change argues that, while in the 'cybernetic mode', organizations will continue to apply behaviours (routines or 'standard operating procedures') in the face of overwhelming

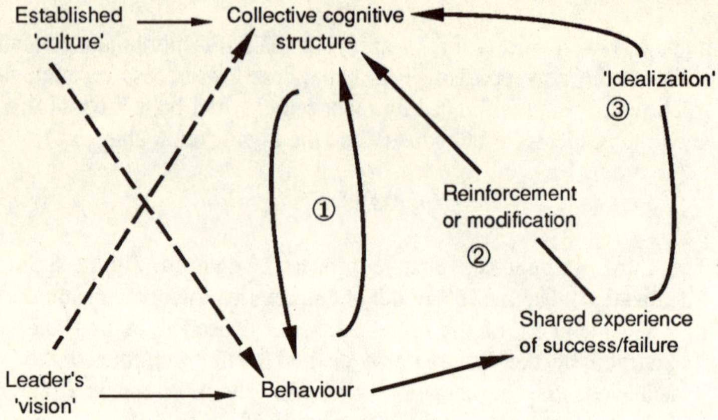

Figure 8.6: A model of the processes of change

evidence of the continuing failure of these behaviours (refer to Chapter 2). The notion of idealization explains why this should be so:

> . . . organizational values can be seen as the idealization of a collective experience of success in the use of a skill and the emotional transfiguration of previous beliefs.
>
> Many authors have observed that success consolidates the belief systems of an organization (Nystrom et al. 1976; Starbuck and Hedberg 1977; Argyris and Schon 1978). However, only the **idealization** of past successes can fully explain why organizations are often unable to unlearn obsolete knowledge in spite of strong disconfirmations. Through the idealization, process beliefs become values, the dichotomy 'sacred-profane' replaces the dichotomy 'true-false' (Bolognini 1984), and the rational acceptance of beliefs gives way to the emotional identification with values (Gagliardi 1986:123).

An example of an idealization of a well-founded belief leading to dysfunctional behaviour is provided by a major international resources company the origins of which lay in the steel industry. Within the context of its original activities, steel making, the belief that enormous care should be taken before making investment decisions was well founded because of the massive investment and technological complexity involved. A central feature of the corporate culture that developed over many years was that a great amount of time and effort should be devoted to analysis before proposing a course of action; no aspect of the issue should be left to chance, and the possibility of error had to be avoided at all costs. This belief became idealized into a core value which meant that this approach to decision making was applied to virtually all the decisions made by the company. Decision making was bogged down, innovation and creative thinking stifled, and managers became risk averse: 'paralysis-by-analysis' set in. A well-founded belief was idealized into a core value which led to dysfunctional decision-making behaviour.

In process ① (refer to Figure 8.6), organizational members behave according to the leader's demands, in order to earn rewards/avoid incurring sanctions, because of the demands of the task/workflow, to conform to peer group pressure, or because of other imperatives stemming from contextual factors. This behaviour may generate dissonance, which will act as a force for a change in beliefs.

In the second process, the experience of success will result in either those beliefs being reinforced or earlier beliefs being modified. Behaviour is initially driven by the leader's 'vision' and the power to demand behavioural conformity. As beliefs change, the new cognitive structure becomes the primary driving force.

The third process, idealization, leads to the beliefs becoming embedded in the collective cognitive structure as core values as a result of the continuing, shared experience of success. It is now the culture of the organization that is guiding thinking and behaviour in the organization. By driving these processes of change a visionary leader is able to create a culture that will continue to act at the cognitive and behavioural levels. The processes become self-sustaining.

In organizations that lack both a culture (a collective cognitive structure) and leadership, these processes will not operate. Inconsistencies between beliefs and values and behaviour will exist, success and failure will be inconsistently defined and rewarded, and core values will not emerge.

The driving mechanisms of change

Much of the work in the area of the management of strategic or cultural change is descriptive. Checklists of change mechanisms and techniques are offered with little or no attempt to provide theoretical explanation or understanding. The model of change developed here allows us to examine the change mechanisms available to managers within a conceptual framework, which explains why the mechanisms work.

The basic mechanisms available to managers to drive the change process are depicted in Figure 8.7.

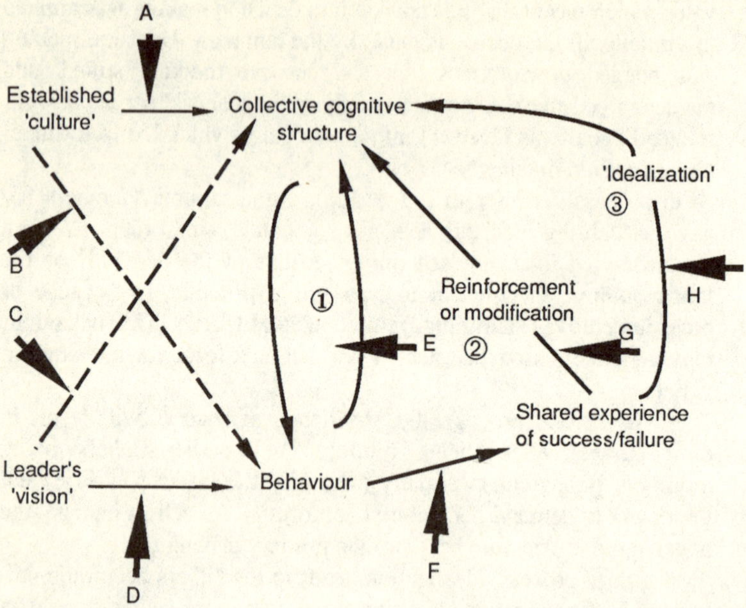

Figure 8.7 The basic mechanisms available to drive change

A & C: Factors that directly influence beliefs. Mechanism A relates to the maintenance of an established culture rather than to change, but acts in the same way as mechanism C. Our interest here is in change, and so we will focus on mechanism C. These mechanisms primarily involve 'instrumental' communication — informing, telling, convincing, persuading, showing, demonstrating, teaching.

This is a crucial, but often overlooked change mechanism in organizations, perhaps because it is taken for granted by managers. The use of information, analysis, and argument can act powerfully to shape cognitive structures. Quinn (1980) discusses this aspect of 'instrumental communication under several headings: 'Amplifying Understanding and Awareness: They seek data and arguments sufficiently strong to dislodge preconceived ideas or blindly followed past practices' (1980:5).

The BRS research indicates that if this mechanism is to be effective in developing new common cognitive structures, the process must be taken outside the formal decision-making structure because this will be locked into the 'cybernetic' mode of behaviour. While in this mode, information will be monitored selectively and interpreted within the established cognitive structure.

Some other researchers have discussed this mechanism. Schein argues that 'the leader needs both vision and the ability to articulate it and enforce it' (1985:317). Clear and consistent messages must be persistently and patiently communicated. Baker (1980) suggests that inconsistent signals often cancel each other out, particularly where the leader's behaviour is inconsistent with what is being said. The message conveyed by behaviour appears to be communicated more powerfully than the spoken or written word. Tunstall suggests that it is essential that leaders 'articulate the value system explicitly — it is critically important to communicate to all employees in specific terms precisely what the corporate value system is, especially in periods of change'(1983:23).

B & D: Contextual and interpersonal factors that influence behaviour. Mechanism B relates to the maintenance of an established culture rather than to change, but acts in the same way as mechanism D.

The very wide range of devices available to managers are listed earlier in this chapter. The application of these devices is well covered in the literature and will not be discussed here. In general terms 'the leadership externalizes its own assumptions and embeds them gradually and consistently in the mission, goals, structures, and working procedures of the group' (Schein 1985:317).

It is often only when beliefs and values are translated into behaviour that they take on real meaning. Kanter talks about 'action vehicles' — 'mechanisms that allow the new action possibilities to be expressed. The actions implied by the changes cannot reside on the level of ideas, as abstractions, but must be concretized in actual procedures or structures or communication channels or appraisal measures or work methods or rewards'(1983:25).

One device that should perhaps be emphasized is role modelling. This is stressed in most of the literature on organizational culture change (Baker 1980; Quinn 1980; Kanter 1983; Sathe 1983; Tichy 1983; Pascale 1985; Pettigrew 1986). The essence of this device is that behaviour should be consistent with, reflect, and reinforce the beliefs and values being espoused. As discussed earlier, behaviour will usually communicate more powerfully than words — behaviour makes the ideas tangible.

Changemakers must find and use role models who can 'walk the talk', thus effectively demonstrating the behaviours and attitudes required by the new culture (Pettigrew 1986). Tunstall talks about 'setting the example': essentially modelling behaviour and ensuring that behaviour is consistent with the desired beliefs and values. 'The chief executive officer whose behavior is consistent with the norms or values he or she has articulated for the company has an enormous head start'(1983:23).

It should be noted that role modelling can also influence cognitive structures directly. Individuals and groups will model referent persons' beliefs and values as well as their behaviour. The role of 'heroes', 'champions' and 'prime movers' has been discussed in the literature (Sathe 1983; Kanter 1983; Schein 1985).

E: Mechanisms that reinforce the behaviour → beliefs link associated with cognitive dissonance. Communication can be used to reinforce the connections between behaviour and beliefs. The various mechanisms used by individuals to dissociate behaviour and beliefs can be negated. Sathe suggests that managers seeking to produce culture change must 'remove external justifications for the new behaviour' (1983:19). These 'justifications' are essentially coping mechanisms that individuals use to deal with the dissonance they face. Sathe suggests further that cognitive changes can be effected more readily if managers do not place too much emphasis on financial rewards and other extrinsic forms of motivation (1983:19). This is consistent with the research on cognitive dissonance (see Hilgard, Atkinson, and Atkinson 1971:530) that greater change in belief takes place in situations of forced compliance if the behaviour change is reinforced with small, rather than large, rewards. It is conformity to the beliefs that is required, not just behavioural compliance.

F: Mechanisms that reinforce/make real the experience of success or failure. These mechanisms appear to have been somewhat overlooked in the literature on the management of change. Perhaps like instrumental communication it is too obvious and tends to be taken for granted. Baker (1980) suggests performance appraisal as a 'less formal channel' of change.

The celebration of success and the public denouncement of failure are important devices readily available to managers. The more interpersonal, and perhaps mundane, techniques of setting personal goals, discussing performance, and coaching are more important in managing change than the literature recognizes.

G: Mechanisms that link the experience of success or failure with certain beliefs (cause-effect relationships). Festinger's well-known study (Festinger et al. 1956) of a religious cult whose experience of the failure of their prophesy led them to reinforce rather than question their beliefs demonstrates that the success/failure → beliefs link is not straightforward. There is an important social dimension to this link that should not be overlooked. Groups will engage in 'collective autistic restructuring' in the face of a shared experience of failure rather than change collectively held beliefs: sometimes too much is at stake personally and socially to accept the evidence of reality at face value.

By translating cognitive abstractions into tangible behaviours and artefacts managers are able to strengthen the link between experience of success or failure and beliefs. The more tangibly the beliefs are translated into expectations of behaviour, and performance, the more powerfully managers can use this mechanism. Schein's (1985) stress on developing and articulating the criteria for the allocation of rewards and status is consistent with this view.

Rewards for success, and sanctions for failure, should be related not to behavioural issues but to the more fundamental association with beliefs. 'You have succeeded not because of behavioural conformity, but because the cause-effect relationship is true':

> The architects of change have to operate on a symbolic as well as a practical level, choosing, out of all the possible 'truths' about what is happening, those 'truths' needed at the moment to allow the next step to be taken. They have to operate integratively, bringing other people in, bridging multiple realities, and reconceptualizing activities to take account of this new, shared reality (Kanter 1983:28).

H: Mechanisms for facilitating idealization — the 'emotional transfiguration' of beliefs into core values. Much has been written about the role of symbolic and affective communication in the management of cultural change (Baker 1980; Quinn 1980; Kanter 1983; Sathe 1983; Tichy 1983; Pascale 1985; Schein 1985; Pettigrew 1986). Schein describes 'stories, legends, myths and parables about important events and people' as secondary articulation and reinforcement mechanisms (1985:237).

Quinn (1980) and Tunstall (1983) discuss the role symbolic communication plays in the process of strategic change. Quinn discusses this under the heading of Changing Symbols: Building Credibility: 'some executives purposely undertake highly visible actions which wordlessly convey complex messages that could never be communicated as well — or as credibly — in verbal terms' (1980:7).

* * * *

Strategy is about change. Strategic decisions require management to 'reframe' their perceptions of the industry, their enterprise, and the relationship between the two; that is, cognitive change is involved. Implementation requires that these new perceptions be translated into action; that is, behavioural change is involved

The management of change is perhaps the most difficult task facing managers. Some managers are extraordinarily successful at it. Many fail. Most are unsure what the successful management of change is and are left uncertain about what their own impact has really been.

Strategic change involves a complex web of technical, cognitive, and political factors. There exists little by way of relevant theory or useful analytical frameworks to guide a manager's actions. This book provides a framework that is based upon an established theoretical foundation. Cognitive theory provides the foundation for a metamorphic model of organizational change, which clearly distinguishes between the everyday, incremental adaptation organizations undergo and the dramatic transformations associated with strategic change. It identifies how managers can trigger an organization from one mode to the other.

Cognitive theory also provides a conceptual model of the process of change. The various change mechanisms and devices available to managers are explained in terms of this model. Hopefully this will allow managers to be more discriminating, and confident, in the application of change techniques.

Notes

1. The term 'leader' will be used to identify this central figure in the change process. It is important to distinguish between the leadership role and position in the authority structure even though the two will often equate in practice.

2. It is conceivable that the development of a new collective cognitive structure may not require change in some individuals because their cognitive structures happen to be able to accommodate the new collective cognitive structure.

3. In the context of this model 'success or failure' is a subjective experience that is affected by internal and external factors, including the leader. Gagliardi suggests that 'In cultural change, then, the role of the leader is, above all, to create conditions under which success can visibly be achieved, even if only in a limited or partial way, and to rationalize positive events after they have happened, even if accidental' (1986:132). Success or failure is a social construct and can be an experience shared by individuals and groups.

4. Thinking controlled more by a person's needs and desires than by reality (Sartain et al., 1973:69). From the perspective of the interpretive paradigm (Burrell and Morgan 1979), this definition raises the interesting question of whose reality?

Appendix 1
THE KEY CHARACTERS

Outlined here are brief resumes of the people who played an important part in the events described in the book. The positions shown are those held at the time that the events took place.

David White — Group Managing Director, British Road Services

Appointed in January 1976 following the promotion of Peter Thompson to the position of chief executive of the NFC. Previously managing director of Eastern BRS: one of the five district managers to be appointed managing director following Thompson's reorganization in 1972. Before joining BRS, White was a Master Mariner with a major oil company.

As group managing director he played the central role in the development of the new general haulage strategy, which was the focus of the research undertaken in BRS during the period 1977-79.

As discussed in the preface, general haulage strategy was only one of many issues of strategic importance that David White was managing at this time. His record of achievement in effectively dealing with these issues and in building BRS's financial performance is not discussed in the book.

Peter Thompson — Chief Executive, National Freight Corporation

Promoted from the position of BRS group co-ordinator in January 1972. Previous experience was in the senior management of the transport/ distribution operations of several major corporations.

James Watson — Finance Director, National Freight Corporation
Previously Thompson's finance controller at BRS group, he moved to the NFC when Thompson became chief executive.

The BRS Regional Company Managing Directors

Steve Abel — Midlands BRS
Abel was appointed managing director of Midlands BRS in July 1976. He had extensive experience in the road transport industry. Born in Scotland where his father started a family haulage business, which operated until it was acquired under the Nationalization Act in 1949. Started work with BRS at the age of fifteen. After National Service, he rejoined BRS as a management cadet. Worked in management positions with several major transport companies before joining Stoutish Road Services as a senior branch manager. Thompson was instrumental in his appointment to the position of managing director of Midlands BRS.

Bill Atkinson — Eastern BRS
Atkinson had joined BRS as a driver and for a number of years was a TGWU shop steward. He subsequently became a branch manager before managing the marketing function for David White, then Eastern District Manager. He was for a time truck rental controller for BRS group. When White was appointed to the position of BRS group co-ordinator in 1976, Atkinson became managing director of Eastern BRS.

Wilf Bates — North Western BRS
Bates was a man of fifty-nine years at the time of the introduction of Thompson's strategy in 1973. He had spent virtually his whole life in the transport industry and before his appointment to North Western BRS, he had been operations manager at the BRS headquarters, at that time under the direction of Mr C. Christensen. Bates was the only older district manager to be made a regional company managing director following Thompson's reorganization of the management structure in 1972. He retired from BRS in early 1978.

Ian Blundell — North Western BRS
Blundell was engineering manager of North Western BRS before being appointed to the position of managing director following the retirement of Wilf Bates in 1978.

John Copland — Scottish Road Services

Before his appointment as managing director of Scottish Road Services in 1973, Copland had been managing director of Tankfreight Ltd, another NFC company. Until 1972 he had been employed in senior management positions with Tayforth. He had originally joined the Scottish division of BRS in 1951. In 1954, he left BRS when parts of this organization were acquired by private interests that later became part of the Tayforth group.

John Farrant — Southern BRS

Farrant was appointed to the position of managing director of Southern BRS in 1976. He had extensive experience in the transport industry, including operations management in BRS headquarters and managing part of NFC's continental operations.

Ron Fortune — North Eastern BRS

Formerly South East district manager, Fortune had been appointed managing director of North Eastern BRS at the time of Thompson's 1973 reorganization.

Ron Irons — Western BRS

Iron's father had been the managing director of a London-based private haulier, and at the age of sixteen he joined the company, just before Nationalization. He worked in BRS for several years before being selected for the management cadet scheme, and then worked for Pickford's for a number of years. In 1969 he was made South Western district manager, and was appointed managing director of Western BRS by Thompson in 1972.

Eric Shortland — Morton's BRS

Shortland was closely associated with the company from the days when it was a family business. He joined Morton's in 1944 and later became general manager: his brother was company chairman. Shortland's association with BRS started when they purchased Morton's in 1967. He was appointed managing director at the time of Thompson's major reorganization of the management structure of BRS.

BRS Group Managers

Clive Beattie — Planning Controller (to 1977)

He joined BRS from British Steel to work for Peter Thompson on the development of a new BRS strategy. He continued in this role when David White became BRS group co-ordinator. In late 1977 he was appointed assistant managing director of Eastern BRS.

Mark Bedeman — Corporate Planning Manager/Membership Products Controller
Bedeman was one of the 'new breed' of BRS managers who joined the company as a university graduate and became a branch manager. He was appointed to the Group corporate planning role after Kieren Fielding took over the planning controllers position in 1978. In 1979 he was appointed membership products controller following several years of discussion between White and the company managing directors regarding the need for group product management of general haulage.

David Cutler — Finance Controller (to 1978)
Cutler was appointed to the position at the time White became BRS group co-ordinator and resigned from BRS in 1978 to accept a position with British Leyland.

Kieren Fielding — Marketing Controller/ Planning Controller
Fielding had worked as head of marketing for Thompson and became marketing controller when White was appointed to the group role. In White's reorganization of group management in 1977, Fielding was made planning and development controller.

Hugh Mellor — Finance Controller (from 1978)
Mellor joined BRS from another NFC company when Cutler resigned in 1978.

Harry Osborne — Group Personnel Manager (to 1978)
Osborne was appointed group personnel manager at the time of the 1976 changes to group management following White's appointment. Osborne retired from BRS in 1978.

Gerry Simmons — Truck Rental Controller/Marketing Controller
Simmons joined BRS in the truck rental area after experience in the car rental industry. He was appointed truck rental controller when Atkinson became managing director of Eastern BRS following White's appointment as BRS group co-ordinator. In the 1977 reorganization of group management, Simmons was appointed marketing controller when Fielding was made planning and development controller.

Charlie Williams — Group Personnel Manager (from 1978)
Williams had formerly been personnel manager for Scottish Road Services. He was appointed to the group role following the retirement of Harry Osborne in 1978.

Appendix 2
THE REGIONAL COMPANIES

The various responses of the regional companies to Thompson's strategy of diversification constituted regional strategies. These strategies were an attempt to accommodate the demands of BRS group while protecting the companies from the potentially grave financial and organizational consequences of the accelerated decline of general haulage. Traditionally, the regions had tended to simply respond to the demands of the market as the branches sought to fulfil local requirements for road transport. The emphasis of management had been predominantly operational, and little initiative was taken to influence the types of services demanded by transport users. Thompson's strategy involved a change in emphasis from general haulage to contractually based activities, but underlying it was a market oriented philosophy that implied basic changes in the organization and, to some extent, in the nature of the market itself.

The increased autonomy granted to regional management at the same time as the strategy of diversification was introduced added a new dimension to the issue of regional response to the market. Previously the overriding power of central headquarters had meant that the power of regional management to intervene strategically between central policies and the response of branches to the market was very limited. With the formation of the regional companies, implementation of the central strategy was subject to a greater degree to the regional management philosophy as an intervening factor.

Some of the regional company managing directors responded to the strategy of diversification and continued general haulage decline by actively seeking out new ways of dealing with general haulage;

some sought to maintain a more traditional approach; some adopted relatively passive postures and reacted by attempting to minimize the impact of the new strategy on their company. Some were prepared to be innovative and adopt completely new approaches; others tended to stay very largely within traditional activities.

Scottish Road Services Ltd

In 1978, the degree of diversification from general haulage by the Scottish company was, for reasons predominantly associated with the historical background of the company, considerably less than that of any of the English companies.

The background of Scottish Road Services was very different from that of the other companies in the group because it had undergone major organizational changes after the creation of the regional company structure in 1972. At that time Scottish Road Services was formed from the BRS Scottish District. The newly appointed managing director, John Copland, divided the company into three areas, because of the wide geographical spread of the company. The National Freight Corporation retained other road transport interests in Scotland (a company called Tayforth Ltd), however, which at that stage were not part of BRS or the other major NFC groups. It was not until 1977 that these interests were merged with the BRS group. The history of Tayforth and the way it was merged with BRS group had a direct influence on the composition of Scottish Road Services's business activities in 1978.

Tayforth was a reasonably large, successful and highly diversified private road transport company when it was acquired by the Transport Holding Company in 1965. A policy of national rationalization of activities was embarked upon following the formation of the NFC in 1968. As a result, Tayforth was dismantled progressively and absorbed by the major NFC groups. By 1975, Tayforth had become a fairly narrowly based haulage company, but it continued to be managed separately and had retained, to a large extent, its own structure and management philosophy and style. In that year a holding company, Tay-Scot, was formed to integrate Tayforth and Scottish Road Services under a single management structure. There was a feeling at that time within Tay-Scot that it would be the basis for a 'Scottish Freight Corporation'. In 1976, however, following the retirement of a key person, who held the positions of chairman of Tay-Scot and managing director of Tayforth, the BRS group absorbed Tay-Scot, thus bringing Tayforth within the group. Early in 1977, the two companies were reorganized to form a single Scottish Road Services company (see Figure A2.1).

In 1978, the two component organizations were still going through a period of change and adaptation and were not fully integrated into the BRS group. Tayforth had been much the stronger of the two organizations, and its culture continued to have a powerful influence within the new company. Almost all the top management of the new company were ex-Tayforth people, including John Copland who had worked for Tayforth before joining BRS. Further, some lingering resentment remained, largely because of the way that NFC had gone about rationalizing the Scottish interests.

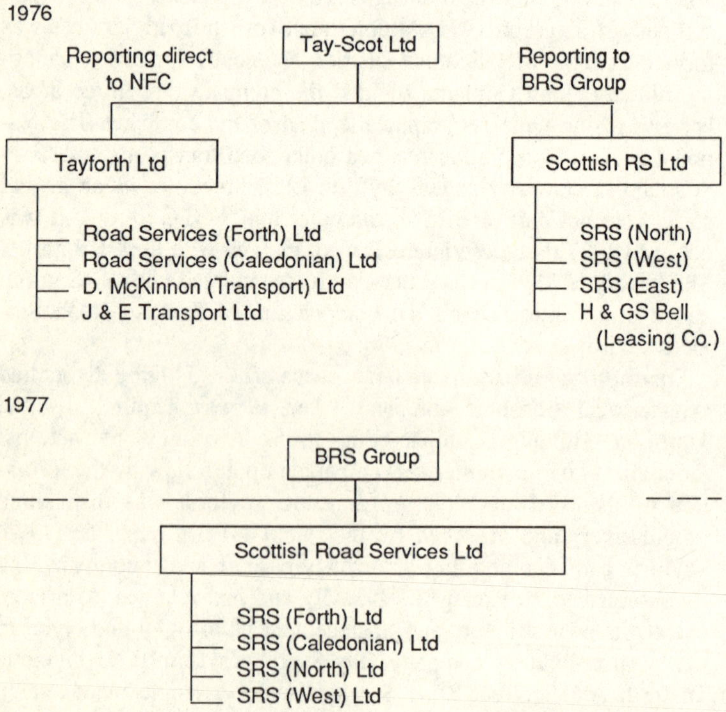

Figure A2.1: Changes to the structure of Scottish Road Services

The Tayforth management philosophy was reflected in the decision to maintain the Tayforth model of a subsidiary company structure. BRS group opposed this structure and argued that Scottish Road Services should adopt the same structure as the other regional companies. The subsidiary company structure remained a major issue within the BRS group throughout 1978, when David White brought great pressure to bear on Copland to reorganize Scottish Road Services to conform to the BRS 'model'.

The strong traditions, and the confused and difficult recent history of Scottish Road Services, meant that the company maintained a culture very different from that of the rest of the BRS group, and this affected both the strategy and the structure of the organization. Thompson's strategy of diversification was compatible with the decentralized structure he had established. Branch autonomy was a key feature of this decentralization. Tayforth had been managed on the basis of a very different philosophy, which gave a great deal of autonomy to subsidiary companies, but which considered branch managers to have a role limited to the operational aspects of the business. Hence the implementation of the strategy of diversification was not feasible until Scottish Road Services was integrated with the rest of the group in a fundamental way. This incompatibility between structure and strategy was recognized by the managing director John Copland:

> The four company structure provided barriers to the product structure, the headquarters has the product managers but the company general manager is responsible for profitability, this leads to communication problems ... it stems from the product manager concept versus decentralized management.

In 1978, Scottish Road Services were enmeshed in changes, involving both the structure and the strategy of the organization, that were imposed by BRS group. The company was under considerable pressure to conform to the strategy of diversification away from general haulage and, in 1977 and 1978, the general haulage activity was declining dramatically. By 1978, Scottish Road Services was smaller than either of the companies from which it had been composed only one year earlier.

Because of these organizational changes, the company was five years behind the rest of the BRS group in the implementation of Thompson's strategy, and a balance between the imposed strategy and the regional management philosophy and business environment had not yet been found. The response of the company was essentially to resist any change imposed from above and, when change could no longer be avoided, accommodate it within a traditional approach to general haulage.

North Western BRS Ltd

This company also had a relatively high proportion of general haulage in 1978, but in its case the dependence on the traditional activity was clearly a result of the policies adopted by the managing director, Wilf Bates. Bates was a man of fifty-nine years at the time of the introduction of Thompson's strategy in 1973. He had spent virtually his whole working life in the industry. Before his appointment to the position in the North West, he had been operations manager at the BRS headquarters, then under the direction of Mr C. Christensen. With the promotion of Len Payne to the position of managing director of BRS, Wilf Bates was made North West district manager. He was successful in the district management role and was the only older district manager to become a regional company managing director following the 1972 reorganization.

Bates was described as a traditional haulage man who maintained close links with the owners of local haulage companies. As a firm believer in general haulage, he was content to leave the management of the contract hire activity to his contracts director, Jack Armitage. Armitage had headed the activity for many years under a number of organizational arrangements that had given him varying, though usually high, degrees of autonomy.

When the strategy of diversification was announced, Bates rejected the new activities and, initially, he refused outright to conform with group policy. The company was at that time highly profitable. Evidently because of this, there existed a degree of mutual respect between Thompson and Bates, and this sustained the relationship in spite of Bates's refusal to conform to the diversification strategy. The situation was further ameliorated by the traditional strength of North Western BRS in the contract hire activity and by the success of the initially opposed truck rental.

By applying severe capital expenditure constraints, Thompson would have eventually forced the company into line with the strategy. Before this situation was reached, however, David White was appointed group co-ordinator. As he became established in the role, White used the planning and control system to try to force Bates to conform to the policy of divestment from general haulage. They often clashed in Group Policy Committee meetings, and quarterly review discussions were frequently tense. The new general haulage strategy was still in the early stages of implementation in North Western BRS when Wilf Bates retired in April 1978.

North Eastern BRS Ltd

According to the figures in the Table 4.2, North Eastern BRS had responded to Thompson's strategy of diversification as rapidly and conscientiously as any of the regional companies. The figures, however, capture little of the actual response of the company to the Thompson strategy. North Eastern BRS was characterized by a reluctance to adopt the strategy of diversification: essentially the company remained wedded to general haulage.

These aspects of the company were revealed by many issues, the most obvious of which was the process of adopting truck rental. The truck rental product was taken on by the company very reluctantly and, for several years after its introduction, the level of commitment to the new activity was very low. The way the product was managed and organized in North Western BRS illustrated a basic resistance to change and eventually led to difficulties in 1978, when the performance of the activity fell well behind budget.

The introduction of truck rental into North Eastern BRS reflected the character of the company and the philosophy and style of its managing director, Ron Fortune. The activities and style of the company, the comments of many members of its management, and Ron Fortune's behaviour and role in the Group Policy Committee were all consistent with a managerial philosophy oriented to the avoidance of any change that involved uncertainty or risk.

Fortune had joined a private haulage company at the age of fifteen and, following war service, rejoined the company shortly before it was acquired under the 1947 Act. He stayed within BRS for his entire career and became South East district manager in 1971 before being appointed managing director of North Eastern BRS, when the regional company structure was established. Ron Fortune's traditional approach to general haulage reflected this background.

A second feature of Fortune's philosophy was his strong attachment to the concept of regional company autonomy. He operated his company as independently as was possible, and he spent a good deal of time attempting to manage the boundary relationship between his company and BRS group. He opposed initiatives or direction from White to the extent that was possible without damaging the relationship and worked actively to secure resources from group for his company. Fortune's strategy vis-à-vis group appeared to be one of maintaining isolation to the maximum possible extent while maintaining a good relationship with David White: in this way he attempted to minimize the impact of any changes imposed by group.

Eastern BRS Ltd

When Eastern BRS was established as part of Thompson's 1972 reorganization, David White was promoted from the position of East Midland's district manager to that of managing director. Also appointed to the board of the company was Bill Atkinson, in the position of marketing director. Atkinson's previous positions in BRS were varied. He had joined BRS immediately after leaving school and, for a number of years, worked as a driver, and later he was a TGWU shop steward. In 1979 he was branch manager of Nottingham contracts branch and then moved to the marketing function in the district office under White.

White was managing director of Eastern BRS from January 1973 until January 1976, when he was appointed BRS group co-ordinator. His philosophy and style in Eastern BRS were largely reflected in the approach he later adopted at BRS group. A crucial aspect of David White's approach was the way he dealt with the problem of general haulage profitability in Eastern BRS. Like all the regional companies, Eastern BRS was initially heavily dependent upon general haulage and, like all of the newly appointed managing directors, White was under pressure from Thompson to decrease this dependency and increase overall profitability.

Towards the end of 1975, White had established within Eastern BRS a working party to examine the general haulage activity. The tactics embodied in the working party essentially revolved around the theme, 'stop-the-bleeding'. Through a branch-by-branch, customer-by-customer evaluation of general haulage, loss making business was identified and either rectified or abandoned. White's experience of the Eastern BRS general haulage working party undoubtedly had a direct influence on the approach he later adopted to the group general haulage problem. The theme 'stop-the-bleeding' was used frequently by White when in the role of group managing director.

Under the managing directorship of Atkinson, the general haulage strategy remained essentially the same. The policy of 'stop-the-bleeding' was actively pursued. As the general haulage activity continued to shrink in terms of revenue its profitability improved significantly.

Midlands BRS Ltd

Midlands BRS response to the Thompson strategy of diversification differed from that of the other regional companies in several important respects. By 1978, Midlands BRS was generally about as diversified as the group, on average, but several important differences were evident. A significantly smaller proportion of the company's revenue was derived from contract hire than in any of the other regional companies. The reasons for this were several and varied: the historic relative weakness of the contract hire activity in the company; the accounting classification between contract hire and other products; the nature of the industrial and commercial environment in which the company operated; and, perhaps most importantly the relatively strong orientation towards general haulage throughout the company. This last point was reflected in one of the significant differences in the company's trading profit profile. Although in terms of revenue Midlands BRS was less dependent upon general haulage than the group, on average, a significant proportion of its trading profit came from this activity. Indeed, it was one of the only two regional companies making a profit from general haulage. Underlying this aspect of the company were important issues of management philosophy.

The management philosophy and style of Midlands had gone through three distinct periods associated with the three managing directors running the company following its inception in 1973. The style of the incumbent managing director, Steve Abel, was forceful and direct. This style, along with his philosophy on general haulage, was consistent with his background and experience in the haulage industry. He had a strong inclination towards operations management that came from his belief that general haulage could be profitable if properly managed at the operational level. He cited his experience in 'turning around' the Glasgow branch as proof that good operational management could make general haulage profitable.

This philosophy was also reflected in his attitude to the development of branch managers and his orientation to group. While recognizing the need for group, he felt its involvement should be limited to co-ordination and specialist advice with no line or product responsibility. His attitude to group was similar to that towards his own company: a strong emphasis on line management, with some support from specialists in staff roles with very limited product line responsibility. Steve Abel said that if he were in David White's position he would run the group as he ran his company. He would strengthen the role of the line managers and grant them a higher degree of autonomy as long as businesses were operating successfully, but with full and direct involvement of the next level of line management if performance began to deteriorate.

Abel's philosophy and style were reflected in a product strategy that revolved around the maintenance of the company's general haulage operations. The strategy had three main elements:

- to maintain the profitability of general haulage through good operational management and marketing in order to attract capital and thereby keep the average fleet age low;
- to retain the substantial volume of British Leyland business at least until other general haulage business could be found to replace it; and
- to encourage the growth and development of new activities such as contract hire, truck rental, distribution, but under the clear operational authority of the branch managers.

Abel operated two major policies in order to implement this strategy. The first was a strong emphasis on operational management at branch level and the selection and promotion of managers with demonstrated ability in this area, supported by his own involvement in the detail of branch operations where necessary. The second was an accounting treatment of overheads and inter-product charging that favoured general haulage. This tactic was used by a number of other managing directors but, in the case of Abel, it was clearly part of a proactive strategy to keep the traditional general haulage business vital. Abel also used the power derived from the relatively high profitability of the company in his dealings with White. This was especially true for the general haulage capital allocated to Midlands BRS.

Although Midlands BRS adopted a traditional general haulage strategy, the activity was managed in an extremely active and enterprising way. Considerable initiative was taken to ensure the traditional activity continued to be successful in the belief that vigorous operational management would result in a profitable product that would grow.

Western BRS Ltd

In 1978, the percentage of revenue derived from each of the various activities in Western BRS was almost identical with that for the BRS group as a whole. That the company had come from a position of very high dependence on general haulage (74 per cent of revenue) in 1974 to a fairly high degree of diversification only four years later indicated a high degree of compliance with the Thompson strategy.

Western BRS was atypical of the group, however, in two important respects. First, its overall revenue growth was significantly lower than the rest of the group (apart from Scottish Road Service, which was a special case), and second, the profitability of the company's general haulage was considerably lower than the group average. These differences once again raise the interesting issue of how much the performance of the company (in terms of growth and profitability) was a function of the business environment in which it operated, and how much it was a function of the effectiveness of regional management strategy. The general haulage strategy adopted by Western BRS was to a great extent an expression of the way in which these two factors had been resolved within the pressures and constraints imposed by the overall Thompson strategy.

The area in which the company operated unquestionably had some unique characteristics, although it would be wrong to imply that the Western BRS region was necessarily more 'difficult' than the other regions. The company had been formed in 1973 from three BRS districts — the South Western District (of which Ron Irons, the managing director of Western BRS, had been district manager since 1969) formed the core of the new company, to which branches from the old South Eastern and South Wales districts were added. The integration of these branches, particularly those from the South Wales district, which was divided and absorbed into the Western and Midlands companies, created some problems. As Irons explained, these branches 'didn't like being managed from Bristol'.

By 1978, it was very clear that substantial integration problems had been encountered: for example, of the twelve South Wales branches absorbed into the company in 1973, six had been closed and a further three were at the bottom of the company's gross margin ranking. It was rather symbolic of the differences that remained within Western BRS that the gross profit margin table prepared by the chief accountant listed the branches not as a 'league table' of gross margin (as in the case of other regional companies), or in alphabetical order, but according to the old district division, with the former South West district branches at the top followed by the former South Wales district branches. The lack of success of the company in terms of revenue growth and profitability can partly be attributed to the problems associated with these South Wales branches and, to a large extent, these problems were a function of the area in which the company was operating.

Irons's philosophy towards general haulage and his management style were obviously influenced strongly by his background in the industry. His father had been managing director of a London-based private haulier and, at the age of sixteen, Ron Irons left school to join a haulage company just before nationalization of the industry. As was the case with all of the BRS managing directors, Irons had a great diversity and depth of experience in the haulage industry, and his management style was similar to that of a private haulier. He accepted, at least superficially, the constraints that group placed upon him but guarded very jealously the management prerogatives related to the internal functioning of the company.

The specific general haulage policies adopted by Ron Irons contained elements that reflected both his philosophy and style, and the constraints and problems of the region. During 1978, the performance of general haulage in Western BRS was considerably worse than the other English BRS regional companies in terms of profitability. Irons appeared to have developed a range of tactics to deal with the problems of general haulage and to alleviate the pressures being applied by group:

- Carefully presenting management accounting information in order to present the performance of general haulage in the most favourable light, which involved transfer pricing between products and the allocation of overheads which favoured general haulage.[1]
- The short-term hiring of vehicles outside group guidelines in order to upgrade the general haulage fleet.
- Actively increasing the level of subcontracting to offset revenue lost by own vehicle operations.

The apparent object of the strategy was to maintain general haulage at some minimum level, with a profitability sufficient to continue to attract some capital. The strategy was highly reactive in the sense that it was a rather desperate short-term response that clearly did not provide long-term solutions to the company's general haulage problem. The fundamental nature of the strategy was revealed by a paragraph in the company 1978-78 Strategic Review:

> With the exception that major consideration will be given in 1978 to change the nature of the product (general haulage) rather than just opting out of it. As this has not yet been shown to be feasible, the figures illustrate the original (strategy).

In his dealings with group, Irons tended to adopt an attitude of accommodation, accepting the constraints that White placed upon him and his company. There is a good deal of evidence, however, that, within his own company, Irons sought ways of circumventing these constraints while appearing to work within them. This tactic effectively constituted an important element of Western BRS's general haulage strategy. Irons was well aware that the criteria White was using to judge general haulage performance was resulting in Western BRS being pressurized to withdraw general haulage from a number of branches. Irons continued to adopt a conciliatory role, and his strategy seemed to be to gain space and time. By placating White and outwardly accepting group policies and constraints, he gained the freedom to act within his own company.

Southern BRS Ltd

Southern BRS had traditionally been in a slightly different position from the other regional companies in that, in 1974, the major proportion of its revenue was already derived from contract hire. There was a strong tradition of contract hire in the London area, and before to 1972 a separate London Contracts District had existed. By 1978, Southern BRS was the most diversified company, as shown by the percentage revenue figures in Table 4.2. By 1979, the proportion of revenue derived from general haulage had fallen to 30 per cent, and in absolute terms was less than in previous years. In terms of the implementation of Thompson's 1972 strategy, Southern BRS was performing well. The problem was that general haulage in Southern BRS was continuing to lose money in spite of the drastic contraction of the activity. Like all the companies, if Southern BRS were to achieve a satisfactory level of profitability, some solution to the general haulage problem had to be found.

The solution proposed by Southern BRS involved establishing a brokerage service between consignors of general traffic and small hauliers, using the Southern BRS vehicle fleet to provide a back-up service. The new brokerage activities were actively marketed under the name 'clearfreight'. The aim was to reverse the proportion of own-vehicle operations and subcontracting, accepting that the former would possibly make a loss knowing that the good margin on subcontracting would ensure overall profitability.

The things that were to distinguish clearfreight from the well-established, existing subcontracting and clearing house operations were the marketing and transport management skills that would be applied, the use of the Southern BRS network of branches to obtain and control traffic, and the use of a relatively large own-vehicle fleet to provide a back-up service. The intention was to market and manage the product in an aggressive and professional way as had been done with other BRS products such as truck rental and rescue. The clearfreight concept was unique to Southern BRS. John Farrant, managing director of Southern BRS, argued that it was a solution to a problem peculiar to the Southeast[2] and would prefer it not to be identified as a national product.

A crucial aspect of the clearfreight strategy was that it was based fundamentally on Farrant's beliefs about the nature and future of the road transport industry. In contrast to the popular view that the sharp increase in the cost of vehicles was leading to the demise of the smaller haulier, Farrant believed that the efficiencies and entrepreneurial drive of the small hauliers would ensure their continued dominance of general haulage in spite of the severely depressed rate structure. Farrant described clearfreight as 'a service designed to assist general haulage operators and users by matching loads to available vehicle capacity ... the concept of linking widespread resources with the smaller operators.'

Clearfreight was Southern BRS's general haulage survival strategy. It was designed to make it possible to maintain, or even expand, the company's fleet of general haulage vehicles. The strategy was therefore directly, if not explicitly, opposed to Thompson's strategy and to the existing official National Freight Corporation and group general haulage policies. The justification that Southern BRS used for the continuation of own-vehicle operations was that these were essential to the successful subcontracting operation. In order to sustain clearfreight, and hence the strategy of general haulage survival, the performance of own-vehicle operations had to be linked directly to the overall success of clearfreight. For these reasons, Farrant resisted demands from group to report clearfreight and own-vehicle operations separately.

The clearfreight reporting issue revealed the strategy underlying the new activity; a strategy based upon a determination to maintain, at least at some minimum level, general haulage as an aspect of the company's operations. The strategy stemmed from Farrant's philosophy about the industry, and particularly about the role of BRS vis-à-vis small hauliers. Another important factor influencing Farrant's approach was something shared by all the regional company managing directors: the difficulties associated with managing the final demise of general haulage. Although greatly reduced, general haulage continued to support many jobs at both the managerial and nonmanagerial levels and was critical to the viability of a number of marginal branches in the company. Farrant was not, either by background or inclination a 'general haulage man', but he was a pragmatist and was sensitive to the grave financial, organizational and industrial relations problems associated with attempting to manage the coup de grace of general haulage. Within this context, his management philosophy guided the development of an innovative approach to the general haulage activity.

Mortons BRS Ltd

Mortons BRS was an anomaly within the BRS group. It was anomalous in terms of its size[3] and also because of its 'specialist' rather than 'regional' base. In terms of product diversity, Mortons BRS was also very different from the regional companies because of its heavy dependence upon general haulage, distribution and warehousing activities associated with the motor industry. The position of Mortons was a direct result of the background of the company and the history of its association with BRS.

Mortons was a long-established family business which had been acquired by BRS twice: once at the time of nationalization and again in 1967. The company traditionally had very close links with the motor industry in the Midlands, and this specialist role was maintained even after the 1967 acquisition of BRS. Len Payne, indeed, insisted that Mortons divest most of its non-haulage activities. Thus under BRS management Mortons went from being a highly diversified company specializing in the motor industry to a narrowly based haulage company.

Given this background, it is rather difficult to discuss in a useful way the response of Mortons to Thompson's strategy of diversification. The manner in which the company's managing director, Eric Shortland, spoke in the Group Policy Committee and quarterly review meetings indicated that he had embraced the Thompson strategy wholeheartedly but that he felt he was constrained by the limited resource and market base of the company. He seemed nevertheless to be making every effort to divest general haulage and build the other BRS activities.

Mortons apparent eager compliance with the strategy of diversification is somewhat misleading because underlying it was a more fundamental issue, the survival of the company not just in the industry, but within the BRS group. The anomalous nature of Mortons put the company in an uneasy position in the group, and with the economic decline of Coventry and the difficulties associated with the motor industry, Shortland was extremely concerned that his company would be absorbed by the other BRS companies. If Mortons could not succeed as a motor industry specialist, then the legitimacy of the company within the group came into question. Geographically, Mortons was 'caged in' and was forced to defend its territory against the much larger and more 'properly' constituted BRS companies with which it shared borders.

Notes

1. To a greater or lesser extent this treatment of information concerning individual activity performance was common within BRS, but always within the constraints of what the auditors considered to be proper accounting practice.

2. The large imbalance between traffic into and out of the area, particularly following the decline of the London docks.

3. Mortons represented only about 3 per cent of group revenue and was, in revenue terms, only one-quarter the average size of the other BRS companies.

Appendix 3
A CHRONOLOGY OF CRITICAL EVENTS IN THE DECISION-MAKING PROCESS

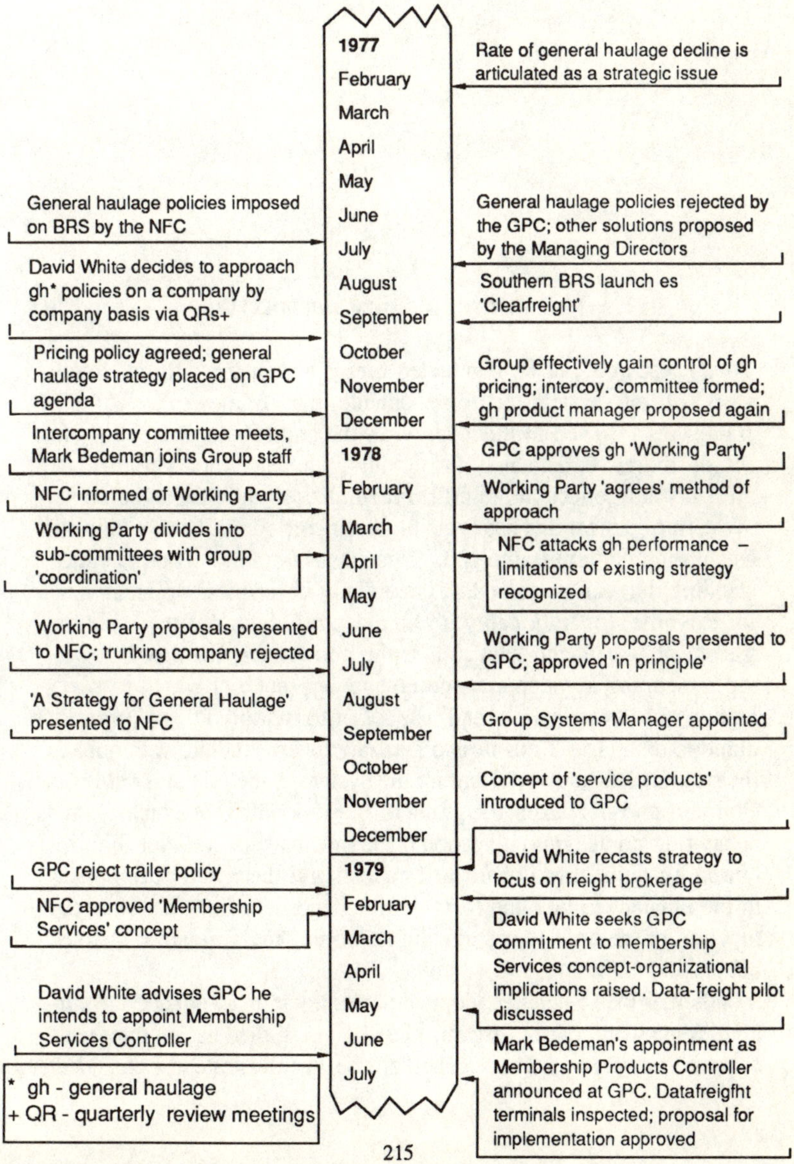

1977
February
March
April
May
June
July
August
September
October
November
December
1978
February
March
April
May
June
July
August
September
October
November
December
1979
February
March
April
May
June
July
Rate of general haulage decline is articulated as a strategic issue
General haulage policies imposed on BRS by the NFC
General haulage policies rejected by the GPC; other solutions proposed by the Managing Directors
David White decides to approach gh* policies on a company by company basis via QRs+
Southern BRS launch es 'Clearfreight'
Pricing policy agreed; general haulage strategy placed on GPC agenda
Group effectively gain control of gh pricing; intercoy. committee formed; gh product manager proposed again
Intercompany committee meets, Mark Bedeman joins Group staff
GPC approves gh 'Working Party'
NFC informed of Working Party
Working Party 'agrees' method of approach
Working Party divides into sub-committees with group 'coordination'
NFC attacks gh performance – limitations of existing strategy recognized
Working Party proposals presented to NFC; trunking company rejected
Working Party proposals presented to GPC; approved 'in principle'
'A Strategy for General Haulage' presented to NFC
Group Systems Manager appointed
Concept of 'service products' introduced to GPC
GPC reject trailer policy
David White recasts strategy to focus on freight brokerage
NFC approved 'Membership Services' concept
David White seeks GPC commitment to membership Services concept-organizational implications raised. Data-freight pilot discussed
David White advises GPC he intends to appoint Membership Services Controller
Mark Bedeman's appointment as Membership Products Controller announced at GPC. Datafreigfht terminals inspected; proposal for implementation approved
* gh - general haulage
+ QR - quarterly review meetings

Appendix 4
THE RESEARCH PROCESS

The anthropological perspective

Social research can be conducted either within the cultural framework of the system or from outside that framework. 'Cultural framework' is used in this context in the anthropological sense of a set of shared beliefs and values and the behaviour patterns and artefacts that reflect and re-affirm them. Research into contemporary Western organizations has typically been carried out from within the established cultural framework. This places limitations on the understanding that can be gained. It is common in business organizations, for example, for 'rationality' to be a central feature of the espoused system of beliefs and values. It is the notion of rationality that provides meaning to much managerial activity, much of which revolves around the examination and use of information in the form of numeric data. Yet, if business organizations are studied from outside their cultural framework, that is, the system of beliefs and values is explored and not taken for granted, the rationality of much of this behaviour comes into question. The means/ends relationship required by rationality is hard to establish and these activities appear to the outsider to take the form of ritualized behaviour patterns, the function of which is to sustain and reinforce the dominant system of beliefs and values.

Whether the researcher adopts a position within or outside the cultural framework of the organization being studied is an important methodological issue. This can perhaps best be illustrated by considering an example from a cultural setting different from our own. Consider the case of a North American Indian raindancer. A researcher adopting a position within the cultural framework would study the situation in terms of rationality — the link between the raindancer's behaviour and atmospheric precipitation having been subsumed at a higher conceptual level, that is, within the established belief system. The important research questions would then take the form of ascertaining the levels of recent rainfall, the need for rain, threatened crop failure, the moral or spiritual failings of the community that have resulted in the Raingod's ill-favour and the need for intercession by the raindancer. These are all rational issues from a perspective within the cultural framework of the community. The anthropologist, however, would not examine these issues, but would instead try to develop an understanding of the system of beliefs and values underpinning the culture. Similarly, a researcher can ask 'rational' questions about the particular method of financial analysis adopted by an organization or can examine this feature of the organization as a reflection of the established system of beliefs and values.

Katz and Kahn (1966) have argued that there is a need to adopt this approach to the study of organizations:

> In spite of the obvious differences between the cultures of organizations performing essentially the same type of functions it is not easy to specify the dimensions of such differences. Though the subculture of the organization provides the frame of reference within which its members interpret activities and events, the members will not be able to verbalize in any precise fashion this frame of reference. They will be clear about the judgments they make but not about the basic standards or frames they employ in reaching a judgment. The many subtle and unconscious factors which determine a frame of reference are not susceptible to direct questioning. The technique of participant observation has thus been more revealing about organizational climate (culture) than the typical survey. What is needed ideally for the study of organizational climate (culture) is participant-observation to supply the insightful leads, and systematic depth interviewing of appropriate population samples within the organization to ensure adequate coverage (Katz and Kahn 1966: 66).

If an organization is to be studied from outside its cultural framework, a particular methodology and specific techniques must be employed. This is more than just an issue of what research technique will be employed, it involves a much broader issue concerning the basic methodological approach. One way a researcher can study an organization from outside its established culture is by adopting an anthropological perspective.

Edgerton and Langness (1974) discuss how the emergence of modern anthropology has been based upon the adoption of a methodological approach called 'fieldwork':

> The core of fieldwork is participant-observation — the anthropologist lives intimately as a member of the society . . . but also remains detached from their life. Complete involvement is incompatible with the anthropologist's primary goals, but complete detachment is incompatible with fieldwork (Edgerton and Langness 1974:2).

Fieldwork is based upon a number of implicit methodological principles:

- tests, questionnaires, etc., may provide a large amount of data, but in order to be able to interpret these data and understand what lies behind them the cultural code must be learned;
- the culture must be seen through the eyes of those who live it, as well as through the eyes and techniques of the scientific observer.

People's lives must be understood in the terms that they understand them. This approach is referred to as 'emic' in contrast with the 'etic', the outsider's understanding. To see life as others do requires involvement, participation and empathy. Yet some intellectual detachment must be maintained if this insider's view is to be analysed and reported.

Pelto and Pelto (1978) have similarly made this distinction between between the etic (outsider's) and emic (insider's) approach:

> According to this view cultural behaviour should always be studied and categorized in terms of the inside view — the actor's definition of human events. Conceptualizations in anthropological theory should be discovered by analysing the cognitive processes of the people studied rather than imposed from cross-cultural (hence ethnocentric) classification (Pelto and Pelto 1978:54).

Pelto and Pelto (1978) and Pike (1954) raise a second, related methodological issue: that of discovering a conceptual framework within the research setting as opposed to applying a predetermined generalized conceptual framework. This methodology underlies Glaser and Strauss's idea of 'grounded theory' (1967). They regard 'qualitative research — whether utilizing observation, intensive interviews, or any type of document — as a strategy concerned with the discovery of substantive theory' (1967:289). This approach of developing and discovering low-level theories through the systematic collection and analysis of data, rather than testing preconceived theories, is at the centre of anthropological methodology.

This methodological approach has implications in terms of data-collection techniques. Survey techniques cannot be used to establish the link between organizational behaviour and belief systems because these techniques must be developed within a conceptual framework that has an implicit belief structure. Either the belief system coincides with that of the organization, and so the researcher is by definition within the cultural framework, or it does not coincide, in which case data collection instruments would be couched in terms that are either meaningless or misleading to the respondents. The anthropological technique of participant-observation seems to overcome the problems inherent in survey techniques. The researcher places himself or herself physically within the social system under study and attempts to gain an understanding in terms of the actors' view of their world.

This technique has been used typically by anthropologists to study cultures very different from their own, and although a number of methodological problems have been recognized, the value of the technique is now well established. Participant-observation has only rarely been applied to the study of modern Western social systems where the broad cultural framework of the researcher is the same as the system being studied. An exception is Whyte's *Street Corner Society* (1943). The insights developed in this research demonstrate the technique can be successfully applied in the researcher's own cultural setting.

Studying the strategy process

The interdependence of theory and research method has been well established in the literature (for example, Pettigrew 1973 and more recently, Van Maanen 1979). The central theoretical concern of the BRS research, the strategy process, dictated both the research design and the data collection methods: 'Since the choice of method should be suggested at all times by the subject matter, and the subject matter in our case was process, the choice of participant-observation as the principal way of investigation seemed a good choice. Our rationale was that the best way to understand a process was to become part of it (Olesen and Whittaker 1968:19).' A vital weakness of studies of the strategy processes in organization has been the failure, often because of practical difficulties associated with gaining access or resource constraints, of appropriate research methods. Pettigrew's (1973) study is a notable exception. Longitudinal studies based upon retrospective case descriptions (for example, Mintzberg et al. 1976) are only a partial solution to this methodological problem because the actual processes involved can only be inferred ex post facto.

Much of the popular recent literature (for example, Quinn 1980; Peters and Waterman 1982; and Deal and Kennedy 1982) is based upon interview data, which, although providing interesting and useful insights into strategic options and behaviour, provides ultimately little understanding of the strategy process itself. An understanding of the strategy process hinges on the direct study of that process, and this demands both a longitudinal research design and real-time data collection. Given the present status of the behavioural sciences, this means that the researcher is limited to qualitative research methods.

Qualitative methods are still burdened by a poor image compared with the more 'rigorous' quantitative approaches, but the methodological foundations of these methods are gradually becoming more established:

> The label qualitative methods has no precise meaning in any of the social sciences. It is at best an umbrella term covering an array of interpretive techniques which seek to describe, decode, translate and otherwise come to terms with the meaning, not the frequency, of certain more or less naturally occurring phenomena in the social world. To operate in a qualitative mode is to trade linguistic symbols and, by so doing, attempt to reduce the distance between indicated and indicators, between theory and data, between context and action. The raw materials of qualitative study are therefore in vivo, close to the point of origin. Although the use of qualitative methods does not prohibit a researcher's use of the logic of scientific empiricism, the logic of phenomenological analysis is more likely to be assumed since qualitative researchers tend to regard social phenomena as more particular and ambiguous than reputable and clearly defined (Van Maanen 1979:520).

The collection of data — the role of participant-observer

> Because the relationship between the research worker and the persons in the field is the key to effective observation and interviewing, much depends on the initial field contacts (Dean, Eichhorn, and Dean 1969:68).

The longitudinal, real-time data collection element of the research was composed of a number of discrete, though partially overlapping steps:

1. Process of formally gaining access to the organization — April 1977 to July 1979.
2. Organizational entry — 14 July 1977.
3. Establishing the research role at Group Policy Committee, group and company managing director level — July 1977 to September 1977.
4. Broadening the scope of data collection to include one of the regional companies and the quarterly review meetings — September 1977 to June 1978.
5. Data collection in the regional companies in addition to the Group Policy Committee and quarterly reviews — June 1978 to February 1979
6. Data collection at Group Policy Committee, group, and quarterly reviews — February 1979 to May 1979.
7. Scope of data collection reduced to attendance of Group Policy Committee meetings only — in conjunction with formal analysis of data — May 1979 to September 1979.
8. Final interview — 27 September 1979.

Access to the organization was gained through an established relationship between the researcher's PhD supervisor (Dr Stuart Timperley, London Business School) and the top management of BRS. A period of four months was required nevertheless before top management agreed that the researcher could attend policy meetings in the role of observer. The established credibility of the researcher's supervisor clearly played a decisive role in obtaining access.

Dean et al. (1969) indicate five principles guiding entry into the field:

1. General field contacts should move from persons in the highest status and authority positions down to the actual participants in the field situation one wants to study.

As access was gained through the group managing director and the Group Policy Committee, virtually blanket approval had been given to the research. Care was taken, however, to 'negotiate' access at successively lower levels as discussed by Kahn and Mann: 'When the researcher has gained acceptance from the people at that level, he asks only that they allow him to talk to their subordinates, and so on' (1969:48).

BRS was one group of several comprising the National Freight Corporation and hence it was desirable that some access upward from David White, the group managing director, was gained. In fact, this was limited to attendance at the formal planning and review meetings and, because of the sensitive nature of the relationship between White and the chief executive of the NFC, no attempt was made by the researcher to broaden this upward access. On the one occasion that the researcher's supervisor arranged a meeting with the chief executive of the NFC, David White very nearly brought the research to an end.

One of the difficulties associated with access sponsored from above is that many people suspect that the researcher will report upwards, and even that he is under contract to do so. The researcher was careful to explain the nature of the relationship between himself and the organization and its members and also the form that the reporting of the research would take. The fact that the researcher had not undertaken to provide a formal written report to the organization at the end of the research eased this problem considerably.

Confidentiality of individuals, groups, and the organization was assured, but the real issue was demonstrating over a period of time that confidences were respected absolutely. This was largely a question of developing the research role and building relationships based on trust.

2. The field worker needs to have a plausible explanation of the research, that makes sense to the people whose co-operation he seeks.

The researcher had a brief speech which he recited the first time he met people in the field. After a short period, the group managing director and company managing directors 'assumed ownership' of the research and made this introduction themselves. The researcher was careful to follow these formal introductions with informal chats over drinks or meals where the occasion arose. The issue was one of building the relationship rather than explaining the research. Few of the managers were very interested in the research itself, but they were interested in the researcher as a person. 'Who is he? What's he doing? Why is he doing it? Who is he doing it for?' were the questions that needed to be answered.

3. The field worker should try to represent himself, his sponsors, and his study as honestly as possible.

This can, of course, only be done if the work is honestly conceived and openly presented. Extended, intensive fieldwork is bound to result ultimately in the exposure of any misrepresentations, and this would make continuation by that researcher, and very possibly other researchers, practically impossible.

4. The field worker should have in mind some rather routine fact-gathering that makes sense to those in the field.

The approach I adopted was to open an interview with questions about the historical background of the organization (or organizational subunit) and the individual. This provided extremely useful contextual material, developed the researcher's general knowledge of the organization and the industry, and provided the respondents with a subject they could discuss in a knowledgeable and relaxed way. The discussion of personal background proved to be a very useful technique: it established a personal relationship, indicated that the researcher was genuinely interested in the individual and not just 'wringing him for information', and established a climate of professional confidence and trust. Typically at least half a day was devoted to each interview; with the top management group the interview situation quickly changed to regular contact.

5. The researcher should sacrifice initial data in order to speed acceptance.

The quality of the data collected was to a large extent a function of the quality of the relationship between the researcher and the field, and hence it was crucial that the research role be carefully established and managed.

Gold (1969) has observed that the participant-observer role can take four forms:

- complete participant, where the true identity and purpose of the researcher are not known to those being observed;
- participant-as-observer, where the researcher develops relationships with the informants through time and both the researcher and the informant are aware that there is a field relationship;
- observer-as-participant, where social interaction is limited to short-term contact such as in a one-visit interview;
- complete observer, where the researcher is removed from the social interaction with informants.

In this research, the role of participant-as-observer was used. Gold points out that two problems commonly associated with this role are the development of 'non-field' relationships, that is, ordinary friendships, and 'going native', that is, over-rapport with informants or the setting. Both of these problems were encountered in the research. Regular contact with people over a period of more than two years created pressures for the development of friendships. This was countered by avoiding non-organizational contacts and meant that on a number of occasions invitations to an informant's home had to be put off. Fortunately most of the people concerned developed an understanding of the researcher's role and accepted the distinction between a field relationship and friendship. This was assisted by the considerable social activity associated with the managerial activity observed — frequent lunches and dinners acted as a form of catharsis.

A more difficult problem was the danger of bias associated with the differential affective attitude that developed towards various individuals. The researcher was aware, and noted in the fieldnotes, that towards the end of field research unbiased observation became extremely difficult. This was partly a result of 'going native' in the situational as well as relationships sense, that is, familiarity with the issues, relationships, perceptions and preferences of individuals meant that the researcher was doing more than observing. The tendency to confirm the rapidly developing analysis of the situation must have biased the data considerably towards the end of the field research.

The quality of the data collected varied with time as indicated in Figure A4.1.

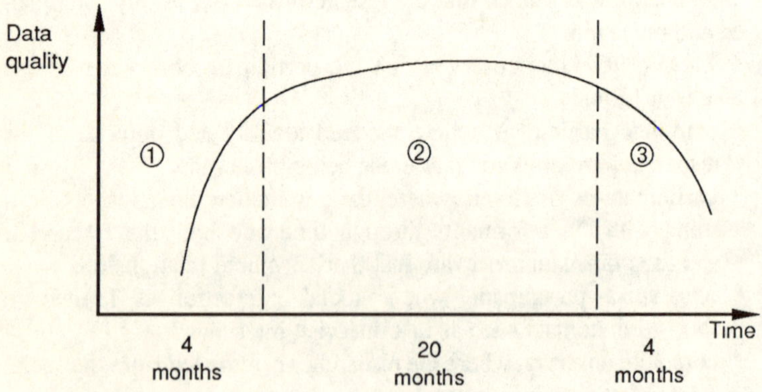

① Poor quality due to ignorance of the individuals, issues and context.

② Maximum data quality.

③ Declining data quality because of over-rapport and the changing focus of research activity, that is, increasing concern with analysis rather than collection of data.

Figure A4.1: Quality of data collected

The development and maintenance of the participant-as-observer role required the researcher to develop a viable, acceptable participant role in the social system of the organization, while avoiding completely any participation in the task system. On several occasions, attempts were made to give the researcher task-related roles. This was initially a result of the uncertainty about the researcher's role, and then subsequently a problem of over-rapport, of the informants wanting the researcher to come fully on-board. The latter problem was eased considerably by the presence of the researcher's supervisor who continued his established research relationship. As well as acting in the valuable role as a second observer, the researcher's supervisor was able to be more involved in the task system by acting as a consultant and confidant, while the researcher maintained a pure research role. The dual participant-observer method proved extremely effective, and it is doubtful whether the researcher could have maintained the pure researcher role for such an extended period without the consultant-observer operating in parallel.

The geographical dispersion of the organization was a further advantage because the researcher could spend time with one group without the other groups being aware. The amount of time spent with various individuals or groups was not known to others, and therefore not a source of anxiety. It also helped maintain a slight air of mystery about the role and made it easier for the researcher to remain equally marginal with all the organizational groupings.

Establishing the role took approximately six months. This time was required before top management was comfortable with the researcher as participant-observer. It varied, of course, from place to place, and individual to individual but, for the central individuals and activities, a period of six months was required.

The development of the role involved gaining the trust and confidence of managers by demonstrating that the researcher was completely non-judgmental and prepared to view situations from the perspective of the managers, rather than from some external 'academic' point of view, and totally outside the communication network of the organization (and the industry). Both elements were tested repeatedly during this initial period. As mentioned earlier, the role was explained in detail to each of the managers, but ultimately it was the passing of their 'tests' that led to acceptance.

These tests took the form of publicly seeking opinions on issues — 'What do you think?' — to which the researcher had to restate his position publicly of being 'just an observer, I'm just trying to understand what happens, I don't want to feed anything back'. Since this test was usually applied by the senior manager in the group, often the group managing director, this rebuff necessitated a subsequent private re-explanation of the role. A similar stance was adopted in discussions with individuals. By refusing to comment, it became clear throughout the organization that the researcher was not a source of 'leaks'. The researcher did not attempt to distinguish between 'hot' and neutral information, but simply did not repeat anything heard or observed. With time this became a source of humour: managers would intervene after a question had been directed at the researcher and say, 'Oh, don't bother, he doesn't say anything.'

The pure participant-as-observer status was assisted by adopting a certain pattern of neutral, predictable behaviour in all meetings, for example:

- avoiding eye contact with individuals and writing fieldnotes regardless of the issues under discussion or the dynamics of the group;
- sitting at the meeting table with the rest of the group, although always being the last to choose a place (but not in a set position);
- only occasionally helping with the serving of tea or coffee in meetings, that is, avoiding the 'tea-lady' role;
- reflecting the emotional climate of the meeting, that is, laughing, serious or whatever, as appropriate; and
- treating the fieldnotes as confidential, that is, not leaving them where they could be casually observed.

Initial emphasis was placed upon establishing the role rather than collecting data: interesting issues were left unpursued, and relevant documents remained uncollected. To an extent this approach was retained throughout the research, and in a sense data collection was 'passive', with the researcher following the ebb and flow of the organization and the decision-making process, rather than rigorously applying a programme for collecting specific material. When the pursuit of material threatened the role, in most cases, the role was given priority. This form of passive data collection had advantages and disadvantages. The primary advantage was that the researcher's preconceived ideas about what was important were prevented from determining the scope of data collection. The primary disadvantage was that certain relevant data, particularly written material supporting discussions and meetings were not collected. The researcher found, however, that once the role was established most relevant material was offered and that patience was rewarded: the disadvantages were partly offset by the length and continuity of the field research.

Some relevant data were forfeited, however, and the analysis thereby weakened. Group Policy Committee minutes, for example, were not regularly made available to the researcher, and no attempt was made to obtain them. In retrospect, this was a weak point in the data collection. More quantitative data could have been collected to support the analysis of the qualitative data. This was particularly necessary where the researcher's analysis questions the objectivity of certain arguments or analyses presented as part of the decision-making process.

The passive approach to data collection matched the exploratory methodology of the research; decisions about what material was relevant could not be made using the operationalization of some preconceived conceptual framework, as is the case with the hypothetico-deductive approach. Sensitivity to the organization and its members was the best guide to what was important, and once again the extended and intensive nature of the field work made this a practical research strategy. The other important guide was, of course, the general area of theoretical interest. The broad parameters within which the strategy process of the organization was structured and operated were apparent once the researcher became familiar with the organization, and these parameters guided the data collection process. Certain activities and individuals were obviously central to the strategy process and, by following these activities and individuals, the overall pattern gradually unfolded. Many hours of contact with members of the Group Policy Committee ensured that the important issues, relationships, and emotions eventually emerged from one source or another.

Sources of data

The following sources of data were used:

Observation of meetings

1. Group Policy Committee — every meeting between July 1977 and September 1979 (22 in all, of which 8 were 'overnight meetings'). A total of 172 meeting hours observed.
2. Group and company planning and control meetings (quarterly reviews) — almost all those held during the period February 1978 to March 1979. A total of 55 meetings observed (approximately 250 hours).
3. Group controllers meetings — 27 meetings observed.
4. Functional meetings (truck rental, marketing, personnel,

finance, planning) — a total of 12 meetings observed. The engineering meetings were scheduled to coincide with Group Policy Committee meetings and were therefore not observed.

5. Company management or policy committee (formerly company board) meetings — a total of 21 observed (at least one from each regional company, excluding Mortons BRS).
6. National and company management conferences, which were attended by all managers — 9 attended.
7. Company joint (management/union) committee meetings — 10 attended.
8. Ad hoc/working party meetings.
9. Branch review meetings — 15 attended.

Interviews/discussions with:

1. All members of the Group Policy Committee.
2. Most group management staff.
3. Practically all regional company senior management.
4. Twenty-eight branch managers (usually a full day spent with the manager at each branch).

Documents

A wide range of documents were obtained for analysis, including:

1. Group strategic reviews, corporate plans, budgets, and quarterly review documents.
2. Regional company corporate plans, budgets and quarterly review documents.
3. The general haulage working party reports.
4. Reports, projects and miscellaneous papers submitted to the Group Policy Committee.
5. Miscellaneous group, company and branch documents.
6. Company personnel records.
7. Company annual trading Returns by branch for the period 1973-77 (excluding Scottish, North Western and Mortons).

Sources of data for the historical analysis included:

1. Books and articles about the organization and the industry.
2. Annual reports 1963-80.
3. BRS company diaries listing branches and names of managers (1969-78).
4. Discussions with informants who had been members of the organization for many years.

The quality of this historical data was inherently not as high as that collected on a real-time basis, but was sufficient to provide the necessary understanding of the context of the strategic issue being studied and the decision-making process. Considerable effort was devoted to the collection and analysis of this historical data because it was felt that the strategy process could only be understood in terms of the context of earlier events. This approach is strongly supported by Pettigrew (1985).

Data collection techniques

The techniques used for data collection revolved very largely around note-taking during and immediately following meetings, discussions and interviews. These fieldnotes were accumulated in chronological order in A4 spiral bound notebooks. In all some half a million words of notes were collected during the twenty-seven months of fieldwork. A decision was made early in the research not to tape-record meetings, because it was felt this would have an effect on the process under study. A second, more practical consideration was that tape-recording would have generated such a large volume of material that the time and expense involved in transcription would have been prohibitive. Both of these problems have been referred to by other researchers: Strauss (1969:73) concludes that 'In the majority of contexts, therefore, the most practical recording procedure is note-taking by the researcher.' Strauss goes on to suggest:

> Furthermore, overt and continual note-taking during an observation or interview frequently gives rise to reactive effects similar to those created by mechanical recording . . . In light of these considerations, most experienced participant-observers generally prefer to make only mental notes during observation or interviewing, committing these notes to paper immediately after leaving the situation (Strauss et al. 1969:73,74).

The experience of this researcher was rather different. The constant taking of notes became one of the hallmarks of the role. It was initially the subject of curiosity: 'What do you write down?' and subsequently the butt of jokes, but assisted to legitimize the researcher's role (he actually did something). Further, most people were rather flattered that someone valued what they said enough to actually write it down. Obviously sensitivity had to be exercised, and there were occasions when note-taking would have been inappropriate. One trade union official actually placed his hand on the page of the fieldnotes at one point in a discussion. On these occasions the technique suggested by Strauss was employed.

Strauss also points out that note-taking should not be allowed to interfere with the process of conducting an interview. This is clearly an important factor, but the researcher quickly developed the technique of note-taking in time-lapsed parallel with listening and asking questions, or in the case of meetings, note-taking 'behind the play'. The note-taking was partly dependent on a form of shorthand that allowed the researcher to take down an interview or meeting largely verbatim. The fieldnotes were usually completed by making further notes after an interview, or during breaks in a meeting — one word memory joggers in the margin were found to be very useful for this purpose.

Initially, the fieldnotes were transcribed on a nightly, or at least weekly basis. As the pace of the fieldwork built up, however, this could not be maintained. Long hours in the field, and the frequency of overnight meetings and travel, made regular transcription of the fieldnotes impossible, and after a few months it was abandoned. Strauss and others warn researchers against this, but it did not create difficulties in this case — the detail with which the notes were originally recorded may provide the explanation. It was felt that any disadvantage of material being lost was more than offset by the researcher not being tempted to develop tentative frameworks early in the research that might have biased later data collection.

Analysing and presenting the data

Data collection over such an extended period of time resulted in a very large amount of material, the major element of which was half a million words of fieldnotes comprised primarily of observational material from meeting and interview notes. The problems of analysing data in this form are considerable, and unfortunately very poorly documented in the literature:

> Qualitative data tend to overload the researcher badly at almost every point: the sheer range of phenomena to be observed, the recorded volume of notes, the time required for write-up, coding, and analysis can all become overwhelming. But the most serious and central difficulty in the use of qualitative data is that methods of analyses are not well formulated (Miles 1979:590).

The process of analysis was in itself a process of discovery, and only in retrospect can it be seen as having a logical structure. The problem of analysis was also related to the underlying methodology as well as the nature of the data. Because of the approach adopted — inductively searching for a theoretical framework that explains observed reality, rather than collecting data specifically to test a preconceived theory — the process of analysis evolved as the material and ideas developed. In practical terms this meant that the analysis had to be built up one step at the time, layer by layer, with increasing conceptual abstraction.

The process of analysis can be summarized diagrammatically as shown in Figure A4.2. This is, of course, a simplification of the actual process of analysis, which involved interactions between the various layers which themselves overlapped considerably. A great deal of the ordering of material was redundant or fruitless and was discarded as not being relevant to the central theoretical concern. Numerous issues that were of potential theoretical interest were ignored or put to one side for subsequent analysis. The process of analysis was a process of discovery, and clearly a single 'right way' to approach the data did not exist. Only by working the material through using the central theoretical interest and the insights gained during the fieldwork as guides and remaining receptive to the data itself could the process of analysis be progressed.

The researcher's experience in analysing qualitative data was similar to that of Miles:

> We found the actual process of analysis . . . was essentially intuitive, primitive, and unmanageable in any rational sense . . . the analysis process is more memorable for its moments of sheer despair in the face of the mass of data, alternating with moments of achieved clarity, soon followed by second-guessing scepticism (Miles 1979:597).

In retrospect, the process of analysing the BRS data did have a logic and a rationality among the false starts, dead-ends and disconcerting volume of data.

Strauss et al. suggest that 'the process of indexing the fieldnotes constitutes a preliminary analysis of the data as well as helping to locate materials' (1969:75). He suggests that an indexing system such as that devised by Whyte (1960) be employed. The indexing of fieldnotes was found to be a crucial first step in the process of analysis: the ordering of the material, the development of data from the mass of material was time consuming and often tedious, but it provided the foundation on which the later interpretations and theoretical inferences were based. A range of indexing systems was employed, depending on the nature of the material; often it consisted of nothing more than making summary notes from the fieldnotes and then underscoring issues or themes in these summary notes. Sometimes the ordering of material involved just a random search for data that the researcher knew to be somewhere in the fieldnotes. In

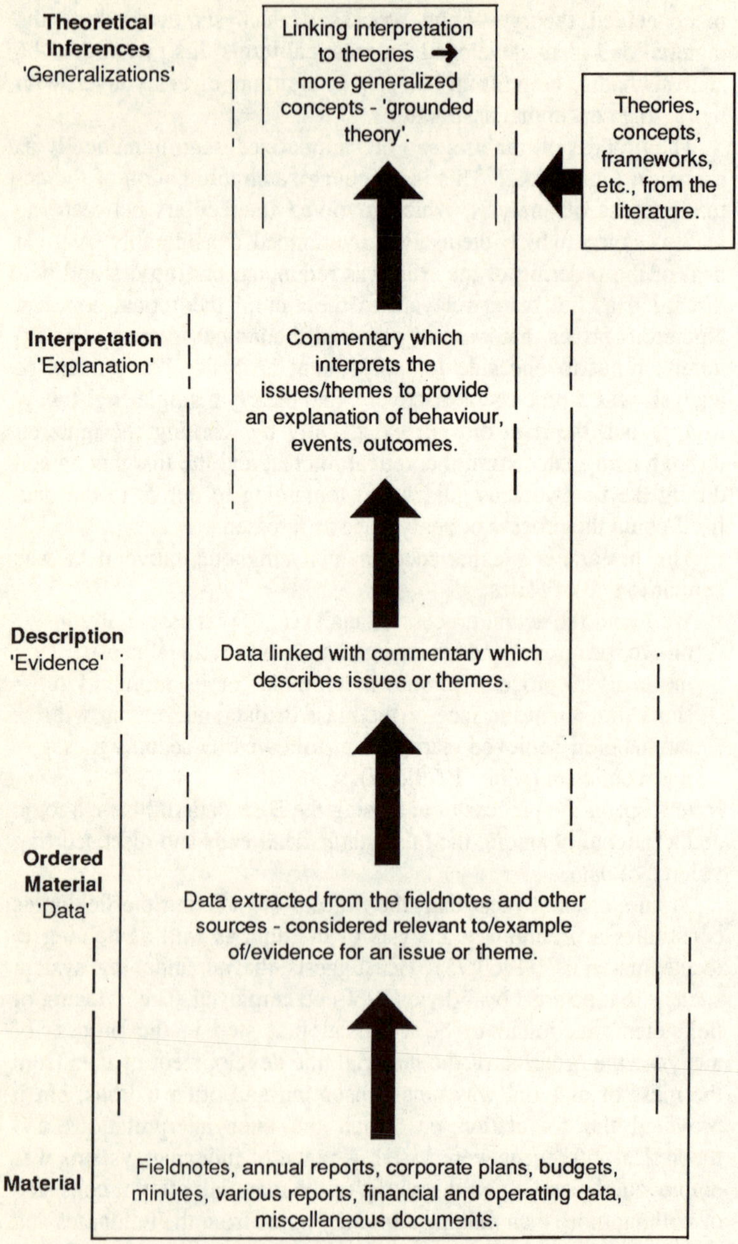

Figure A4.2: The process of analysing and presenting the data

retrospect, a more formal method of indexing would have helped the process of analysis, at least in the early stages.

Problems of bias and validity

The methodology adopted has a number of unavoidable weaknesses. Dean et al. (1969:20, 21) point out that unstructured field methods have two basic limitations:

1. They are not generally useful for statistical treatment because of the non-standardized way the data are collected.
2. A second major limitation flows from the researcher's use of the relationships he establishes in the field, that is, the likelihood of bias.

The second problem was considered more relevant in this research, although the first clearly places a limitation on the form of analysis that could be undertaken. It was felt that given the nature of the theoretical issues under study, statistical analysis would not have added greatly to the insights gained. Such techniques are more useful in testing hypotheses than in generating grounded theory.

The problem of bias in the collection of data is recognized as being generally associated with qualitative, and in particular observational, data:

> By and large, the principal concerns regarding the observational data of the participant-observer can be summarized under three headings:
> (1) reactive effects of the observer's presence or behaviour on the phenomenon under observation, with the result that the observer does not have the opportunity to observe the very thing that he may have hoped to observe and that he may in fact believe he is observing;
> (2) distorting effects of selective perception and interpretation on the observer's part; and
> (3) limitations on the observer's ability to witness all the relevant aspects of the phenomenon in question (McCall 1969:128).

The practical steps taken to minimize the first two of these effects have been outlined above in the section called 'The Collection of Data — The Role of Participant-Observer'. The reactive effect was considered not to have been significant. Careful development of the role, and habitual presence and behaviour over an extended period, was believed to have limited any reactive effects in meetings. Obviously the process of interview or discussion of issues with an outsider has a tendency to make people reconsider their attitudes and perceptions, but again the preservation of a careful neutral stance, and minimal feedback would have limited this effect. It was considered that, in the overall scheme of things, the reactive effect of the researcher was insignificant.

The other problems were minimized by a research design involving multiple methods (observation, interviews, documents) and multiple sources (multiple observers, multiple informants, diverse document sources). The efficacy of this design has been argued by Pettigrew (1973).

Problems of validity, reliability and interpretability remain, however, as an inherent weakness of the methodology. The quality of the data and, therefore, the validity of the inferences drawn from them vary, but the consistent patterns in these data make misinterpretation as a result of selective perception and presentation of the data unlikely. The data concerning the central theoretical issue, the decision-making process associated with the emergence of a new general haulage strategy, was generally of high quality because of the multiple-method, multiple-source design, and the intensity and extensiveness of data collection that was applied to that aspect of the study. Care was taken to support assertions, interpretations, and inferences about these issues with data when possible, so that independent assessment of the reasonableness of such assertions and interpretations can be made by the reader. The limitations inherent in qualitative data, however, are once again revealed. To present all the supporting data would consume an unreasonable amount of space, and would strain the reader's level of interest.

> The analytic framework which emerges from the researcher's collection and scrutiny of data is equivalent to what he knows systematically about his own data . . . This conviction does not mean that his analysis is the only plausible one, but only that the researcher himself has a high confidence in its validity (Glaser and Strauss 1967:294, 295).

The limitations of the research

The conceptual models that have been developed from the BRS research are, of course, subject to the limitations of the research, which as discussed earlier derive from the methodology adopted. Findings based upon a single example are impossible to validate in the scientific sense. Berg (1979) argues that the validity of this type of research can, however, be judged in terms of:

1. The accuracy of the data: the extent to which the description of issues and events is correct.
2. The credibility of the interpretation of the data: is the interpretation reasonable in terms of the overall pattern of data? Does sufficient data exist to support a particular inference?
3. The validity of the theoretical conclusions reached: are the general statements concerning the theoretical issues justified and, to what extent, are these conclusions generalizable?

With regard to the BRS research, the first two criteria of the accuracy of the description and the reasonableness of the interpretation have been discussed and, to a large extent, the material presented in the book speaks for itself. The third criterion is more difficult because it is related to the inherent limitations of the methodology: to what extent does the analysis of one organization justify general conclusions? As Berg (1979) points out, the findings of the study of one organization do not lend themselves to validation in the traditional sense.

> This does not mean that the theories cannot be judged, but rather that the validation must take a different form, oriented more to the credibility of the research process. The task of the researcher is therefore not to show whether his findings, models or hypotheses are right or wrong, but to convince the reader that they are reasonable conclusions, drawn from material, which has been processed by methods which can be explicitly described (Berg 1979:165).

Note

1. For example, problems of validation and bias, in particular the problem of 'going native', where the researcher unwittingly takes on the cultural framework under study.

REFERENCES

Arthur D. Little, Inc. (1974), *A System for Managing Diversity*, Cambridge, MA.

Ackoff, R. L. (1981), *Creating the Corporate Future*, John Wiley and Sons.

Allison, Graham T. (1971), *Essence of Decision: Explaining the Cuban Missile Crisis*, Little, Brown and Company.

Andrews, Kenneth (1971, 1980), *The Concept of Corporate Strategy*, Homewood, Ill.: Dow-Jones-Irwin.

Ansoff, H. (1965), *Corporate Strategy*, McGraw-Hill.

— (1984), *Implementing Strategic Management*, McGraw-Hill.

Argenti, John (1974), *Systematic Corporate Planning*, Nelson.

Argyris, Chris and Schon, Donald A. (1978), *Organizational Learning*, Addison-Wesley.

Ashby, W. Ross (1952), *A Design for the Brain*, New York: John Wiley and Sons.

Axelrod, R. (1973), 'Schema Theory: An Information Processing Model of Perception and Cognition', *American Political Science Review*, 67:1248-1266.

Baker, Edwin L. (1980), 'Managing Organizational Culture', *Management Review*, July: 8-13.

BCG Report: Strategy Alternatives for the British Motorcycle Industry (1975).

Beckhard, R. and Harris, R. (1977), *Organization Transitions: Managing Complex Change*, Reading, Massachusetts: Addison-Wesley.

Beer, Michael (1980), *Organization Change and Development*, Goodyear Publishing Company.

Berg, Per-Olof (1979), *Emotional Structures in Organizations*, Chartwell-Bratt.

Beyer, Janice M. (1981), 'Ideologies, Values, and Decision Making in Organizations'. In *Handbook of Organizational Design*, Vol. 2, Nystrom, Paul C. and Starbuck, William H. (eds), Oxford, New York: Oxford University Press.
Bolognini, Bruno (1984), *Prospettive de cultura organizzativa*, Genova: ECIG.
Boston Consulting Group (1973), *Perspectives on Experience*, No. 135, p. 149.
Bower, Joseph L. (1970), *Managing the Resource Allocation Process: A Study in Corporate Planning and Investment*, Boston: Division of Research, Graduate School of Business Administration, Harvard University.
— and Doz, Yves (1979), 'Strategy Formulation: A Social and Political Process'. In *Strategic Management*, Schendel, D. and Hofer, C.W. (eds), Boston: Little, Brown and Company.
British Transport Commission, *Annual Reports* (1940-62).
Burgelman, Robert A. (1983), 'A Model of the Interaction of Strategic Behaviour, Corporate Context, and the Concept of Strategy', *Academy of Management Review*, Vol. 8 No. 1:61-70.
Burns, T. (1961), 'Micropolitics: Mechanisms of Institutional Change', *Administrative Science Quarterly*, 6 (3): 257-81.
Burrell, G. and Morgan, G. (1979), *Sociological Paradigms and Organisational Research*, London: Heinemann.
Butler, Richard J., Hickson, David J., Wilson, David C, and Axelsson, Runo (1979), 'Organizational Power, Politicking and Paralysis', *Organization and Administrative Sciences*, Vol.8, No.4, Winter: 45-59.

Camerer, Colin (1985), 'Redirecting Research in Business Policy and Strategy', *Strategic Management Journal*, Vol. 6: 1-15.
Chandler, A. (1962), *Strategy and Structure: Chapters in the History of American Industrial Enterprise*, MIT Press.
Christensen, C. Rowland, Andrews, Kenneth R. and Guth, William D. (1965), *Business Policy: Text and Cases*, Richard D. Irwin.
Christensen, C. Rowland, Andrews, Kenneth R., and Bower, Joseph L. (1973), *Business Policy: Text and Cases*, Richard D. Irwin.
Cooper, J. and Croyle, R. T. (1984), 'Attitudes and Attitude Change', *Annual Review of Psychology*, 35:395-426.
Cyert, Richard M. and March, James G. (1963), *A Behavioural Theory of the Firm*, Englewood Cliffs, N. J.: Prentice-Hall.

Darwin, C. (1859), *On the Origin of Species by Means of Natural Selection*, London: Murray.

Davis, Fred (1968), 'Professional Socialization as Subjective Experience: The Process of Doctrinal Conversion Among Student Nurses'. In Howard S. Becker, Blanche Geer, David Riesman, and Robert S. Weiss (eds), *Institutions and the Person*: 235-251, Chicago: Aldine.

Davis, Stanley M. (1982), 'Transforming Organizations: The Key to Strategy is Content', *Organizational Dynamics, Winter: 64-80, AMACOM.*

Deal, Terrence E. and Kennedy, Allan A. (1982), Corporate Cultures: The Rites and Rituals of Corporate Life, Addison-Wesley.

Dean, John P., Eichhorn, Robert L., and Dean, Lois R. (1969), 'Establishing Field Relations'. In McCall, George J. and (eds) Simmons, J. L. *Issues in Participant Observation: A Text and Reader,* Addison-Wesley.

Dell, Paul F. and Goolishian, Harold A. (1981), 'Order through Fluctuation: An Evolutionary Epistomology for Human Systems', *Australian Journal of Family Therapy*, 2:4, 175-184.

Dewey, John (1910), *How We Think*, Heath.

Edgerton, Robert B. and Langness, L. L. (1974), *Methods and Styles in the Study of Culture*, San Francisco: Chandler and Sharp.

Eisenstadt, S. N. (1978), *Revolution and Transformation of Societies: A Comparative Study of Civilizations*, New York: The Free Press.

Eldridge, N. and Gould, S. J. (1972), 'Punctuated Equilibria: An Alternative to Phyletic Gradualism'. In *Models in Paleobiology*, T. J. M. Schopf (ed.), San Francisco: Freeman, Cooper.

Fahey, Liam (1981), 'The Causal Texture of Organizational Environments', *Human Relations*, 18:21-32.

Festinger, L. (1957), *A Theory of Cognitive Dissonance*, Row, Peterson.

—, Rieken, H. W., and Schachter, S. (1956), *When Prophecy Fails*, University of Minnesota Press.

Fox, A. (1971), *A Sociology of Work in Industry*, Collier Macmillan.

Gagliardi, Pasquale (1986), 'The Creation and Change of Organizational Cultures: A Conceptual Framework', *Organization Studies*, 7(2): 117-134.

Galbraith, Craig and Schendel, Dan (1983), 'An Empirical Analysis of Strategy Types', *Strategic Management Journal*, Vol. 4: 153-173.

Glaser, Barney G. and Strauss, Anselm (1967), *The Discovery of Grounded Theory: Strategies for Qualitative Research*, Aldine.
Gluck, F. W. (1986), 'Strategic Planning in a New Key', *The McKinsey Quarterly*, Winter: 18-41.
Glueck, William F. (1976), *Business Policy: Strategy Foundation and Mangement Action*, McGraw-Hill.
Goffman, Irving (1959), *The Presentation of Self in Everyday Life*, Garden City, N.Y.: Doubleday.
— (1961) *Asylums*, Anchor.
Gold, Raymond L. (1969), 'Roles in Sociological Field Observations'. In McCall, George J. and Simmons, J. L.(eds), *Issues in Participant Observation: A Text and Reader*, Addison-Wesley.
Greiner, Larry E. (1972), 'Evolution and Revolution as Organizations Grow', *Harvard Business Review*, July-August: 37-46.
Grinyer, P. H. and Spender, J. C. (1979), 'Recipes, Crises and Adaptation in Mature Businesses', *International Studies in Management and Organization*, Vol. IX, No. 3: 113-133.
Guth, William D. (1976), 'Toward a Social System Theory of Corporate Strategy', *Journal of Business*, July, 49(3): 374-388.

Handy, Charles (1976), *Understanding Organizations*, Penguin.
Harris, D. J. and Davies, B. C. L. (1981), 'Corporate Planning as a Control System in United Kingdom Nationalized Industries', *Long Range Planning*, Vol. 14, February: 15-22.
Harshbarger, Dwight (1973), 'The Individual and the Social Order: Notes on the Management of Heresy and Deviance in Complex Organizations', *Human Relations*, Vol. 26, No. 2: 251-269.
Hedberg, Bo and Jonsson, Sten (1977), 'Strategy Formulation as a Discontinous Process', *International Studies in Management and Organization*, Vol. VII, No. 2: 88-109.
Henderson, Bruce D. (1979), *Henderson on Corporate Strategy*, Cambridge Ma.: Abt Books.
Hickman, Craig and Silva, Michael A. (1985), *Creating Excellence*, Allen and Unwin.
Hilgard, Ernest R., Atkinson, Richard C., and Atkinson, Rita L. (1971), *Introduction To Psychology*, 5th edn, Harcourt Brace Jovanovitch.
Horvath, Dezso and McMillan, Charles J. (1979), 'Strategic Choice and the Structure of the Decision Processes', *International Studies of Management and Organization*, Fall, Vol. IX, No. 3: 87-112.

Hofer, Charles W. and Schendel, Dan E. (1978), *Strategy Formulation: Analytical Concepts*, West Publishing Company.

Kahn, Robert and Mann, Floyd (1969), 'Developing Research Partnerships'. In McCall, George J. and Simmons, J. L.(eds), *Issues in Participant Observation: A Text and Reader*, Addison-Wesley.

Kanter, Rosabeth Moss (1983), 'Change Masters and the Intricate Architecture of Corporate Culture Change', *Management Review*, October: 18-28.

Katz, D. and Kahn, R. L. (1966), *The Social Psychology of Organizations*, John Wiley and sons.

Kiesler, Charles A. (1971), *The Psychology of Commitment*, New York: Academic Press.

Kuhn, T. S. (1970), *The Structure of Scientific Revolutions*, 2nd edn, University of Chigaco Press.

Land, George T. Lock (1973), *Grow or Die: The Unifying Principle of Transformation*, New York: Random House.

Leontiades, Milton (1980), *Strategies for Diversification and Change*, Little, Brown and Company.

March, James G. and Simon, Herbert A. (1958), *Organizations*, John Wiley and Sons.

McCall, George J. (1969), 'Data Quality Control in Participant Observation'. In McCall, George J. and Simmons, J. L.(eds), *Issues in Participant Observation: A Text and Reader*, Addison-Wesley.

McCall, Morgan W., Jr (1977), 'Making Sense with Nonsense: Helping Frames of Reference Clash'. In Nystrom, Paul C. and Starbuck, Willian H., (eds), *Prescriptive Models of Organizations*, Amsterdam: North-Holland.

McCaskey, M. B. (1982), *The Executive Challenge*, Boston: Pitman.

Metcalfe, J. Leslie (1979), 'From Crisis Management to Preventive Medicine', Working Paper, London Graduate School of Business.

Miles, Matthew B. (1979), 'Qualitative Data as an Attractive Nuisance: The Problem of Analysis', *Administrative Science Quarterly* (December), Vol. 24, No. 4: 590-601.

Miles, R. E. and Snow, C. C. (1978), *Organizational Strategy, Structure, and Process*, New York: McGraw-Hill.

Miller, D. (1982), 'Evolution and Revolution: A Quantum View of Structural Change in Organisations', *Journal of Management Studies*, 19 (2): 131-51.

Miller, D. and Freisen, P. (1982), 'Structural Change and Performance: Quantum vs Piecemeal-Incremental Approaches', *Academy of Management Journal*, 25 (4): 867-892.

Mintzberg, H. (1978), 'Patterns in Strategy Formulation', *Management Science*, Vol. 24: 934-948.

— (1979), 'Patterns in Strategy Formation', *International Studies in Management and Organization*, Vol. IX, No. 3: 67-86.

—, Raisinghani, Duru, and Theoret, Andre (1976), 'The Structure of "Unstructured" Decision Processes', *Administrative Science Quarterly*, June, Vol. 21: 246-75.

Mitroff, Ian I. and Emshoff, James R. (1979), 'On Strategic Assumption Making: A Dialectical Approach to Policy and Planning', *Academy of Management Review*, Vol. 4, No.1: 1-12.

Moore, W. E. (1969), 'Occupational Socialization'. In D. A. Goslin (ed.), *Handbook of Socialization Theory and Research*, Rand McNally and Company, 1075-88.

Murphy, Gardner (1947), *Personality: A Biosocial Approach to Origins and Structure*, New York: Harper and Row.

Murray, John A. (1979), 'Toward a Contingency Model of Strategic Decision', *International Studies of Management and Organization*, Vol. VIII, No. 4: 7-34.

National Freight Corporation, *Annual Reports* (1968-69).

Neisser, U. (1976), *Cognition and Reality*, San Francisco: W. H. Freeman.

Notes on Long-Term Planning (1974-78), internal BRS document.

Nystrom, Paul C., Hedberg, Bo L. T., and Starbuck, William H. (1976), 'Interacting Processes as Organizational Designs'. In *The Management of Organizational Design*, R. H. Kilmann, L. R. Pondy and D. P. Slevin (eds), Vol. 1, 209-30, Elsevier North-Holland.

Oleson, Virginia L. and Whittaker, Elvi Waik (1967), 'Role Making in Participant Observation: Processes in the Researcher-Actor Relationship', *Human Organization*, 26:273-81.

Pascale, Richard T. (1984), 'Perspectives on Strategy: The Real Story Behind Honda's Success'. In *Strategy and Organization: A West Coast Perspective*, Glenn Carroll and David Vogel (eds), Marshfield, Ma.: Pitman.

— (1985), 'The Paradox of "Corporate Culture": Reconciling Ourselves to Socialization', *California Management Review*, Vol. XXVII, No. 2: 26-41.

— and Athos, Anthony (1981), *The Art of Japanese Management*, New York: Simon and Schuster.

Paterson, John (1983), 'Bureaucratic Reform by Cultural Revolution', *Canberra Bulletin of Public Administration*, Vol. 10, No. 4, Summer:6-13.

Pelto, Pertti J. and Pelto, Gretel H. (1978), *Anthropological Research: The Structure of Inquiry*, 2nd edn, Cambridge: Cambridge University Press.

Perrow, C. (1973), *Complex Organizations: A Critical Essay*, Scott Foresman.

Peters, Thomas J. and Waterman, Robert H. (1982), *In Search of Excellence: Lessons from America's Best-Run Companies*, Harper and Row.

Pettigrew, A. M. (1972), 'Information Control as a Power Resource', *Sociology*, 6: 187-204.

— (1973), *The Politics of Organisational Decision Making*, Tavistock.

— (1977) 'Strategy Formulation as a Political Process', *International Studies of Management and Organization*, 7(2): 78-87.

— (1979) 'On Studying Organizational Cultures', *Administrative Science Quarterly*, 24(4): 570-81.

— (1980) 'The Politics of Organizational Change.' In Neils B. Anderson (ed.), *The Human Side of Information Processing*, North-Holland.

— (1985), *The Awakening Giant: Continuity and Change in Imperial Chemical Industries*, Oxford: Basil Blackwell.

— (1986), Keynote Address delivered at the Strategic Management Society Annual Conference (Singapore), reported by Bernard Reimann in *Planning Review*, January/February 1987:43-6.

Pfeffer, Jeffrey (1981), 'Management as Symbolic Action: The Creation and Maintenance of Organizational Paradigms', *Research in Organizational Behaviour*, Vol. 3, JAI Press.

Pike, Kenneth Lee (1954), *Language in Relation to a Unified Theory of Human Behavior*, prelim. edn, Glendale, California: Summer Institute of Linguistics, 1954-1960, 3 Vols.

Pondy, Louis R. and Mitroff, Ian I. (1979), 'Beyond Open System Models of Organization'. In Barry M. Staw (ed.), *Research in Organizational Behaviour*, Vol. 1: 3-39, Greenwich, Conn.: JAI Press.

Porter, Michael E. (1980), *Competitive Strategy: Techniques for Analyzing Industries and Competitors*, The Free Press.

Pym, D. (1975), 'The Demise of Management and the Ritual of Employment', *Human Relations*, 28:675-98.

Quick Smith, G. W. (1967), 'Contrasting Concepts in Transport Organization', *Institute of Transport Journal* (May).

Quinn, J. B. (1980), 'Managing Strategic Change', *Sloan Management Review*, Summer: 3-20.

Reid, Graham L. and Allen, Kevin (1975), *Nationalized Industries*, Penguin.

Rumelt, Richard P. (1974), *Strategy, Structure and Economic Performance*, Harvard University Press.

Salancik, G. R. and Pfeffer, J. (1977), 'Who Gets Power — And How They Hold On To It: A Strategic Contingency Model of Power', *Organizational Dynamics*, Winter: 3-21.

Sartain, A. Q., North, A. J., Strange, J. R., and Chapman, H. M. (1973), *Psychology: Understanding Human Bahaviour*, 4th edn, McGraw-Hill.

Sathe, Vijay (1983), 'Implications of Corporate Culture: A Manager's Guide to Action', *Organizational Dynamics*, Autumn: 5-23.

Schein, Edgar H. (1968), 'Organizational Socialization and the Profession of Management', *Industrial Management Review*, 9: 1-15.

— (1983), 'The Role of the Founder in Creating Organizational Change', *Organizational Dynamics*, 12: 13-28.

— (1984) 'Corporate Culture: Constraint or Opportunity for Stragegy', *PA Journal of Management Issue 1*, Vol. 1 No. 1: 4-10.

— (1985), *Organizational Culture and Leadership: A Dynamic View*, Jossey-Bass.

Shell International Chemical Co. Ltd (1975), *The Directional Policy Matrix — a New Aid to Corporate Planning*.

Shirley, Robert C. (1982), 'Limiting the Scope of Strategy: A Decision Based Approach', *Academy of Management Review*, Vol. 7, No. 2: 262-268.

Silverman, David (1968), *The Theory of Organizations*, Heinemann.

Silverzweig, Stan and Allen, Robert F. (1976), 'Changing Corporate Culture', *Sloan Management Review*, Spring: 33-49.

Simon, H. A. (1957), *Administrative Behaviour*, Macmillan.

— (1964) 'On the Concept of Organizational Goal', *Administrative Science Quarterly*, Vol. 9: 1-22.

Slovic, Paul, Fischoff, Baruch and Lichtenstein, Sarah (1977), 'Behavioural Decision Theory', *Annual Review of Psychology*, Vol. 28, 1977: 1-41.

Sproull, Lee S. (1981), 'Beliefs in Organizations'. In Nystrom, Paul C. and Starbuck, William H.(eds), *Handbook in Organizational Design*, Vol. 2: 204-24, Oxford, New York: Oxford University Press.

Starbuck, W. H. (ed.) (1971), *Organizational Growth and Development*, Penguin Books.

— and Hedberg, Bo L.T. (1977), 'Saving the Organization from a Stagnating Environment'. In *Strategy + Structure = Performance*, H. B. Thorelli (ed.): 249-258, Indiana University Press.

Strategic Planning Associates, Inc. (1981), *Strategy and Shareholder Value: The Value Curve*, Washington, DC.

Steinbruner, John D. (1974, 1976), *The Cybernetic Theory of Decision: New Dimensions of Political Analysis*, Princeton, New Jersey: Princeton University Press.

Steiner, George A. (1969), *Top Management Planning*, Macmillan.

Strauss, Anselm, Schatzman, Leonard, Bucher, Rue, Erlich, Danuta, and Sabshin, Melvin (1969), 'Field Tactics'. In McCall, George J. and Simmons, J. L.(eds), *Issues in Participant Observation: A Text and Reader*, Addison-Wesley.

Thompson, A. W. J. and Hunter, L. C. (1973), *The Nationalized Transport Industries*, Heinemann.

Thompson, James D. (1967), *Organizations in Action*, New York: MacGraw-Hill.

Tichy, Noel (1983), 'The Essentials of Strategic Change Management', *Journal of Business Strategy*, Vol. 3(4), Spring: 55-67.

Transport Holding Company, *Annual Reports* (1963-68).

Tunstall, W. Brooke (1983), 'Cultural Transition at AT&T', *Sloan Management Review*, Fall: 15-26.

Van Maanen, John (1978), 'People Processing: Strategies of Organizational Socialization', *Organization Dynamics*, Summer: 19-36.

— (1979), 'Reclaiming Qualitative Methods for Organizational Research: A Preface'. In 'Qualitative Methodology' John Van Maanen (ed.), *Administrative Science Quarterley*, Vol. 24, No. 4, December: 520-526.

— and Schein, Edgar H. (1979), 'Toward a Theory of Organizational Socialization', *Research in Organizational*

Behavior, Vol. 1: 209-64, JAI Press.
Von Neumann, John and Morgenstern, Oscar (1947), *Theory of Games and Economic Behavior*, Princeton.

Walker, G. (1953), 'Transport Policy Before and After 1953', *Oxford Economic Papers* (March).
Watzlawick, Paul, Weakland, John H., and Fisch, Richard (1974), *Change: Principles of Problem Formation and Problem Resolution*, New York: W. W. Norton.
Weick, Karl E. (1979), 'Cognitive Processes in Organizations', *Research in Organizational Behaviour*, Vol. 1: 41-74, JAI Press
Witte, Eberhard (1972), 'Field research on Complex Decision-Making Processes — The Phase Theorem', *International Studies in Management and Organization*, Vol. 2, No. 2, Summer: 156-182.
Whyte, William Foote (1943), *Street Corner Society*, University of Chicago Press.
— (1960), 'Interviewing in Field Research'. In Richard N. Adams and Jack J. Preiss (eds), *Human Organization Research*, Dorsey Press.

INDEX